Books in the FT Press Analytics Series

Enterprise Analytics by Thomas Davenport and the International Institute for Analytics (ISBN: 0133039439)

People Analytics by Ben Waber (ISBN: 0133158314)

A Framework for Applying Analytics in Healthcare by Dwight McNeill (ISBN: 0133353745)

Modeling Techniques in Predictive Analytics by Thomas W. Miller (ISBN: 0133412938)

Applying Advanced Analytics to HR Management Decisions by James Sesil (ISBN: 0133064603)

The Applied Business Analytics Casebook by Matthew Drake (ISBN: 0133407365)

Analytics in Healthcare and the Life Sciences by Thomas Davenport, Dwight McNeill, and the International Institute for Analytics (ISBN: 0133407330)

Managerial Analytics by Michael Watson and Derek (ISBN: 013340742X)

Data Analytics for Corporate Debt Markets by Robert S. Kricheff (ISBN: 0133553655)

Business Analytics Principles, Concepts, and Applications by Marc J. Schniederjans, Dara G. Schniederjans, and Christopher M. Starkey (ISBN: 0133552187)

Big Data Analytics Beyond Hadoop by Vijay Agneeswaran (ISBN: 0133837947)

Computational Intelligence in Business Analytics by Les Sztandera (ISBN: 013355208X)

Big Data Driven Supply Chain Management by Nada R. Sanders (ISBN: 0133801284)

Marketing and Sales Analytics by Cesar Brea (ISBN: 0133592928)

Cutting-Edge Marketing Analytics by Rajkumar Venkatesan, Paul Farris, Ronald T. Wilcox (ISBN: 0133552527)

Applied Insurance Analytics by Patricia L. Saporito (ISBN: 0133760367)

Modern Analytics Methodologies by Michele Chambers and Thomas W Dinsmore (ISBN: 0133498581)

Advanced Analytics Methodologies by Michele Chambers and Thomas W Dinsmore (ISBN: 0133498603)

Modeling Techniques in Predictive Analytics, Revised and Expanded Edition by Thomas W. Miller (ISBN: 0133886018)

Modeling Techniques in Predictive Analytics with Python and R by Thomas W. Miller (ISBN: 0133892069)

Business Analytics Principles, Concepts, and Applications with SAS by Marc J. Schniederjans, Dara G. Schniederjans, and Christopher M. Starkey (ISBN: 0133989402)

Profiting from the Data Economy by David A. Schweidel (ISBN: 0133819779)

Business Analytics with Management Science Models and Methods by Arben Asllani (ISBN: 0133760359)

Digital Exhaust by Dale Neef (ISBN: 0133837963)

Web and Network Data Science by Thomas W. Miller (ISBN: 0133886441)

Applied Business Analytics by Nathaniel Lin (ISBN: 0133481506)

Trends and Research in the Decision Sciences by Decision Sciences Institute and Merrill Warkentin (ISBN: 0133925374)

Real-World Data Mining by Dursun Delen (ISBN: 0133551075)

Digital Exhaust

What Everyone Should Know About Big Data, Digitization, and Digitally Driven Innovation

Dale Neef

Associate Publisher: Amy Neidlinger
Executive Editor: Jeanne Glasser Levine
Operations Specialist: Jodi Kemper
Cover Designer: Chuti Prasertsith
Managing Editor: Kristy Hart
Project Editor: Andy Beaster
Copy Editor: Geneil Breeze
Proofreader: Sarah Kearns
Indexer: Tim Wright
Senior Compositor: Gloria Schurick
Manufacturing Buyer: Dan Uhrig

Upper Saddle River, New Jersey 07458

For information about buying this title in bulk quantities, or for special sales opportunities (which may include electronic versions; custom cover designs; and content particular to your business, training goals, marketing focus, or branding interests), please contact our corporate sales department at corpsales@pearsoned.com or (800) 382-3419.

For government sales inquiries, please contact governmentsales@pearsoned.com.

For questions about sales outside the U.S., please contact international@pearsoned.com.

Printed in the United States of America

First Printing December 2014

ISBN-10: 0-13-383796-3
ISBN-13: 978-0-13-383796-4

Pearson Education LTD.
Pearson Education Australia PTY, Limited.
Pearson Education Singapore, Pte. Ltd.
Pearson Education Asia, Ltd.
Pearson Education Canada, Ltd.
Pearson Educación de Mexico, S.A. de C.V.
Pearson Education—Japan
Pearson Education Malaysia, Pte. Ltd.

Library of Congress Control Number: 2014949792

Contents

About the Author

Dale Neef is a businessman, consultant, speaker, and author specializing in "Big Data" management issues and electronic monitoring and reporting technologies. He has been a technical consultant for the Asian Development Bank, has worked for IBM and Computer Sciences Corporation, and was a fellow at Ernst & Young's Center for Business Innovation. A frequent contributor to journals, and a regular speaker at technology conferences, he earned his doctorate from Cambridge University, was a research fellow at Harvard, and has written or edited seven books on the economics of knowledge and data management and the use of information technology to mitigate risk.

Introduction

This book is for everyone who wants to understand the implications of the Big Data phenomenon and the Internet Economy; what it is, why it is different, the technologies that power it, how companies, governments, and everyday citizens are benefiting from it, and some of the threats it may present to society in the future.

That's a pretty tall order, because the companies and technologies we explore in this book—the huge Internet tech groups like Google and Yahoo!, global retailers like Walmart, smartphone and tablet producers like Apple, the massive online shopping groups like Amazon or Alibaba, or social media and messaging companies like Facebook or Twitter—are now among the most innovative, complex, fast-changing, and financially powerful organizations in the world. Understanding the recent past and likely future of these Internet powerhouses helps us to appreciate where digital innovation is leading us, and is the key to understanding what the Big Data phenomenon is all about. Important, too, are the myriad innovative frameworks and database technologies—NoSQL, Hadoop, or MapReduce—that are dramatically altering the way we collect, manage, and analyze digital data.

The complexity and multi-disciplinary nature of this topic means that any book on the subject needs to remain at a fairly high level. Although it won't provide the level of understanding necessary to program in Hadoop or to set up nodes in a Massive Parallel Processing network, this book will give the reader a good understanding of what Big Data is all about, where those companies are leading us, and why these technologies are going to be so important in the future.

The second challenge to writing a book on Big Data is that things are simply changing very rapidly, with new technologies, start-up companies, and applications emerging, merging, or collapsing on an almost weekly basis. In fact, in the time it has taken to write this book (and conceivably in the time it will take to read it), there were many new announcements, from IPOs to new smartphone versions, which nudged the process of innovation slightly one direction or another. With this in mind, regularly updated editions of this book—and its accompanying web page and e-book—will be made available.

Still, by and large, although the companies, the technologies, the policies and the issues evolve, the major trends behind Big Data and the digital economy are emerging quite clearly: greater power and flexibility in computer analytics, mass digitization of personal data through the global expansion of mobile smartphones and tablets, a focus on cloud-based applications and storage, and collection by companies and government agencies of personal customer and user data. Hopefully, this book will help all readers—technical and non-technical, corporate manager and small business owner, student and interested citizen—to deal with these issues in a more informed way as we plunge headlong into the era of Big Data and the digital economy.

1

The Big Data Big Bang

Key Chapter Points

- Five aspects of the digital economy are converging to create the Big Data phenomenon:
  1. The Consumer Internet
  2. The Industrial Internet
  3. The Internet of Things
  4. A growing digital data collection industry
  5. New technologies for collecting and interpreting unstructured, Internet-based data
- As a result, an unprecedented amount of digital data is being created all around the world.
- That provides opportunities to leverage Big Data in four ways:
  1. To provide unique insight into trends or correlations not previously understood
  2. To collect customer data that can be used to improve sales and service and for targeted advertising
  3. To sell customer data as a separate profit line
  4. To create industrial supply chain efficiencies using mostly machine-to-machine data

The phrase *Big Data* appears a lot in the media these days. It is used to describe a statistical approach to genetics or epidemiological projects, the sequencing of DNA, and also to explain the new search and storage technologies that allow companies to scan different types of online media for "sentiment" data. Many people, hearing the phrase, think of Google, or possibly the NSA, and the implications of collecting and selling personal data on civil liberties and privacy. Others see it manifested in new technologies like Hadoop, or cloud computing, or the coming Internet of Things. Some say Big Data is revolutionary; others that it is all overblown, an unnecessarily capitalized sobriquet for injecting excitement into what is simply the next evolutionary phase in the advancement of information technology. (In a nod to that breathless enthusiasm with which so many talk about the phenomenon, I have capitalized Big Data throughout the book.)

It can be argued that Big Data is all those things, and yet not limited to any one defining characteristic, making it a "big thing" in the sense that all these various interpretations are a reflection of a larger process of technological and economic change that is just now beginning to mature and manifest itself in what I refer to as the Big Data-intelligence complex—a group of wealthy and influential companies and government agencies responsible for the myriad of technological developments powering growth and innovation in the economy and revolutionizing how we communicate, entertain ourselves, and interact with others throughout the world.

Is Big Data revolutionary and transformational? Probably so, by historical standards, although it may not really matter whether it is a process of evolution or revolution, or even whether Big Data (in all its manifestations) qualifies as a transformational technology in the manner of electricity, the telephone, or the internal combustion engine. That debate seems to me to be just a marketer's way of trying to label (and glamorize) an amorphous and rapidly changing group of technologies. But however it is described, it is important to consider where Big Data as a broader phenomenon takes us over the next decade, because the emerging Big Data-intelligence complex is already proving to be both rambunctious and irrepressible, introducing innovation at a rate that is almost impossible to follow, much less regulate. That has implications not just for civil liberties and personal privacy (which are already significant), but for the way in which our businesses, our global economy, our laws, and even the relationships between nations, develop in the future.

The Big Data Ecosystem

In this book, we look at the convergence of five aspects of Big Data, which may at first glance seem to be distinct but in fact are all part of a coalescence of powerful organizations, new technologies, and consumer trends. What are they?

First and most prominent is the familiar consumer technology: the Internet, e-commerce, telematics, social media, and mobile technologies that combine to create a *consumer-driven Big Data industry*. This is all about entertainment and smartphones and instant messaging. We live it and see it around us every day: The quarrels and the mergers and the Initial Public Offering (IPOs), the money surrounding these tools and toys, and the billions being offered for the latest app. The consumer-driven Big Data industry is helpful, and it's entertaining, even distracting, and because of that, we have a tendency to trivialize it somewhat, to see it as being not as serious or as economically important as the normal, productive economy, essential to employment and economic growth. But the consumer-driven Big Data industry is not trivial, even if it involves Tweets, photo sharing, and Angry Birds. This is big business, and big money, concentrating our best and brightest minds on advertising, apps, and games—and ever-more-clever ways of capturing enormous amounts of personal data.

The actual technologies are impressive, if not technologically revolutionary. But what is more likely to be revolutionary is that increasingly the companies that dominate in this consumer-driven Big Data economy—Google, Amazon, Facebook, Alibaba, Twitter, Apple, and the myriad of Internet-related startups that support and feed off these companies around the world—will also dominate (or at least greatly influence) the industrial side of the economy in the next decades. For the foreseeable future, economic growth, not only in the developed economies but in the developing world (if that phrase is even appropriate anymore), will be determined by where these big data giants take us. Some may worry that to have so much of our global economic future tied to a handful of gatekeeping technology companies is at least unsettling if not downright scary.

But the consumer side of Big Data that we see every day is only one aspect of the phenomenon. At the same time that consumer-driven Big Data industry is roaring away, another possibly even more important side of Big Data is emerging. It is the industrial side of Big Data—Big Data applied to what is increasingly seen as the "old" economy. This is because the combination of mechatronics and Internet-based technologies is transforming the collection and analysis of business data in a much more traditional and orthodox—but nonetheless important—way. New self-reporting sensors, components, and systems now can feed performance data into ever-more sophisticated enterprise computing systems, making traditional business functions such as sales, accounting, inventory, and logistics much more efficient (and able to operate with many fewer employees). These innovative machine-based data collection and analysis technologies lie behind the expansion of the *Industrial Internet* and the *Internet of Things*, and together are causing a parallel (and occasionally overlapping) deluge of digital data generation and collection.

And although the hardware may still be manufactured by the "old economy" powerhouses like GE or Siemens or Erikson, the companies that are likely to make the Internet of Things happen—and to control it and profit from it when it does happen—will be the new and powerful young Turks like Google, Facebook, and Amazon. That's because their core competency is mining and analyzing Big Data. Those who once worried IBM would be their Big Brother should think again. When the battle for the Internet is over, chances are that IBM and GE will simply provide the supportive infrastructure to help Amazon, Google, and Facebook control the digital data flowing to and from our businesses, homes, cars, and smart phones.

Again, in themselves these industrial Internet Big Data technologies are not revolutionary. My Saab has been alerting me to (a multitude) of ongoing mechanical and electrical failures for six years. Predictive diagnostics are helpful, but they still don't repair the car. But Google may soon be driving the car for me. And Google will suggest where I should go to have it repaired and how to get there. And the bill will be paid with the Eaze app, activated by my voice command or a nod while wearing Google Glass, after I've scanned the QR code through its camera and activated my virtual Apple Pay or Bitcoin wallet to transfer the payment. And while I'm away, Google will adjust my home's thermostat using Nest technologies while Amazon orders the parts and organizes the repairs, along with my groceries and my dry cleaning. And I will monitor and direct it all from my mobile, running on Google's Android operating system, which will allow Google to monitor and capture all that activity (including sentiment-scraping the e-mails I send to the service center), and add it to the ever-growing digital profile that it has on me, so that I can receive customized advertising (possibly a coupon from a rival auto service center). Google will then record how I react to that coupon, or if I recommend the service center to social media friends through a "like" button, and then Google will follow that cookie onto the accounts of my friends and similar coupons will appear on their Facebook sites inviting them to come to the service center—and the digital data collection will continue and grow and grow.

This apocryphal story about an aging Saab makes a more serious point. When combined, the convergence of these three Big Data trends—the Consumer Internet, the Industrial Internet, and the Internet of Things—begins to take on new significance.

That is in part because in parallel to these major Big Data trends, another powerful industry has emerged—*the digital data collection industry*. It consists of the big Internet players like Google, Yahoo!, Facebook, and Twitter, and online retailers like Amazon and Apple. It also includes the majority of major online and offline retail (former and current bricks-and-mortar) stores such as (in the United States) Walmart, Target, and Walgreens, which collect and sell their customers' personal and transaction data. It also consists of hundreds of online data tracking software and service companies that most people have never heard about but that monitor our everyday online activity, following our digital footprints and selling the data (either in an aggregated or personally identifiable form) to advertisers and employment agencies and debt collectors, and anyone else who will pay for it. And, of course, it also includes the major advertising agencies, and the large data aggregators like Experian, FICO, and Acxiom who had their origins in credit reporting but now maintain colossal databases on the personal and private details of millions of people around the world.

Together, this sometimes competing, sometimes mutually supporting, collective of data-handlers has become a powerful, shadowy, economic force, making a fortune by interpreting and selling consumer-related data and allowing companies to know much, much more about those consumers than they ever thought possible. And the data collectors derive their power from the fact that they have the databases and the tools to control the data everyone wants to get their hands on—to determine how it is distributed, who sees it, and how it is used. They are the drivers, the manipulators, the monetizers of Big Data. They are important—in fact, essential—to the success of a Big Data economy, because they are the ones that spin raw data into the supposed gold of customer-targeted advertising.

The confluence of these four trends has created a frenzy of data production and collection activity—and a surfeit of digital data. In fact, Big Data can mean a Big Data overload for most companies, now enticed by the idea of creating a new profit stream by selling customer-related data on this digital data market and told to collect everything—*everything*—that they can on their customers and their transactions, and to store *all the data* in case they might later be able to extract information that could be useful to advertisers or product sales, or to simply sell that customer data to another company. That has become the mantra in companies (and, for that matter, national intelligence agencies) today—collect everything. That means e-mails, credit card numbers, online purchases, what a customer viewed and rejected on web sites, advertisements clicked on or lingered over, customer complaint calls, Tweets that refer to the company or a product, and on and on. As a result of this Big Data market, expectations about the value, ownership, and sanctity of personal data are changing radically.

This takes us on to a fifth feature of the Big Data phenomena: the *supporting Big Data technologies* that are emerging. To extract value from all that digital data, it needs to be stored, organized, retrieved, and analyzed, and current systems don't handle large, unstructured data sets very well. As those of us who work in IT know, most companies' systems are already stretched to the breaking point under the constraints of conventional database technologies.

That means to benefit from all this digital data, all the parties to this Big Data phenomenon need to ensure the success of new Big Data technologies, which include the following:

- New data search and retrieval technologies that allow mining of large and disparate data sets. These come in the form of NoSQL, Hadoop, and MapReduce-type technologies, the same tools that power the Big Data search capabilities for Google, Yahoo!, Facebook, and Amazon.

- Readily accessible data storage technologies, a need that is, in part, prompting the migration toward cloud-based outsourcing and the massive global data storage capacity being built by the Internet powers like Amazon and Google.
- Improved analytical tools that help to sift through the huge quantities and varieties of data to discover important relationships and correlations.

The development of these new technologies is important, because they have allowed the IT industry and venture capital markets to turn their attention away from the continuous, if uneventful, growth in computing power (better number-crunching capacity with ever-more-powerful computing systems) and to focus on Big Data, which is something very different.

The Defining Features of Big Data

So how is Big Data different from just Big Computing?

First, Big Data is not just about crunching numbers. Big Data is about collecting and utilizing the unprecedented—almost inconceivable—amount of digital data now available and applying new analytical tools to reveal new insight from that data. It is called Big Data because quantity is the key element, and it is premised on the fact that all over the world an explosion of digital data is occurring—every second and nearly everywhere.

Simply to describe this digital explosion enters territory far beyond the meager gigabyte or terabyte thresholds that used to impress; today we talk in terms of petabytes, exabytes, yottabytes, and zettabytes (a zettabyte is a trillion gigabytes). My personal favorite, partly because it sounds like something that the Flintstones might have ordered as a take-out, is the brontobyte (1,000 yottabytes).

For most of us, these numbers don't reveal much. I've worked in data management most of my life, and I have no sense of what it means when IBM estimates that there are an additional 2.5 quintillion bytes of data being generated every day. Figure 1.1 provides a good sense of the explosive nature of this growth of digital data.

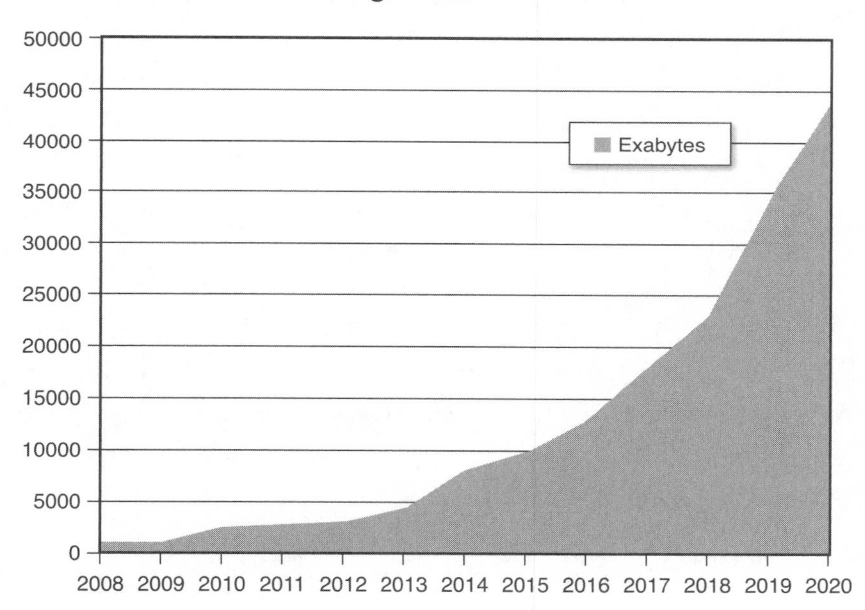

Figure 1.1 An Explosion of Digital Data
Data Source: IDC

Comparisons can help. For example, it is estimated that somewhere around 2011, the amount of data being produced around the world exceeded 1.8 zettabytes (1.8 trillion gigabytes), at which point there were as many bytes held electronically as there are stars in the universe. Or consider that the 25 petabytes of new data entering the Internet every day is 70 times larger than the total of all the collections in the Library of Congress.[1] The IDC estimates that the digital universe will grow by a factor of ten—from 4.4 exabytes in 2013 to 44 exabytes—by 2020.[2]

Better still, we can think in terms of transactions that we are familiar with. For example, every minute, 48 hours' worth of new video is loaded onto YouTube. In that same 60 seconds, 34,722 "likes" are recorded on Facebook, and 571 new web sites are created around the world. In one hour, the point-of-sale systems for Walmart capture more than 1 million customer transactions.[3] Each day there are more than 180 billion e-mails exchanged around the world, and it has recently been announced that the Library of Congress is maintaining a comprehensive collection of the more than 500 million Tweets sent every day; leaving them currently with an archive of more than 180 billion Twitter messages.[4]

More unsettling than the idea of a comprehensive Twitter archive, a single data-aggregating company, Acxiom, now maintains a profile containing some 1,500 data points on each of nearly 190 million people. That database accounts for nearly 126 million households in the United States, and about 500 million people worldwide. Acxiom processes more than 50 trillion data "transactions" a year,[5] and they are only one (albeit one of the larger) of thousands of data aggregators that collect and sell personal data.

This digital torrent is not limited to just the United States and Europe; 70% of all digital data is already being generated outside the United States,[6] and by 2020, the Asian data market alone will be producing more digital data than the United States and Western Europe combined. And this mass digitization process is really only just getting started; 90% of all the world's digital data has been produced in the past two years, and the rate of data generation is growing steadily at 50% year-on-year.[7] That means that there will be nearly 800% more digital data being produced and stored by 2020 than there is now.

The second important feature of Big Data is that it comes from a variety of data sources: online Internet searches, phone recordings, GPS, social media, a car's diagnostic systems. And from thousands of other sensors and self-reporting components that are increasingly a part of our world.

To put this in perspective, consider for a moment the amount of digital data that individuals create every day—not just the web sites visited, or the output from Twitter accounts, or text and e-mail messages. Also include all the data that is generated on the job—through enterprise systems, presentations, and forwarded and group e-mails. Then think about all of the online activity being logged, tracked, and saved in some way. Everything purchased online—music, games, prescriptions—each blog, photo or video, like or dislike. If you glance at a local paper or *The New York Times* online, you can be sure that hundreds of electronic trackers are instantly recording what pages you read, calculating how long you linger, and determining which advertisements interest you and which ones don't. If you use an e-reader, you are monitored for what you have selected to read, how long it takes you to read it, and even the notes you take on each page. Telephone calls to customer service agents may be recorded, digitized, and later "scraped" for keywords or sentiments. When we use a loyalty card to shop for groceries on the way home, the retailer—and anyone else the retailer cares to sell that information to—has a record of our purchases down to the item level. In many stores, smartphones identify the user to in-store tracking systems, and closed circuit TV (CCTV) follows them through the aisles.

Streaming video, TV, and films purchased through set-top boxes and subscription-based cable providers is monitored and logged. Wearable technologies can monitor heart rate, temperature, and blood pressure—and calculate how many calories we've burned. Smartphones transmit who we are and where we are; the GPS systems in our cars provide a constant digital trail of our location and our speed and potentially even our driving and braking patterns. At dinner and as the family prepares for bed, the utility companies monitor the amount of water and electricity we use, and when we use it. If, like me, you have Google's Nest, they have access to a detailed record of your household temperatures.

Each and every day, data aggregators compile a vast record of our financial and personal life taken from both online and offline transactions: employment, income, loans, repayment records. They categorize us by our socioeconomic status and our preferences, selling names and contact information to interested retailers, dentists, car dealerships, or charities. Other online data compilers (some reputable, others less so), for around $10, provide personal information—phone numbers, e-mail addresses, where we live, where we went to school or college, who our relatives are, and even who we associate with—to anyone who has access to the Internet anywhere in the world. Facial recognition software captures photos that we—or others—have posted online, and these are picked up, in turn, by the major search engines. If the photos came from the camera in a mobile phone, there is data showing when and where those photos were initially taken or posted.

And that's just the consumer side of Big Data. Beyond that is all the data being created and exchanged in the Industrial Internet in hundreds of millions of supply chain and financial system transactions taking place in companies and suppliers and their customers all around the globe. And as we move more and more into the world of smart parts and self-monitoring components, hundreds of millions of measurements—from car, jet, and marine engines; pumps; motors; bearings; refrigerators; air conditioners; and hundreds of thousands of other mechanical devices that rotate or create heat or power—will record performance data every second. Then think about all the government data: the census, employment levels, labor statistics, GNP, retail prices, and epidemiological data on disease, or digital sources of statistics on poverty and crime. All that data is being created and to an ever-increasing extent being stored in a digital format.

Some of that data—names and contact information, credit card and social security numbers, product SKUs, and banking transactions—is structured data, easily converted into ones and zeroes and placed in digital tables for searching and retrieval. That has pretty much been standard for digital data in the past 30 years, and although it may strain the capacity of our existing relational database and analytics systems, other than its ever-increasing volume, there is nothing essentially revolutionary about the nature of this type of data.

But much of the data being produced and collected today worldwide (probably as much as 90%) emanates from videos, Internet search tracking, customer service phone calls, and other sources of digital data that is only in a semistructured or unstructured format, which makes search and retrieval using our conventional storage, database, and business intelligence technologies much more difficult. Figure 1.2 reflects the relative growth between structured and unstructured digital data. One of the fundamental contentions of those who see Big Data as a unique new phenomenon is that we need to keep all the data we produce, because it is only when we apply algorithms to a full and complete universe of a single large data set, that computers can discern new patterns or correlations that otherwise would remain invisible.

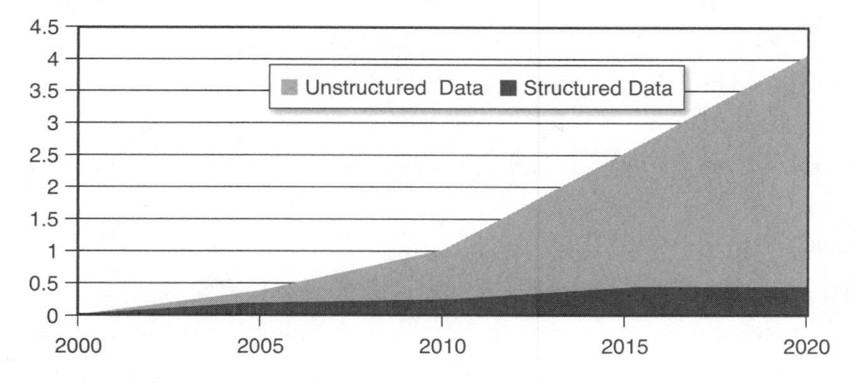

Figure 1.2 The Growth of Unstructured Data

Data Source: IDC

This reflects the number-crunching origins of Big Data in science and engineering, and the assumption that the data in that complete universe of a single, large data set, is clean, uncorrupted, and relevant. Obviously, if 90% of that data comes from such a wide variety of sources and in such varied formats, ensuring that we have a usable data set for analysis is much more difficult. And if we are going to deal with these large data sets, given the sheer volume of data being produced and made available from the consumer and industrial spheres—most of which is in an unstructured format—we need to change our conventional approach to data management.

This brings us to the third important feature of Big Data: the new tools and technologies that now allow us to store and analyze that data in ways that can help draw correlations and conclusions about everyday activities—customer preferences, political positions, purchasing patterns, and personal health—in ways that weren't possible in the past. This is what makes Big Data different from just "more data"—the ability to apply sophisticated algorithms and powerful computers to large data sets to reveal correlations and insight previously inaccessible through conventional data warehousing or Business Intelligence tools.

These Big Data tools consist broadly of new storage systems (mostly cloud computing) and new search and analytical tools such as Hadoop and other MapReduce-type technologies that allow storage and analysis of massive amounts of data from many different formats. Technologies that had their origins in the enormously powerful search engines—Yahoo! and Google—have revolutionized the way we search the Internet. We look at all these things more carefully throughout the book, but the important thing to note is that for the first time these types of technologies—for collection, storage, search, and analysis—are becoming democratized—made available to organizations of any size through a wide variety of cloud-based offerings and enterprise software. Part of the reason that the Big Data phenomenon has captured the imagination of the business world is because now almost anyone can get a piece of the Big Data action.

Those are the fundamental features of the Big Data phenomenon in its narrowest sense: huge amounts of digital data being produced and captured from a variety of sources and new tools to analyze large data sets to extract patterns and correlations that we otherwise could not. That puts us fairly close to the IT research and advisory firm Gartner's long-standing definition that describes Big Data as "high-*volume*, high-*velocity*, and/or high-*variety* information assets that demand cost-effective, innovative forms of information processing for enhanced insight, decision making, and process optimization."[8]

The Key Elements of Big Data

- Very large volumes of digital data, or very large data sets
- A wide variety of digital sources and formats
- New tools and technologies that help to extract patterns and correlations

That definition of Big Data was first created by Gartner (then still the META Group) in 2001. It didn't seem all that revolutionary then, and it certainly didn't make the business and IT world contemplate buying and selling whole new IT platforms. It's now many years on and cloud computing has grown, the MapReduce technologies have become more commonplace, but we've never really seen the explosion of benefits or the transitional effects that were promised. Until now.

The Four Key Benefits of Big Data

As we've said, Big Data and the digital economy is not a new topic; it's been written about in the technical press since the phrase was first introduced in 1997. The three V's—volume, velocity, and variety—widely used to describe the Big Data phenomenon were picked up and enhanced by Gartner as far back as 2001. But only recently has the Big Data discussion evoked the superlatives that we hear so often today. Consider, for example, what recent thought leaders have had to say about the subject.

The professional services group (PWC):

> As its potential becomes more evident, Big Data will transform every aspect of the organization, from strategy and business model design to marketing, product development, HR, operations and more....[9]

GE's Joe Salvo, manager of the Complex Systems Engineering Laboratory at GE Global Research, stated:

> We are at an inflection point. The next wave of productivity will connect brilliant machines and people.[10]

McKinsey's Global Institute estimates that:

> A retailer using big data to the full could increase its operating margin by more than 60 percent.... In the developed economies of Europe, government administrators could save more than €100 billion ($149 billion) in operational efficiency improvements alone by using big data, not including using big data to reduce fraud and errors and boost the collection of tax revenues. And users of services enabled by personal-location data could capture $600 billion in consumer surplus.[11]

Will Big Data really transform every aspect of the organization, deliver $600 billion in consumer surplus by capitalizing on personal-location data, and provide a typical retailer a 60% increase in operating margins?

Really?

If so, we're looking at something important here. But the first step is obviously to understand what, exactly, we are talking about when we use the term Big Data, because it's obvious that not everyone is talking about the same thing when they use the phrase.

The standard definitions and descriptions of the Big Data phenomenon help to understand what Big Data is all about, but don't really help much when it comes to understanding why all this is so important, and why it is beginning to reshape our global economy now. For that, we need to look at the issue not in terms of what Big Data *is*, but rather, what Big Data *does*. And Big Data does four things:

First, Big Data Provides Unique Insight

As we've seen, Big Data is all about analyzing huge data sets to understand things in new ways—by using powerful computers to analyze a wide variety of source data to reveal hidden correlations and patterns in that data. Essentially, the mantra is "let the numbers speak for themselves." There is a lot of evidence—from epidemiologists, economists, and even political pollsters like Nate Silver—that demonstrates that for those who are able to tap into the potential for analyzing large data sets, the insights can be profound.

Take, for example, the hospital looking after premature babies that now can capture data in real-time on every breath and heartbeat of each of the babies being cared for. All that data can be analyzed to predict infections 24 hours before the baby shows any visible symptoms.[12] Or consider the Centre for Therapeutic Target Validation (CTTV) being created by GlaxoSmithKline and other bioscience centers, which shares early-stage research work that combines huge amounts of data on the biological processes behind disease and allows a variety of companies and researchers to analyze the data to look at how genetics can affect disease progression.[13] Similarly, the National Weather Service uses Raytheon software to collect what will soon be as much as 5.4TB of data from US and other nations' weather satellites each day—capturing data for every meter of the globe every four hours. It is a staggering amount of data that then needs to be combined with local information around the globe on temperatures, wind speeds, and barometric pressure, all analyzed using sophisticated algorithms and processed for everything from forecasts to assessments of sea ice concentrations.[14]

Unfortunately, getting this level of insight from huge amounts of data is not for the uninitiated. Numbers might not lie, but they can mislead. The complex algorithms behind large data set analysis are not easy to create and interpret, and statistical and data modelling issues can seriously distort conclusions. As we will see, although larger data sets do allow for more sophisticated analysis, that level of sophisticated analytics still remains largely in the fields of research and science, where data are much easier to control and manage, and skilled data scientists are in place to direct hypothesis generation and testing.

Whether that same level of insight can be easily achieved by the average manufacturer or retailer is yet to be proven. Many organizations should probably accept a much more prosaic reality, which is that most of the benefits that they are seeking—a better understanding of supply-chain costs and profitability or a better grasp of their customers' buying patterns—could be achieved if they simply use their current technologies more effectively and apply more rigorous data-management techniques to the huge volumes of structured transaction data that they already collect.

Still, whatever its limitations, the unique level of insight that comes from complex calculations of large data sets is at the heart of the Big Data, and when academics, epidemiologists, statisticians, or economists characterize the Big Data phenomenon, this insight is almost always what they are talking about.

Second, Big Data Underpins Digital Advertising and Customized Individual Marketing

That same principle—that new technologies can be used to extract insight from large, unstructured data sets—can also apply to the fields of marketing and sales. In fact, when most retailers, advertisers, marketers, or business press columnists describe Big Data, they are most likely not talking about the advanced predictability calculations used by Nate Silver, GlaxoSmithKline, or the Federal Reserve. They are most likely talking about how companies can use large data set analytics and new storage and retrieval technologies to anticipate broader sales trends or as a means of capturing their customers' personal data and creating customized marketing or sales messages. The principle is the same, and the methods and tools are similar, but the focus is different. These Big Data advocates are hoping that by gathering and analyzing huge amounts of information on individual customers they will be able to better target their advertising campaigns to sell more products.

Applying Big Data analytics to customer data has taken the retail world by storm. Consider a recent comment by luxury goods maker Burberry's CEO, Angela Ahrendts: "Consumer data will be the biggest differentiator in the next two to three years. Whoever unlocks the reams of data and uses them strategically will win."[15]

It's an attractive idea. After all, the reasons why groups like Amazon or Google or Facebook have retained such high levels of funding and high stock valuations is that they have a huge advantage when it comes to applying their sophisticated search technologies to the data on millions of users of their systems. Although users may see these platforms in terms of the services they provide—a search engine, e-mail, a news feed, an online store, or a method for sharing photos—the company executives and their financial backers have always seen them primarily as platforms for collecting data and selling digital advertising. It took the world some time to realize that as remarkable as e-commerce and online search is, in reality, for the hugely successful Internet tech companies like Google, Facebook, or Twitter, *it was always about the customer data*.

As John Sargent, the chief executive of Macmillan, recently admitted in a *New Yorker* article about meeting Jeff Bezos at Amazon in the mid-1990s, "I thought he was just a bookstore, stupid me. Books were going to be the way to get the names and the data. Books were his customer-acquisition strategy."[16]

If that strategy was unique to Jeff Bezos then, it certainly isn't any longer. As we will see, the move toward capturing individual customer data and applying predictive analytics is all part of a fundamental change overtaking the advertising world, where the emphasis is shifting toward digital advertising and particularly toward digital advertising for mobile devices. And as more and more advertising revenues shift from print to digital, and from PC and TV to mobile, greater pressure is being placed on advertisers to more accurately target and deliver their ads. There is nothing more frustrating than a badly placed, poorly composed, or worst of all, an irrelevant, advertisement on a mobile device. The advertising world understands that if digital advertising is going to work—and the major media conglomerates and Internet platform leaders are betting their companies' futures that it will—then those advertising messages are going to have to be much better made and targeted. And the best way to do that, they contend, is to understand all they can about individual customers.

There are other benefits. Obvious bottom-line efficiencies come from targeted ads, and particularly digital ads, compared with general, mass print mailings or e-mails. Marketers want to live in a world where the right message for the right product can be delivered to the right person at the right price at the right time—delivered and tracked for success on the customer's mobile device. That, they say, has to mean increased sales and significant savings to an organization's bottom line. And surely, they add, it must be beneficial for the customers themselves.

It all seems to be cause for celebration among the Internet tech companies, mobile app developers, and advertisers. Whether it is good news for brand owners or retailers is yet to be proven. Despite what we're hearing from pro-Big Data marketers, it is difficult to determine yet whether this type of customized advertising really does add to a retailer's top line (that is, more revenues through expanded sales). As we'll see, although it may be more efficient to distribute targeted electronic marketing messages, at this point few studies show that this type of personalized advertising actually prompts customers to buy more, or differently, than before.

Still, advertising has never been an exact science. As John Wanamaker, once famously said, "Half the money I spend on advertising is wasted; the trouble is I don't know which half." Advertisers and marketers are hoping that by collecting extensive amounts of personal data on each of us in the future they will be able to do better than half.

Third, Big Data Creates a Market for Harvesting and Selling Customer Data

Even if a company doesn't advertise and sell directly to customers through retail, it can still profit from Big Data by harvesting and selling its customer data. In fact, an enormous market for personal data has appeared that offers all types of organizations a tantalizing opportunity to sell what they know about their customers to others.

This capturing and selling client data can be eye-wateringly profitable. Walgreens, for example, admitted to the SEC that it sold its customers' prescription and prescribing physician data to big pharma buyers in 2012 for $749 million.[17] That's the kind of money that makes executives sit up and take notice, and in the last few years, most organizations have considered the possibility of capturing and selling their own customers' data. That was reflected well in a recent survey by Spencer Stuart of 171 US-based marketing executives, which found that marketers have widely embraced the idea of Big Data and customer data mining (see Figure 1.3).

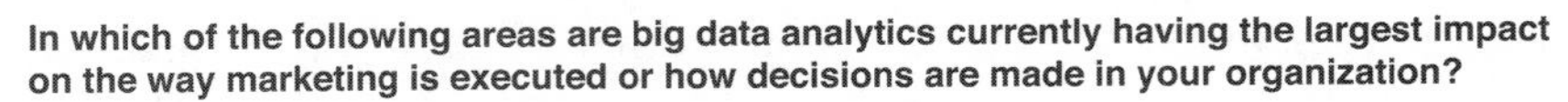

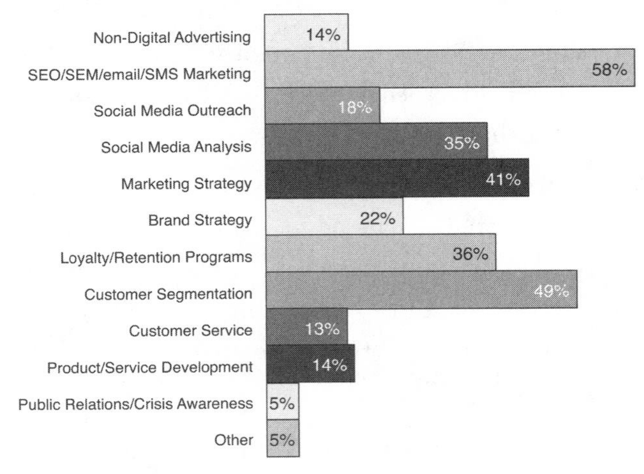

Figure 1.3 Hoping Big Data Will Improve Marketing, Sales and Customer Service

Data Source: SpencerStuart[18]

Still, this type of customer data mining can go very wrong. A spate of lawsuits were filed against Walgreens (as well as CVS pharmacies) by customers angry about the retailer's breach of personal medical data. Target used to boast of how it had been collecting and analyzing customer data for nearly a decade. But despite its efforts to leverage that data to improve customer experience, few Target customers would profess a sea change in their Target shopping experience during that time. Mostly, Target customers were not pleased to find that their personal data—including Social Security and credit card numbers—had been vacuumed up by hackers in a data breach that compromised 40 million payment card accounts. Target's CEO resigned, the company spent more than $60 million in dealing with the breach, and its Christmas revenue went down 5%.[19, 20]

It is early days, and certainly too soon to predict where customers' attitudes toward their data and privacy will go. Many contend that given the myriad and virtually unregulated number of sources collecting and selling our personal data, we might as well simply accede to the inevitable and admit that privacy as we once knew it is dead. But many believe that a customer revolt over data privacy issues is going to be the "blowback" of these customer Big Data policies, and as data breaches continue, we may see, through litigation or boycott or support for alternative privacy-ensuring software, customers create their own revolution when it comes to the use of their personal data. (Privacy issues are discussed further in Chapter 10, "Doing Business in a Big Data World.")

Fourth, Big Data Supports Supply Chain and Industrial Services Efficiencies

A fourth important application of Big Data returns to the theme of insight but has nothing to do with customer profiling. Purists from the "make and move" industries believe that too much of the Big Data discussion is focused on collecting consumer data and developing customized advertising for mobile phones. They contend that instead, the world should be celebrating the ability of Big Data and new mechatronic components to create a revolutionary level of efficiencies in product development, production, or delivery. Industrial leaders from companies like Siemens or GE are interpreting Big Data as something very different from the marketers and advertisers, the research scientists or the economists. They see Big Data as new technologies to collect and analyze mostly machine-to-machine digital data throughout the supply chain, the Industrial Internet, and the coming Internet of Things.

The real benefit of Big Data, they say, comes from new machine-based self-monitoring and reporting technologies now appearing throughout the global supply chain. As these sophisticated sensors and interconnected diagnostic networks eventually merge with the Internet of Things, they contend that they will result in huge efficiencies (see Figure 1.4).

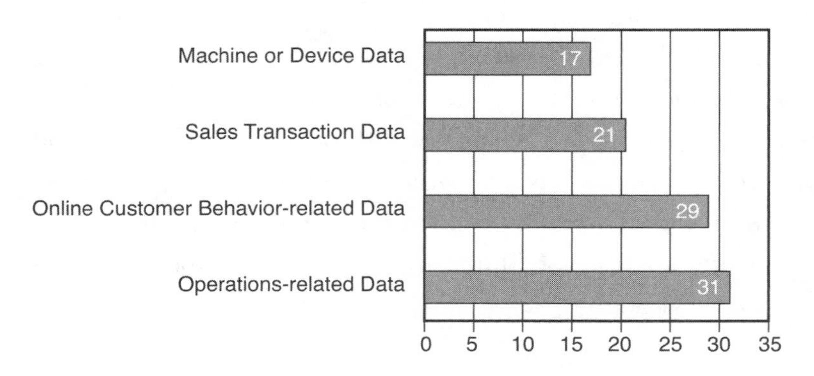

Figure 1.4 The Origins of Big Data Projects

Data Source: IDC's 2012 Vertical IT and Communications Survey

Unquestionably, a lot is happening in the realm that GE dubbed the Industrial Internet, and advocates are right to say that early returns show that Big Data projects focused on reducing costs (the bottom line) through increased efficiencies have so far been a lot more effective than Big Data collection focused on expanding revenues (the top line) through customer profiling and customized advertising. In fact, bolstered by improvements in artificial intelligence and machine learning, the Industrial Internet might prove to be the most revolutionary in its outcome, because it will almost certainly have a profound impact in the coming years on productivity, employment, and the continued polarization of the economy.

Lost in the Big Data Universe

Skeptics at this point might say that much of what is being called Big Data by any of these definitions is just a logical extension of what we've been doing for years with enterprise systems (ERP) and business intelligence software. And they would be right. In fact, so great is the interest in this burgeoning opportunity, that we are almost in danger of making the Big Data market the equivalent of the IT market itself—redefining Information Technology as Big Data Web 2.0. That may be where we're moving, because if we go back to our definition of Big Data—large amounts of digital data being captured and sold from a wide variety of sources, and the tools and technologies to store, retrieve, and analyze that data for greater insight—that does put Big Data right at the heart of the digital economy and IT platforms of the future.

But Big Data is not just about technology. If nothing else, public acceptance of personal data being captured and sold without consent or compensation marks something of a cultural revolution. Even if Big Data is just an evolutionary step, it is an important one because businesses of all stripes will find it hard not to be sucked into the vortex as a participant. It's hard for any organizational leader to resist the temptation of this type of "revolutionary" technology because the sales pitch promises real opportunity: Every retail company is being told that it can sell its data for huge profits and analyze that same data to provide uniquely successful advertising to customers; doctors can help patients, policemen can catch criminals, insurers can revolutionize their underwriting and actuarial services, and bankers can use advanced algorithms and computerized trading to better understand the market and their customers to make a fortune.

Most importantly, Big Data involves big money. Record-high technology stock valuations, mega-profile acquisitions, and enormously profitable public offerings in this area are fueling an unprecedented digital stock boom on both sides of the Atlantic and in Asia. Gauged by any measure—IPO valuation, investor capital, merger and acquisition activity—the arena is a gold mine. Because the boundaries of the Big Data market are unclear, estimates to its value vary, but at its most narrow interpretation, Wikibon estimates that "pure play" Big Data vendors (independent hardware, software, or services vendors whose Big Data-related revenue accounts for 50% or more of their total revenue) will expand in the United States alone from $18 billion in 2013 to more than $50 billion by 2016 (see Figure 1.5).[21]

The International Data Corporation (IDC) predicts that the market for Big Data will grow six times faster than the overall IT market.

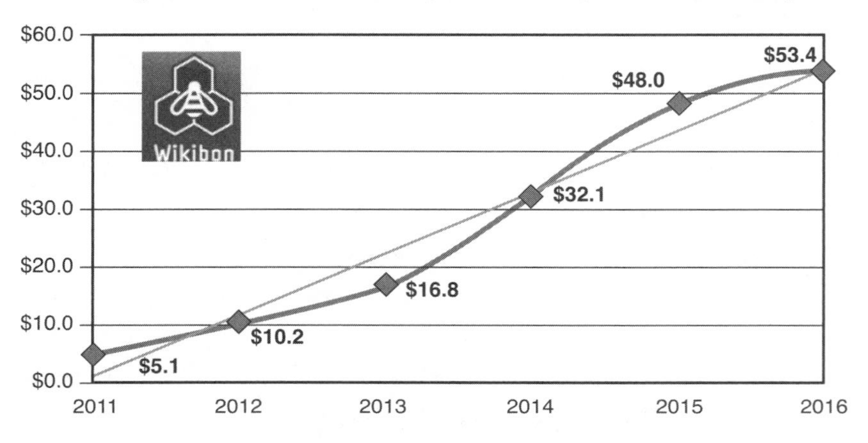

Figure 1.5 Overall Big Data Market Growth

Source: Wikibon

But if we look at a broader interpretation of the Big Data market that includes global tech companies, media, and telecoms (which in the following chapters we see are quickly becoming more of a single, consolidated industry dependent upon digitized data and the Internet), that number climbs enormously. Big Data-related mergers or acquisitions racked up a record $54 billion in transactions *in the first three months* of 2014 as the industry's powerhouses scrambled to buy up the important digital technology products of the future. If we include media and telecoms, mergers and acquisitions activity in those areas was an astonishing $174 billion in that single quarter.

Big Data Without Borders

So Big Data is about huge volumes of data from a wide variety of new sources. It's also about business intelligence and analytics, storage capacity, and new search capabilities. It is all that and much more. As we see in this book, it is both helpful and harmful, good and bad. Big Data is part of an innovation continuum, and yet it seems to cross a red line into revolution. It can bring us extraordinary new insight into research, medicine, and customer buying patterns, and yet at the same time it potentially poses serious threats to long-cherished personal freedoms. It can create tremendous supply chain efficiencies and yet contributes to IT sprawl that threatens to overwhelm company IT departments. It will be the basis for the Internet of Things, but security breaches and data losses could cost companies huge amounts of money and compromise the personal data of millions of customers.

In the end, maybe a strict definition will always elude us. After all, when enterprise resource planning (ERP) systems came on the scene, they evolved and changed, adding functionality and modules, altering their focus, consolidating, and bringing out new products. It didn't matter much whether we could describe what was happening at the time within tight definitional boundaries. If we accept that Big Data means various things to different constituents, and if we take all the effort associated with the four key benefit areas we discussed previously, the one thing we can say for certain is that the Big Data phenomenon becomes something that is remarkable in its scope and effect.

Whether we call this phenomenon Big Data, the Digital Revolution, mass datafication, or the birth of the digital-industrial complex, it is still all about digital data: producing it, capturing it, storing it, retrieving it, making sense of it, making money from it. And whether it is revolution or evolution, it is still going to be the focus of economic activity for the foreseeable future. There is going to be a whirlwind of activity with a few of the biggest Internet and retail players in the world being feted like queen bees by supportive smaller companies. There will be significant winners and significant losers, both in the business realm and in society as a whole.

That's why even those who don't have a Facebook account, never plan to program with Hadoop, and don't care much about Cloud computing will still want to have some level of appreciation for what Big Data is and why all this is happening. For those who are in the midst of it all, for those wishing to be, or for those who worry about it but don't quite understand what it is, the following chapters should help explain what Big Data is, who wants it to happen, and how it is likely to change all our lives. Because there can be no doubt that mass datafication and the era of data-driven innovation—and data dependency—means that the world our children live in will be very different from today.

2

Big Data and the Battle for Control of the Consumer Internet

Key Chapter Points

- The development of the PC and mobile phone democratized technology and shifted the focus of information technology investment and power away from business and toward the consumer.
- Consumer demand led to a rapid expansion of the Internet and huge improvements in data handling and storage.
- A handful of Internet-based companies have become highly valued on world markets based on their ability to cater to this consumer market and, particularly, to capture vast amounts of consumer data.
- Cash rich, these Internet tech companies are now vying for control over as many Internet channels—from search and messaging to streaming video, TV, and cloud storage—as possible.
- The business model for these companies relies on a Faustian Bargain made with their users—to provide free services in return for personal information.

Consider what it was like in the early 1990s, just 25 short years ago. Back then, the information technology marketplace was still almost exclusively the domain of the business world. There were still only a few token rivals to IBM in the mainframe marketplace—ICL, Amdahl, Olivetti—mostly small, nationally-sponsored rivals to Big Blue. The IT world consisted mostly of mainframes and batch work; companies had only begun, reluctantly, to move toward distributed computing. Most importantly, data management—access to digitized data—was still pretty much exclusively in the hands of the hardware and software giants. Even in the early 1990s, most of the PCs in the world were owned and used by businesses. And despite the fact that most computing involved large companies and large mainframe computers, data storage and memory were still infinitesimally small by today's standards, mostly recorded on reels of tape. In 1986, 99% of all data storage was analog. Four years later, only 3% of the world's information was kept on emerging digital technologies like optical disks or hard drives.

1990 was also the year that Tim Berners-Lee invented something he called a networked hypertext system, or the World Wide Web, for government and academia. The public wouldn't have access to it for another year, and the nascent Internet then bumped along slowly for several years, impeded by dial-up connections running at 56 kilobits per second, bland web sites, and limited bandwidth. Apple made personal computers, but no one could have imagined the iPod, much less the iPad or smartphone. Google wouldn't even register its domain name for another seven years. No one had even dreamt of technologies like Facebook or Twitter (Mark Zuckerberg was six years old). Even as late as 2000, for most people the Internet was still just a frustrating curiosity. Discussions about the Internet revolution at that time centered on how we were moving from Web.1 (static web pages) to Web.2 (interactive web pages).

On the consumer media side in the early 1990s, we had audiocassettes for music and VHS format VCRs for films. Almost no one had a mobile phone, and those who did carried them around with heavy battery packs. Mostly driven by an innovative market in the Nordic countries, they were cumbersome first generation (1G) systems based on analog technology.

Power to the People: The Democratization of Technology

By 2000, with the boom in personal computers and the rise of Apple, Dell, HP, Compaq, and Acer, we began to see the rapid commercialization of digital technology and for the first time nonbusiness users—people in their homes—began to take control of the creation and ownership of digitized data. IT was shifting away from the impersonal world of business to the personal world of the "me-machine"—technology that could benefit individual consumers. In a matter of a few short years, the combined take-up of home-based PCs, music CDs, and the digital camera all combined to drive home digital storage away from the original floppy discs and into the improved 3½-inch disks (which could hold up to a mind-boggling 20 MB). These would soon give way to DVDs; hard, flash, and zip drives; and memory cards that captured and stored personal digital data in quantities inconceivable only a few years before. By 2002, digital storage passed analog data storage for the first time—most of that driven by digital data being created by nonbusiness users.

Flash forward now to 2015, and the world looks very different. The Internet, with its high-capacity fiber-optic cables, routers, and data centers, has expanded into the remarkable global, public, and private network of networks that it is today. Three billion people are now on the Internet worldwide, and more than seven billion people use mobile phones. Facebook boasts 1.2 billion users worldwide. And although IT and the Internet are a core feature of most businesses today, an enormous market for IT, mobile, telematics, and Big Data-related products and services in 2015 lies not only with businesses but also with consumers—old, young, married, single, rich, poor, rural, and urban—all around the world, who are surfing the Web; watching streaming TV programs, films, and videos; playing games; emailing; texting; posting photos; and buying things online. All this, increasingly, is being done on a mobile device like a tablet or a smartphone. That is a different paradigm from 1990, but it is also a different paradigm from 2000, or for that matter, 2010 (see Figure 2.1). If current rates of storage improvement continue, a micro-memory card in 2050 could conceivably have the storage equivalent of three times the brain capacity of the entire human race.[1]

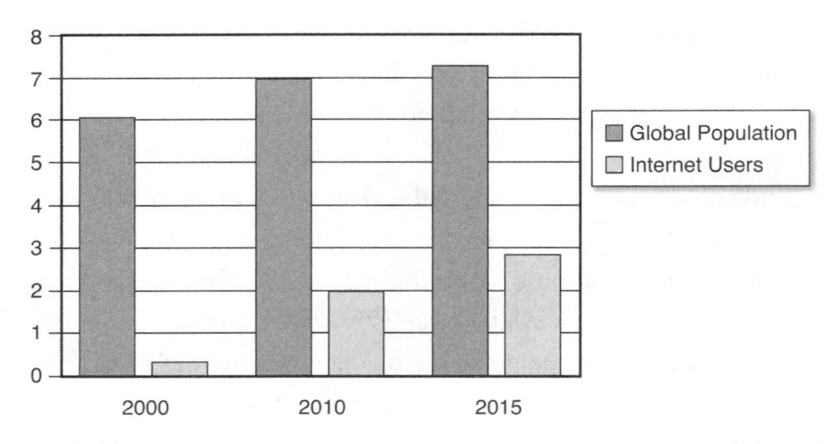

Figure 2.1 Internet for All

Data Sources: Internet Live Stats, Infoplease, US Census Bureau, and Microsoft

Of the once-dominant IT manufacturers, only IBM survived relatively unscathed among the mainframe manufacturers of the day, and it is now a global services company mainly focusing on analytics and cloud-based applications and storage (to a large extent in support of consumer Big Data). Once feared because they were so large and powerful, IBM is, like the rest of the business-focused IT and software houses, in some way only a bit player, important and supportive, but following the major Internet technology companies on the ever-expanding consumer Internet side of the market. Not even the PC makers, such as Dell or HP, who for a fleeting moment potentially owned the gateways—the user interface—to the Internet, managed to become dominant players in the consumer Internet marketplace.

This is in part because the consumer Internet and the data that flows over it are not fundamentally about sophisticated technology—hardware or software, or even networks (new non-relational database and Hadoop technologies and cloud computing are designed to use shop-grade computers). And, as we'll see, the Internet is less and less about PCs. All these groups essentially missed the train on the consumer Internet side, and for the most part remain focused on the industrial Internet, with its occasional intersections and overlaps with the consumer data world through the Internet of Things (both of which we look at more closely in the next chapters).

To get into the world of Facebook and Twitter—with IPOs worth billions of dollars—companies need to have a unique way of accessing and controlling Big Data on the consumer side. That's where almost all the commercial momentum lies, and that's why the big, traditional hardware and software services groups are finding it difficult to elbow their way back into the mainstream of that market. For many, the best that they can hope for is to provide the tools necessary to help store and analyze consumer-derived digital data. In some ways, it's a real comedown for the once mighty giants of IT.

And that's also why, for the most part, when the press, politicians, businessmen, Wall Street investors, and venture capitalists talk about Big Data, they are talking about *big consumer data*, not big business data (and certainly not, whatever its merits, big science data, big finance data, or big engineering data). And they're talking about a specific set of relatively new powerful companies riding the growing swell of that wave of consumer digital data.

The Emergence of the Internet Tech Giants

So if the Big Data market and the consumer Internet do not belong to IBM or SAP or Oracle, who does it belong to? The key rivals for control of the consumer Internet today are just a handful of innovative, popular, well-run companies, names we have all come to know (see Figure 2.2):

- With 215 million active account holders, and sales growing at around 20% a year,[2] Amazon has become the largest online retailer in the world. Amazon also produces mobile devices, including the Kindle e-books and the Kindle Fire tablet, has begun creating original video content, and provides online payment services through its "login and pay" system and Simple Pay, a PayPal-like service that allows consumers to use their Amazon account platform to pay for purchases on other web sites. They compete with Netflix and Hulu for steaming video through the Amazon Prime offering and Fire TV, an Android-powered instant video streaming and gaming set-top box. Amazon recently announced the release of its own smartphone, running on a customized Android operating system. These various offerings had a combined revenue of more than $50 billion in 2013. The company is also the world's largest cloud computing infrastructure holder, with Amazon Web Service generating $1.8 billion in revenue last year, and with what Gartner estimates to be five times the capacity of 14 other cloud computing companies (including IBM) combined. Its Web Services (cloud) clients include organizations as varied as Netflix, Shell, and the CIA.[3] Amazon was valued at around $150 billion in 2014.[4]
- At more than $500 billion in 2014, Apple, the most valuable company in the world (by market valuation), makes personal

computers and its OSX operating system software, as well as iPad tablets and iPhones, which run its widely popular mobile operating system iOS.[5] Apple also has the iPod portable digital music players, tied into the Apple iTunes store, where customers can download digital music and video, and the Mac App store for software, apps, and peripherals. It also has Apple TV, a set-top box for downloading iTunes, and iWatch, their long-awaited and still unannounced wearable computer. The Apple iPhone's fingerprint sensor system, Touch ID, opens the gateway for its own online purchasing platform. Apple also has its own cloud storage service, iCloud, which allows all Apple products to be managed online without a computer, as well as a cloud storage service for documents, music, movies, TV programs, or books.[6] The company recently announced its intention to move into the household Internet of Things with its home automation ecosystem offering.

- Still the predominant search engine with both Google and the Google Chrome browser, and number one in digital advertising, Google has a market capitalization of somewhere around $400 billion. Google provides its popular Gmail, Google+, a dominant news filter, travel scheduling, Google maps, traffic and location tracking, online shopping, a social network, video and photo sharing, YouTube, and a messaging system. The company also makes Google e-readers, owns the Android operating system, and partnered with Samsung to produce the Galaxy mobile phones and tablets. In the home, Google has a TV set-top box and has invested heavily in Google Fiber, its high-speed fiber-optic service scheduled for installation in 34 US metropolitan areas. It also has investments in satellites and wind farms, and own a number of drone design and manufacturing companies, the Nest home monitoring system, six massive data centers, and the second largest cloud computing service in the world.[7]

- At a market valuation of $175 billion, Facebook stands out among the large Internet tech companies vying for control of the consumer Internet, because of its massive user base, ready cash supply, and its willingness to build on the same key elements of its consumer Internet platform. Facebook has its social network, of course, with more than 1.28 billion users worldwide, and it moved into the mobile marketplace, modifying its desktop software for both the Android and iOS mobile markets, and with apps, including a wide variety of alliances that provide music and video downloads. Facebook is branching into search with its newly announced Graph Search and it has a cloud-based payments system; the Facebook Audience Network, a powerful, multipurpose digital advertising exchange service; a popular mobile photo-sharing framework with Instagram; and WhatsApp, the global instant messaging system.
- Microsoft has its globally dominant Windows software, and in July 2014 announced its intention of combining its mobile and desktop operating systems after moving into the world of mobile hardware with the recent purchase of Nokia. Microsoft has the Bing search engine (which also powers Yahoo! search); Azure, its cloud analytics and storage platform; Skype; the social network Yammer; and ownership of 18% of the MSNBC cable news channel.
- A relative newcomer to the big league, Twitter is now valued between $25 and $70 billion due to wild share price fluctuations. Twitter boasts more than 250 million users worldwide. It has moved into mobile advertising through its MoPub advertising exchange and is experimenting with video sharing.
- With more than 270 million users, Yahoo! is still a consumer Internet giant. It took some time for the company to realize that it could no longer attract users simply through a news and entertainment web portal, and it recently spent $200 million on nearly 20 new startups, including its purchase of Tumblr, the

blogging network, for $1.1 billion. Unlike Google, Facebook, Amazon, or Apple, Yahoo! doesn't make mobile devices or control them through an operating system. It does, though, have an Internet advertisement sales system (known as Panama), and offers a variety of online shopping services such as Yahoo Shopping and Yahoo Travel, and has a faithful following and a strong presence globally.[9]

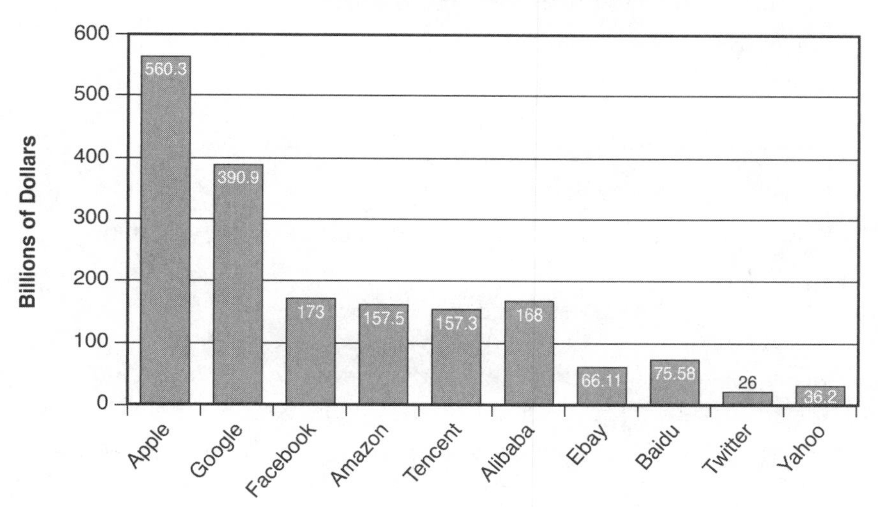

Figure 2.2 Market Capitalization of the Largest Internet Technology Companies

Sources: Bloomberg, company filings, and Yahoo Finance[8]

It would be wrong, though, to think of all this as a purely Western phenomenon;, challenges to dominate the consumer Internet aren't just coming from Silicon Valley. There is also IndiaMART (India) and ECPlaza (South Korea). And with Taobao, its billion-product eBay-like online shopping site, and Alipay, its online payment service, China's Alibaba had sales of $170 billion in 2012, making it a rival to both Amazon and Google. Weibo (the Chinese word equivalent of microblog) provides a service similar to Twitter and plans to list as an IPO in New York with a valuation of $7 to $8 billion. Baidu, the Chinese-language search engine and encyclopedia, also provides video music and multimedia files and is moving quickly into mobile search. Tencent, the massive Chinese investment company, offers everything from online shopping and games to instant messaging. It has a market capitalization of $157 million, making it larger than companies like McDonald's, Boeing, and Cisco.[10]

These companies are making headlines in the financial and business press every day, spending vast amounts of money to buy up the most important new technologies that will give them the ability to control (or at least administer) the flow of data to and from consumers on the Internet.

Alibaba and Tencent

The Alibaba group is China's largest online business conglomerate, combining many similar elements of today's Western Internet giants: It has an Internet-based news and information portal, an online shopping search engine, consumer online shopping sites (Taobao and Tmall) that rival Amazon and eBay, and a massive business-to-business trading portal (Alibaba.com) to allow Chinese companies to trade with overseas partners. It also owns Alipay, an online payment system, and recently began offering a wide variety of cloud computing services.

Tencent is its chief rival in China, with a broad portfolio of Internet-based services including Internet and mobile phone services, instant messaging (Tencent QQ), and the mobile chat service (WeChat), which already has 355 million users—including 100 million users outside China. Tencent also has a social networking site that earned $2 billion more than Facebook in 2012, a web portal, online shopping, a number of powerful online gaming companies, and a cloud-based storage facility.

Tencent is listed on the Hang Seng Index, and Alibaba is hovering for a much-anticipated listing in New York.

Much More to Play For: The Battle for Control of the Consumer Internet

The pattern is probably already obvious. Each of the groups listed previously—as diverse as they are from Facebook to Apple—is seeking a strong portfolio of offerings that will help them capture the gateway to the Internet with a platform that includes some, or all, of the following:

- An attractive core function funded predominantly through the collection of customer data and the sale of digital advertising
- A focus on mobile devices, including mobile hardware, and if possible, a close affiliation with, or ownership of, a mobile operating system
- A capacity for instant messaging
- A social media offering
- A multitude of apps and a competitive arrangement with other major operating systems (iOS, Android)
- Location, mapping, and GPS services
- Online shopping, integrated within their platform
- An intermediary TV offering (between the customer and the Internet service provider or cable/satellite company) to redirect TV, streaming media, and other content toward their own in-home service platform
- Some mechanism for integrated, online payment (mobile wallets)
- Outsourcing storage and software through massive cloud-based service platforms

This comprehensive approach—owning or controlling offerings in as many of these key areas as possible—allows these companies not only to leverage their core services but also to intercept and collect as much consumer data as possible from as many different sources as possible. Becoming the principal interface between the consumer and the Internet gives these companies the ability to dominate the crucial gateways to our lives: telecoms, the media (books, music, TV, gaming), Internet search, online shopping, banking, and data storage. We have to turn to this handful of Internet Tech companies and examine what they are doing in these important areas in order to understand why Big Data as a topic and a movement is so powerful, because what these companies are doing not only excites investors, but it also makes civil libertarians blink in horror at the sheer size and span of influence that these few companies will soon have over our everyday lives.

User Data and the Faustian Bargain

Although these powerful new Internet technology companies are all now competing for this same broad set of online consumer services, their origins are diverse: from Internet search to smartphones, selling online books to providing social media and chat apps. A few years ago, not many people would have thought that Apple, Microsoft, Google, and Facebook would be competing in the same market to control the gateways to the consumer Internet. So what do all these Internet tech companies have in common that makes them stand apart from other powerful companies?

The answer, obviously, is that they all have access to huge amounts of personal customer data and are good at *collecting and analyzing that personal data* to sell their products and services (Apple and Amazon) or to provide targeted advertising (all the rest). This ability to capture and manipulate customer data provides them—as diverse as their core offerings are—with an underlying business model that is unique and different from the former Fortune 100 powerhouses: IBM, SAP, GE, Procter & Gamble, and so on. In short, these Internet tech companies, whatever else they are about, are all about collecting Big Consumer Data.

Sharing our personal, sometimes even intimate, data with technology companies is also not something most of would have considered 20 years ago. So what's the deal?

It's more of a bargain, really: the *Faustian bargain*. It is the arrangement we have been living with since we first marveled at the free search offerings from Google or Yahoo! all those years ago. In short, these companies provide a free service in return for which users voluntarily give up personal data and accept advertising—a sort of, they'll show you theirs (service or content) if we show them ours (personal data) arrangement that forms the basis of the business model for Facebook; Yahoo!; Twitter; Google's Search, Earth, and mapping; Gmail; YouTube; and many other services offered for free over the Internet.

The Faustian Bargain

The story of Faust and his pact with the devil has its origins in medieval times but has been used in various literary works, including those by Christopher Marlowe and Johann Wolfgang von Goethe. In these tales, Faust reaches an agreement with the devil in which he gives up his soul to Mephistopheles in return for wealth, power, or some other type of diabolical favor. Today a Faustian bargain simply means a contract or pact agreed to with a view of immediate gain without regard for potentially disastrous cost or long-term consequences.

In this arrangement, the company's service (search or email) or content (short video, news links, stock prices, and so on) serves as the bait to entice users to allow the Internet company to monitor their online activities, track their preferences, elicit their opinions, and send them targeted advertisements. That arrangement is the basis for these companies' business model, and the reason that those services are free. And although most of these companies keep a low profile when it comes to revealing the extent to which they capture customer data, for the most part their intentions are stated (if not always clearly) in their Terms of Service agreements.

This Faustian bargain seemed almost acceptable as long as the data that was being collected could not be associated with us personally. In that regard, there is some good news and some bad news, because these companies collect that personal data in two formats: anonymized and personally identifiable (PI).

Anonymized Data

Much of the data being collected about our everyday activities is anonymous—that is, not personally identifiable data. As long as we're not logged in to a particular service, a search on Google or Bing or Yahoo!, for example, usually only reveals that someone at a particular IP address searched those sites or was interested in a particular advertisement. That is still valuable information for companies, because they can apply Big Data analytics and extract trends for themselves or for interested third-party marketers and advertisers—even if they don't know precisely who completed an online search, or who watched a particular video.

But advertisers always want to know specifics—age, sex, income, likes, and dislikes—on an individual basis. Some of that information (again, using computer analytics) can be inferred from other data collected on a particular IP address. For example, it is most likely, but not by any means certain, that if the IP address repeatedly buys women's clothing, at least one of the PC's users is probably a woman. But those types of inferences won't always be accurate. Collecting information from an anonymous IP address is helpful, but matching that data against specific names provides a much richer return.

What Is an IP Address?

Every computer and mobile device that communicates over the Internet uses a communication protocol known as TCP/IP (Transmission Control Protocol/Internet Protocol) and is assigned a numerical label (four sets of numbers separated by dots: 123.45.67.890) known as an Internet Protocol address (IP address), which provides the network with the device's unique identity and location. That IP address can either be *dynamic* (changes each time you log on to a site) or *static* (is permanently assigned to the user when registering, and so on). Unless a user is required to log on or register, the IP address normally doesn't contain any personally identifiable information (PII) but can sometimes be used to *infer* the user's identity.

No one appreciates this more than the investors, eager after many years of patience for a higher return, who have increasingly pressured Internet tech companies like Facebook and Twitter to prove that their side of the Faustian bargain will turn a profit. They know that the more data that can be collected against a personal profile, the more valuable that profile is to a broader variety of brands and advertisers. And the premium for those targeted ads is high: In 2013, an anonymous, untargeted online ad paid an average of $1.98 per thousand viewers. A targeted ad (where the recipient was already known through a personal profile) paid $4.12 per thousand viewers.[11] That means that an Internet tech company like Facebook or Google or Yahoo! can get twice as much in digital advertising revenues if they can collect personally identifiable information on a user. That's quite an incentive.

Personally Identifiable (PI) Data

For that reason, the real prize for companies like Google or Facebook or Yahoo! is personally attributable data—data that can be related directly back to a user's personal profile and that reveals that the user searched particular sites or was interested in a particular advertisement. The best way to find out who a user is, is simply to ask, which is why most of the major Internet groups have now moved toward mandatory registration for many of their services (particularly with mobile or e-mail accounts), because once a user registers for a service (Gmail, an app, or a Facebook page), the user's online activities from that point forward are matched directly against a personal profile. This is where companies (and investors) believe Big Data will pay off—by applying sophisticated analytics to that personally attributable data (particularly as it accumulates over the years), they believe they will be able to predict what the user, very specifically, will be interested in doing or buying in the future. And the more comprehensive the personal profile, the more they can charge for targeted advertising.

Even in the recent past, this level of comprehensive data collection was difficult, because most Internet companies only owned one or possibly two data channels—messaging and a chat line, search and e-mail, and so on—and so could only amass a limited amount of data on a particular user. But by expanding their offerings to a wide variety of services that require registration—from streaming video to instant messaging—these companies are now capturing an increasingly rich trove of personally attributable data. That's why the largest and most successful of this group are assembling the full set of services listed previously, and why in the first quarter of 2014, the technology, media, and telecommunications (TMT) sector accounted for almost a third ($170 billion) of all merger and acquisition activity in the United States.[12]

3

The Battle for the Internet Gateway into the Television

Key Chapter Points

- Most of the huge growth in digital data comes from online music, video, and games, which people increasingly want to access via the Internet on their home TV.
- The Internet tech companies want access to that home-TV online market.
- Traditional cable/satellite Internet service providers (ISP)s in America have bundled services to try to protect their telephone, broadband, and pay-TV offerings.
- This has led to a battle between ISPs and the major Internet tech companies for domination of the Internet gateway to the online TV.
- Both groups are moving toward monitoring and collecting viewer data and providing targeted advertising.

When I edited *The Knowledge Economy* in 1996, I and many others envisioned the television as the data center for each household, delivered via the Internet through powerful new fiber-optic cables. Although TVs themselves never turned into the computers we assumed they would (although it's likely that the next generation of TVs will always include Internet connectivity) and the fiber-optics (at least in America) aren't as ubiquitous as we expected them to be, the television/telephone cable still remains the most effective way of delivering Internet broadband to most households.

In the United States, at least, delivery of that broadband Internet service is reserved for the Internet service provider (ISP), which is almost always also a cable or digital subscriber line (DSL) provider that wants to sell its customers some type of bundled package that includes telephone, Internet, and pay-TV.

With their relatively meager use of data, telephone calls have become a mere commodity, almost incidental to the arrangements, and as broadband take-up expanded, more and more revenue has become associated with digital program streaming and Internet services.

At first it was not an easy sell, because for many years both the content and the quality of delivery for Internet streaming into the home was a poor second to programming from satellite/cable providers or even broadcast analog TV. Even as late as 2010, the larger Technology, Media, and Telecommunications (TMT) discussions were more about cable TV and telephones than about broadband and streaming games and media. But as consumers became more familiar with video and music delivered over the Internet (at first on their PCs and then on their mobile devices), they began to expect to receive those same services on a wider screen—to be able to play games or watch TV programs and films on demand, and to choose what they want to do or see through their mobile device.

A recent Nielsen survey found that American adults watch more than 33 hours of television a week (children about 24 hours each week). For the average day, an adult spent an additional hour at home on the Internet, an hour and seven minutes on their smartphone, and nearly three hours listening to the radio. Not only are adults spending more time on the Internet and their smartphones, but increasingly they are opting for Internet-based streaming services—from

YouTube to Hulu—instead of watching cable or satellite-provided television programming (see Figure 3.1). Netflix, for example, gained 630,000 subscribers in a three-month period in 2013, as more and more viewers opted for online programming.[1]

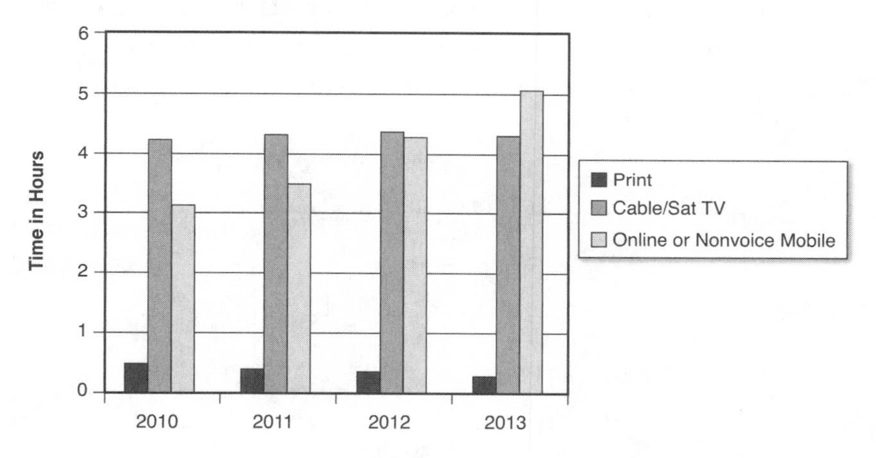

Figure 3.1 Spending Time on the Internet
Data source: eMarketer

In fact, nearly a million American homes dropped their pay-TV services in 2011, and more than a half million more in 2012.[2] By 2014, Comcast, America's largest cable Internet provider, for the first time had more subscribers to its Internet broadband service than its cable television offering (see Figure 3.2). In 2014, there should be nearly 200 million US digital video viewers (77.3% of American Internet users).[3]

Everything Is Moving Online

Needless to say, this dramatic shift to online viewing (and listening) hasn't gone unnoticed by either the traditional cable and satellite carriers or the Internet tech companies, because each minute a viewer spends on the Internet is a potential opportunity not only to target that person with advertising but to collect personal information. Both the cable/satellite providers and the Internet tech companies know that controlling the Internet gateway into the television provides a two-way digital access in and out of the houses of millions of customers, a single digital pipeline that can provide those who control it with unparalleled insight into a user's lifestyle and interests. And both groups also know that in the future, *all data going in or coming out of a house is going to be through that Internet pipeline.*

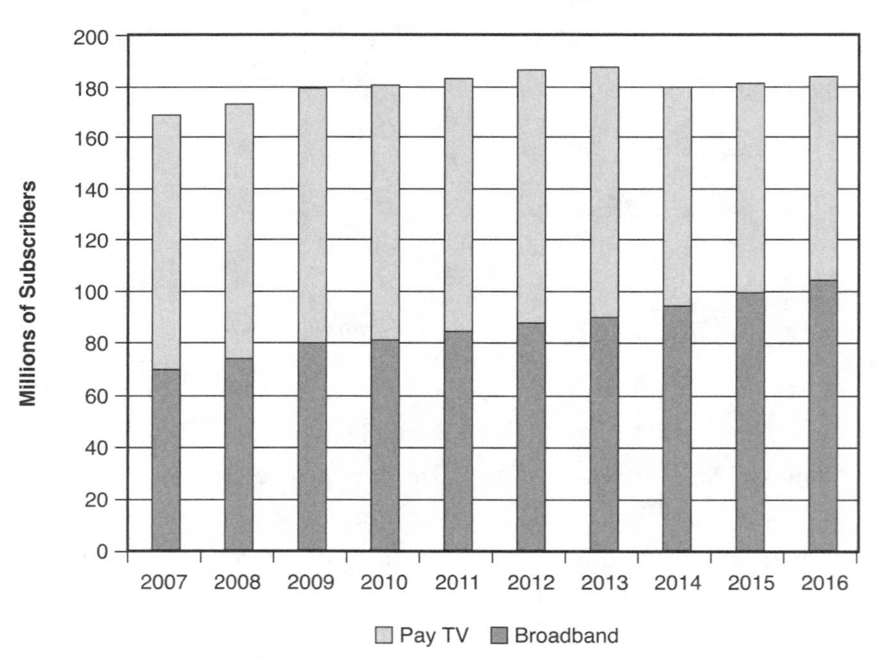

Figure 3.2 Pay TV is Losing Ground to the Internet
Data Sources: IHS Screen Digest Research and Leichtman Research Group

That's why for several years, broadband providers in America—Comcast, AT&T, Verizon, Sprint, T-Mobile—have been "bundling" their offerings to try to gain a more comprehensive control over the various digital content going into the home—Internet, TV, telephone, radio, streaming media. It is also why AT&T purchased DirectTV in

2014 for $49bn and is the rationale behind Comcast's offer to pay $45bn for Time Warner (in the hopes of securing some 40% of the high-speed Internet market to households in America). These traditional phone and cable providers want to control the Internet in the home because they own and maintain the cables and don't like the idea of ceding their near-monopoly on pay-TV to the Internet tech companies (which can provide their services—and the same TV and music streaming content—using the ISP's network).

What's more, recognizing a lucrative business model and hoping to leverage their close ties to viewers, the traditional cable and satellite providers are also trying to get into the consumer data collection market. Comcast's original efforts to collect and sell customer data began with passing new subscribers' phone numbers to telemarketers, but now the company has taken the plunge with NBCUniversal's announcement in 2014 of its new NBCU+ Powered By Comcast offering, a platform designed to capture video-on-demand subscribers' viewing habits and sell them targeted ads based on their anonymized data. Comcast was straightforward about its motivation and intentions: It will use the data collected from monitoring these viewer patterns, combined with other data purchased from subscribers' store loyalty cards and movie ticket purchases, as well as data held by the large data aggregators like Acxiom and Experian (see Chapter 8, "The Data Collectors") to get into the game of digital data collection and user profiling.[4]

Comcast is not alone among the ISP cable groups beginning to collect and sell subscribers' data. Verizon Wireless says it has begun to sell aggregated consumer data to advertisers, providing detailed demographics and location analysis of its subscribers as well as the foot-and-mobile traffic habits (from subscribers' mobile devices) so that advertisers can determine where their "target consumer segment lives and works."[5] AT&T has adopted the same policy, selling anonymized user data that includes its subscribers' web browsing history, mobile app usage, and location data.

Still, Big Data is not really the core competency of these telecom giants; their focus has always been more on controlling the digital data flow into the house (and getting paid for it) rather than collecting data coming out of the house. But if these attempts at Big Data monitoring are a sideshow for Comcast or Verizon, it's what groups like Google and Amazon are all about. And they have a real advantage, because they have a more intimate relationship with their customers and already have a long-standing arrangement; users have been allowing them to collect personal data for years. The fact that Google or Amazon can track the programs or films that users order and make recommendations for others that they believe they might like, doesn't seem unusual at all; it's what Amazon always does when consumers buy online. Extending that arrangement into the home through targeted advertising has hardly been noticed.

Unlike most other countries around the world, there is less opportunity for competition in use of the telephone line or television cable that runs into houses in America, and unless Federal Communications Commission (FCC) rules change in the future, these will remain in the hands of the cable/satellite and telephone providers like Comcast or Verizon.[6] Google has its forays into optic cabling with its broadband and fiber-to-the-premises service, Google Fiber, around the United States, but those efforts have been limited geographically.

Apart from remedying the poor bandwidth offered by many cable providers, though, Internet tech companies like Google and Amazon don't really need to own the cables themselves. If they can *capture and reroute the Internet connection after it enters the house*, they can make the TV into a virtual computer, riding for free on the Internet service provider, while luring users onto their own platforms, making the TV itself little more than a projection screen. This is particularly true if they can convince users to access their TV and video content through their home Internet using their own mobile phones and tablets.

Their efforts at essentially hijacking TV programming have been largely focused on providing a variety of streaming TV peripherals—mostly set-top boxes or plugin "dongles"—that provide the user with direct control of the Internet over the TV screen. Google's efforts to capture the home Internet TV market began as far back as 2010 with its Google TV set-top box, which provided an interface between the user and all the video sources streaming in from the cable/satellite box. In 2013, Google simplified its approach, bringing out Chromecast, its Web-to-TV streaming dongle, a low-cost stick that plugs directly into a TV's HDMI port and then permits users to project onto the TV the streaming programming that is passing first through Google's Chrome browser on their smartphone or tablet.

Google also announced Android TV, which allows users to stream video and live broadcasts to home TVs using a set-top box or through the Android operating system on their mobile or tablet. YouTube videos are accessible on a user's home TV through Google Chrome, and through the Android operating system. In fact, owned since 2006 by Google, YouTube is one of the greatest contributors to data volumes over the Internet, combining video-sharing and a mass media Internet portal. More popular among the 18- to 35-year-old bracket than any cable or TV network (according to Nielsen), YouTube boasts of more than a billion unique user visits each month—100 hours of video uploaded every minute—and now supports more than a million different advertisers worldwide using Google's own ad platforms.

Apple, too, wants a share of these home Internet revenues and the consumer data that come with them. Already the dominant provider of online music through iTunes, Apple offers a set-top box—Apple TV—that provides an interface between online content providers and a user's home TV, so that users can listen to iTunes or watch video downloads, TV programs, and movies. Although Apple TV only accounted for $1 billion in revenues to Apple in 2013 (about 1% of Apple's total revenue), it puts a stake in the ground for Apple to control more of the Internet media content going into the home. Some suggest that Apple will soon make a bid for Netflix outright.[7] Yahoo!, too, recently announced Yahoo Smart TV, which openly boasts of a recommendation engine—taken from user preferences—for online TV and video programming.[8]

With Fire TV, Amazon has also pushed its way into the video streaming marketplace, adding its online retail capabilities to the TV set or the home tablet. Amazon, uniquely, can provide to home users everything they could want in a single service: online shopping, video games, music, television, films. Amazon's new voice recognition system ties directly to a user's online profile, so that the user never has to type in an order. A microphone built into the Fire TV remote records not only direct user requests but also other sounds in the viewer's room—babies crying, music playing, or simply conversation. All of that "noise" is uploaded to the user's profile for the set-top box and can be analyzed for sentiment data. Ingeniously, the Fire TV box doesn't even have an on-off switch, ostensibly so that Amazon can send updates at any time, but with the practical effect that unless it is unplugged, it is the primary interface between a user and his TV.

If users sign up for Amazon Prime—which means providing direct identification for program selection and watching patterns—they get to stream for free. In return, as with the Kindle reader, Amazon can monitor what a user orders and understand viewing preferences, so it can make suggestions with its highly successful recommendation engine. Amazon's ASAP feature even anticipates what programs a user will want to watch and sets them up for instant streaming. In fact, Amazon may revolutionize the "home shopping channel" approach to TV sales, replacing the soul-destroying amateurism of current shopping channels with a direct link between its system and sensors in the home, anticipating and compiling shopping lists of everyday necessities that will be transmitted to the local store and delivered directly to your door.

Watching Your TV Watching You

What the Internet gatekeepers would really like is to not only monitor what programs are being watched but actually monitor the people watching the programs.

In fact, several companies are already putting a toe into the water of this more intrusive type of monitoring. Verizon, for example, in 2011 applied for a patent for a system that would reside in set-top boxes and would use cameras and microphones to monitor conversations, activities ("such as eating and drinking"), and even the "moods" of the viewers—with the view to then providing them with targeted advertisements. The system would detect and interpret sounds and body movements in the room, and then select commercials accordingly. Word recognition technology would match spoken words with associated products and (according to the patent application): "If detection facility detects one or more words spoken by a user (e.g., while talking to another user within the same room or on the telephone), advertising facility may utilize the one or more words spoken by the user to search for and/or select an advertisement associated with the one or more words...."[9] The surveillance system would even be able to detect two people "cuddling on a couch" and deliver "a commercial for a romantic getaway vacation, a commercial for a contraceptive, a commercial for flowers, a commercial including a trailer for an upcoming romantic comedy movie, etc." Wherever Verizon was going with those patent applications, it has now turned to Intel's former OnCue Web TV service (which Verizon bought in 2013), which included (at least in Intel's prototype) a camera integrated into the set-top box intended for facial recognition software that could be used for targeted advertising for viewers. Verizon hasn't yet said whether it will use the cameras in its version of the set-top box.[10]

As Orwellian as that sounds, Verizon is hardly alone in its monitoring aspirations. Microsoft applied for a similar patent that same year for a system that could be placed in its Kinect video gaming box to track TV viewer activity, offering potential rewards for viewers who manage to sit through commercials, and prompting an upgrade if too many people come into the room.[11] As we've seen, Amazon's new Fire TV records voices through a microphone button pressed on the remote control. Google TV applied for a patent using the video and audio recorders to gauge the number of people watching the screen, and Comcast patented a similar set-top monitoring technology as far back as 2008.[12]

Even the TV manufacturers want a piece of the action. In the United Kingdom, LG, the Korean TV manufacturer, was found to be monitoring households directly through its television sets for their TV viewing patterns—including videos played independently and every selection of the remote control—to collect viewer data and sell targeted advertising.[13]

Even the social media and messaging giants are getting in on the monitoring market. Facebook just bought an auto-recognition app for its site that will use the built-in microphones in Android and iPhone devices to identify music and television playing in the user's background. It signed contracts with more than 160 television stations in the United States and claims that the system can recognize music or programs in the user's background within 15 seconds, allowing Facebook to relay that information to those interested in sending the user targeted advertising through those channels.[14]

Even Twitter is getting into the TV monitoring field in its own way with its $100 million acquisition of Bluefin Labs in 2013, which allows Twitter to scan Tweets and other social media during TV programs and advertisements and analyze them for product interests and sentiment analysis. They can then also provide advertisers with the Twitter IDs of those who reacted positively to their advertisements or brands, so that they can follow-up with further marketing targeted directly to those users. In Twitter's words, this allows advertisers to "continue the conversations they start with their TV advertising."[15]

4

The Battle for the Gateway into the Mobile Internet

Key Chapter Points

- Tremendous worldwide mobile phone, smartphone, and tablet growth has occurred in the past four years.
- Apple's iOS and Google's Android operating systems dominate the mobile marketplace.
- The utility and profitability of apps caused an explosion in development and the emergence of the "app economy."
- The need to make online payments from mobile phones as simple and as safe as possible led the Internet tech companies to develop mobile online payment systems.
- As more people access the Internet from their mobile phones, advertisers are shifting their efforts away from print, TV, and PCs, and toward mobile devices.
- To retain control and capture as much advertising revenue as possible, Internet tech companies are building and buying their way into the online advertising exchanges and markets.

Despite this frenetic activity, traditionally the home TV has never been the main source of Internet access. For many years it was the PC, but with more than six billion mobile phone users around the world, the future gateway to the Internet—inside or outside the home—is going to be through the mobile device in the form of a smartphone or a tablet.

In fact, the advent of the mobile smartphone and tablet is arguably the single consumer trend that contributed most to the Big Data Big Bang. The fact that so many people worldwide now carry around what a decade ago would have been considered a super-computer opened up a global market for transferable mobile technologies and a race for faster, less expensive processors and new, universally appealing applications. The International Data Corporation (IDC) reports that vendors shipped a total of just over a billion smartphones worldwide in 2013 alone.[1] The United States (which in many ways lags behind other nations) has grown to more than 300 million users today. In New Zealand, there are now more mobile phones than there are people.[2] Worldwide, the number has grown to more than six billion subscriptions (which, according to a UN study, means that more people have mobile phones available to them than the 4.5 billion who have access to working toilets).[3]

As smartphones have grown in power and flexibility, they have begun to supplant the PC as the principal source of our interaction with the Internet, and 2010 marked the first year that the sale of smartphones and tablets was larger than the sale of PCs worldwide (see Figure 4.1): As of 2014, 6% of the global population owns a tablet, 20% owns a PC, and 22% owns smartphones.[4] In China, the world's largest mobile phone market, mobile Internet shoppers overtook PC shoppers in as far back as 2012.[5]

All this means that if the Internet tech companies want to control the gateways to the Internet for data collection and advertising to users, they need to be as integrated as possible with mobile phone technologies.

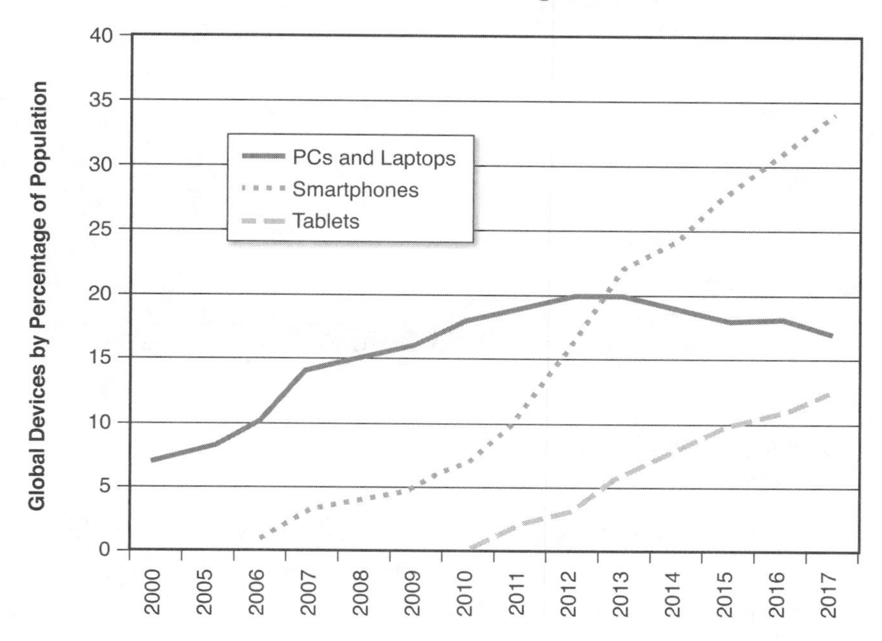

Figure 4.1 The Move Toward Mobile

Data Sources: IDC, Strategy Analytics, Gartner, World Bank, eMarketer

M-Commerce

The Apple iPad was the brainchild of Steve Jobs, and Apple rightly inherited the mantle of key innovator and controller of the smartphone through its iOS mobile operating system. But by 2005, as the leading Internet Big Data company, Google moved quickly to secure the Android operating system, which proved enormously valuable in ensuring Google a transition from the PC to the mobile market. Until now these two tech companies have dominated the mobile operating system market; together, Apple's iOS and Google's Android systems account for more than 90% of all smartphone operating systems sold in 2013 (see Figure 4.2).[6]

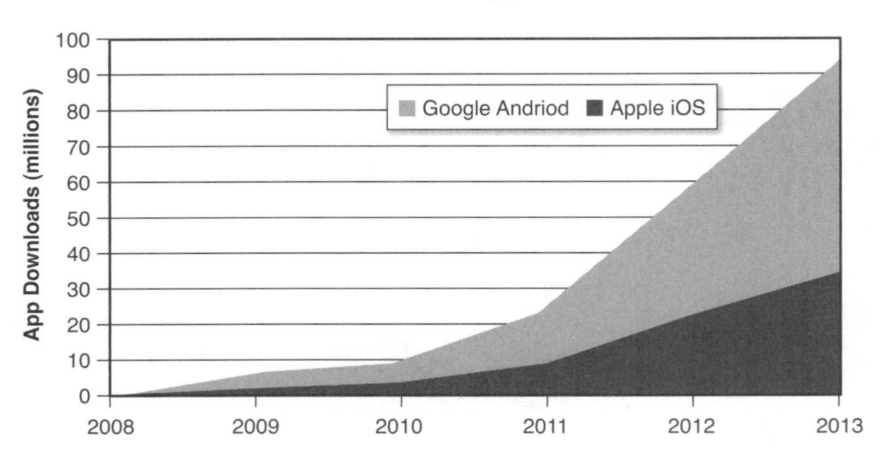

Figure 4.2 Dominating the Mobile Operation Systems Market
Data Sources: Entropy Economics, App Annie, and Tech-Thoughts

Originally thought of as a mobile computer with a primary interface with the iTunes store for downloading digital music, Apple's focus for the early versions of its iOS mobile operating system was to provide a direct and easy link to product offerings and supporting sales through its iTunes Store. But with Android, Google was more ambitious. Google could immediately see the potential for controlling the gateway to the Internet through services that worked well on a mobile device—Google Maps, a GPS locator system, and so on.

But Google's real insight came in appreciating the broader implications of m-commerce—online purchasing with mobile devices—which, according to Forrester Research, is expected to grow by about 30% each year, making up about a quarter of all retail purchases by 2016 (see Figure 4.3).[7]

In this arena, Google and Apple had a head start, because this global shift away from the PC proved initially to be difficult for groups like Microsoft and Facebook, neither of which had (until recently) a mobile offering (neither an operating system nor hardware). Even Microsoft was slow to realize the implications of the rise of the smartphone, only belatedly moving into the m-commerce space with its

Surface tablets and by buying Nokia's phone business. Microsoft also recently announced that Windows and its Office suite would now work on tablets or smartphones, including on iPads. The fact that, after years of restrictive bundling and ring-fencing, Microsoft has chosen to now run on Apple's iPad, shows how important the company views the mobile marketplace. In its attempt to catch up with Google and Apple, Microsoft is even giving its Windows mobile phone software away free, hoping to encourage app developers to include its platform in the future.

Amazon, too, is driving toward capturing a dedicated slice of the mobile Internet channel, taking the middle road between e-reader and tablet with its Kindle Fire, a mini-tablet version of its e-reader. Although it is not as powerful as the iPad or the Galaxy tablets, it is more affordable and is linked directly (and more exclusively) to Amazon's online store. Amazon also released its own smartphone, Amazon Fire, running on a customized Android operating system, in July 2014.

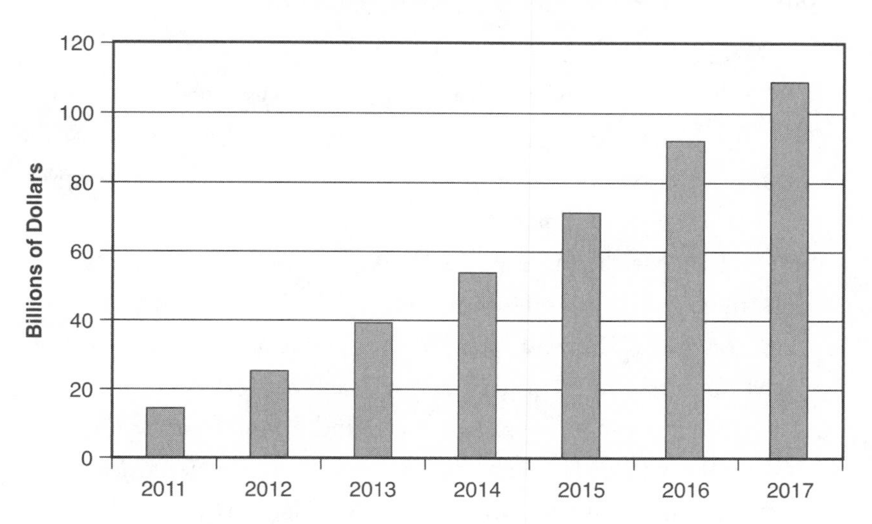

Figure 4.3 Moving Toward a Mobile Economy: the Shift to m-commerce

Data Source: eMarketer

But m-commerce doesn't begin and end with online ordering from a mobile device. Retailers and banks know that to make m-commerce work, they need to make it easy for users to pay with their smartphones. This is particularly true for the millions of small transactions every day around the world that account for apps or games—often initiated by teenagers—which could be impractical with credit cards.

The solution is to move away from credit cards and toward a platform where the smartphone becomes a digital wallet, able to download prepaid cash or even swipe directly from the user's savings account like a debit card. That's why many of the most powerful Internet tech companies—Amazon, Google, Facebook, Alibaba—have all focused on acquiring or building *mobile payment platforms* that allow users to pay in shops using their smartphone apps.

These online payment systems put the companies that run them in the unique position of being able to cut in between the customer and the normal payment route with banks and credit cards and act as a middleman in the transaction. It not only makes the transaction easier for the customer but it ensures that all the transaction data is captured directly by the Internet tech provider.

Accordingly, these types of online payment systems have become popular for groups large enough or savvy enough about the Internet to set up such a platform. They are springing up everywhere. Apple has said the development of the Touch ID fingerprint recognition system was in part because of its interest in mobile payments, and in September of 2014 announced its Apple Pay product. Amazon has Amazon Local Register, a mobile payment app, and a new card reader, announced in 2014, that allows small businesses to take payments through smartphones, Amazon Kindle, or tablets, and competes directly with offline card reader platforms like Square, Inuit's GoPayment, and PayPal. Microsoft announced partnerships that allow its Surface tablets to act as point-of-sale solutions. Vodafone has an e-money license for Europe, and Google has registered in the United Kingdom for the right to issue electronic money, including through Google Wallet, an app for Android that allows users to download prepaid credit. The Paym and Zapp systems released in 2014 in Britain, allow customers to use their mobile phone number to withdraw money directly from their bank accounts. Alibaba in China has Alipay Wallet, an offering it wants to market in the United States and Europe. Tencent has Tenpay, as part of WeChat. Facebook is experimenting with various offerings in the United Kingdom and Ireland, from electronic money that can be stored on the user's site to international money transfer services that can be done online via smartphones. In 2013, Facebook served as the online financial conduit for more than $2 billion of game-related transactions, for which it received fees that came to nearly 10% of its total revenues.[8]

The App Economy

Then, of course, there is the app economy. The application software, or "apps," available on these smartphones and tablets are what make these devices so versatile and attractive to young and old alike. In many ways, the app is the prodigy of Apple, which first understood the idea that these software applications would make the iPhone more attractive to customers and at the same time draw in unaligned, innovative developers to help create an entire smartphone "ecosystem" involving "killer apps," an online store, and eventually even cloud storage.[9] Typically coordinated by the owner of the hardware or the operating system in an *application hub* on the device (in Google's case, a Samsung Galaxy tablet would have application hubs sponsored by Google, Samsung, and Android), some apps are given away free, others are sold for a small fee, and typically the revenues are split between the application developer and the hub owners.

Apart from entertainment and games (known as *virtual goods*), these apps provide a multitude of services from banking and accounting to theater ticket purchasing and airline tracking. Some collect data on the state of the user's health (activity levels, blood pressure, temperature), or even provide security programs based on facial, iris, or fingerprint recognition.

There has been an explosion of these apps since 2010 (Gartner estimates that there were more than 100 billion downloaded in 2013).[10] Most Americans download between 30 and 40 apps on their smartphones or mobile devices, so the Internet tech companies want to have as many applications as possible on their platforms, and the more interesting the application the better (see Figure 4.4).

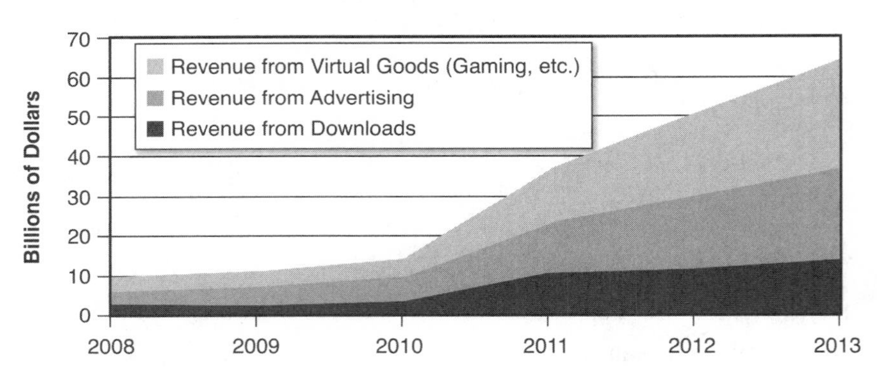

Figure 4.4 The Growth in App-Based Revenue
Data Source: Strategy Analytics

Setting aside their entertainment value, utility, or novelty, these apps serve as a way of collecting specific user data and delivering personalized online advertising. Along with the GPS location tracking inherent in the technology, the combined digital data flowing from these apps/phones relay information at all times about who we are, where we are, and what we are doing—including the purchases that we make online by credit card or through a mobile payment system. They also frequently upload the names from a user's address-book. And, of course, which apps we choose and use reveals a good deal to the developers and platform owners about our interests too.

The app economy is big business, and employment in the development of mobile apps in the United States now accounts for three quarters of a million people (up 40% from 2013).[11] Developer Economics estimates that one in every eight software developers worldwide in 2013 were involved with smartphone application design. According to AppNation, the combined value of paid apps, in-app advertising, and app-enabled purchases will reach $151 billion in the United States alone by 2017.[12]

From AppMen to AdMen

Although apps tend to make smartphones attractive to users, the advertising makes them attractive to the providers. As mobile phone sales have grown, there has been a huge shift away from traditional print and PC-read online advertising toward developing advertising for smartphones and tablets. The mobile device is particularly revolutionary when it comes to targeting personalized ads, because not only are mobile phones ubiquitous—found in the hands of shoppers and merchants and students all over the world at all times of the day and night—but their mobility means that a user's idle time is spent scrolling through pages, ripe for targeted advertising. In fact, a recent study by comScore found that the uptake in smartphones and tablets has almost doubled the amount of time an average user spends online over the past three years (see Figure 4.5).[13]

And unlike a PC or a TV, the smartphone is by its nature a personal device, almost invariably owned by a single, identifiable individual, something that provides advertisers with a tantalizing new level of customer intimacy. The combination of Big Data analytics and mobile advertising, runs the latest marketing riff, means being able to advertise to millions of potential customers on an intimate, one-to-one basis.

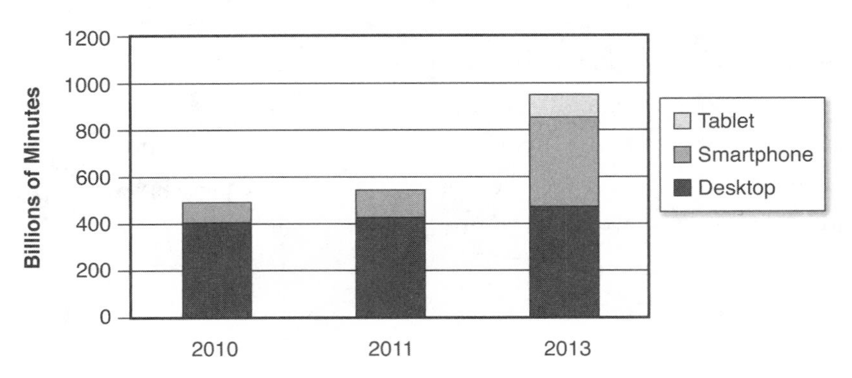

Figure 4.5 More Time Online Means More Opportunity for Advertising
Data Source: comScore

For the past several years, much of that digital advertising revenue has been captured by Google, which has dominated the digital advertising economy because of the revenues that come from its search advertising (see Figure 4.6). After all, that's how Google moved from being a small also-ran search engine in 1998 (listed that year at number 13) to the global powerhouse it is today.[14] Yahoo!, with a similar business model and similar technologies, was the company with the second largest online advertising revenues, only to be overtaken by Facebook in 2014.

But even these giants can't ring-fence their own digital advertising market anymore, as competition for domination of the Internet comes from all sides. Part of that competition comes from online retailers like Amazon (and in a more limited way, Apple), both of which are less dependent on advertising but no less interested in their users' personal data. Amazon has multiple opportunities to become one of the dominant owners of our Internet Gateway—not only through the home but by pursuing an integrated "anywhere, anytime" platform through the mobile market. Amazon just announced its own Fire smartphone, confirming not only Amazon's important role in the Internet infrastructure battles but bringing shopping apps that provide users with a pre-integrated, direct interface that reaches directly into Amazon.com. Building on the Fire TV set-top strategy and the Kindle e-reader, Amazon also announced Amazon Dash, a mobile bar-code scanning technology that features the same voice recognition capabilities of Fire-TV—making it possible for mobile users to order products directly through Amazon.com, including groceries through the delivery service AmazonFresh, which the company hopes will soon become an integral part of the Internet of Things (which we explore later in the chapter).

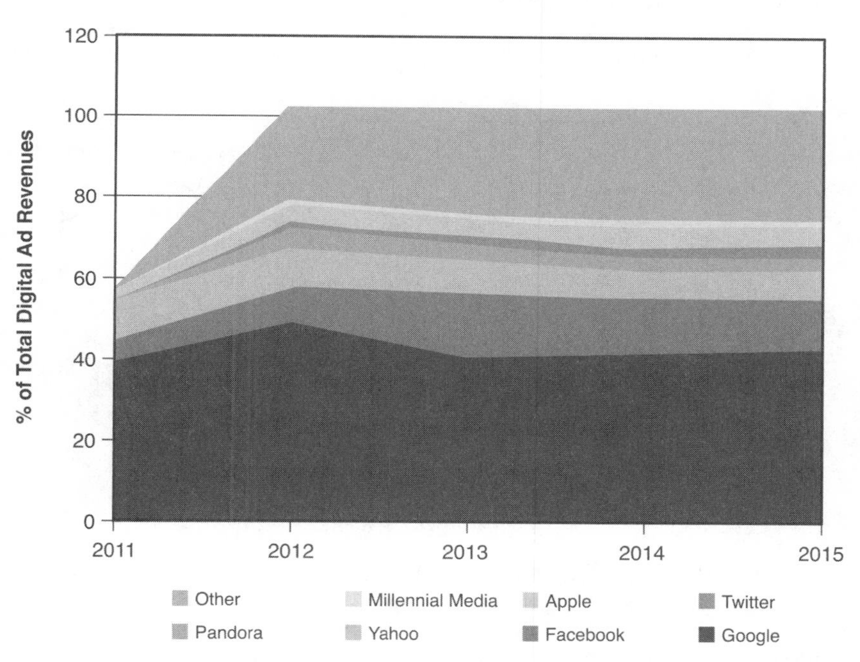

Figure 4.6 It's All About Advertising

Data Sources: Company filings and eMarketer

Apple, too, is still sitting on the fence, not certain whether to commit to a broader move away from a focus on its own products and get into the maelstrom of digital advertising business. The company has been waging a not-so-subtle war against Google's advertising revenues for some time. Apple made Microsoft's Bing its default search engine for Siri voice-activated software in 2013, and in 2014 announced that its own local search function, Spotlight, would strip out search-related ads and only deliver web results—thereby undermining Google's ad revenue (although Google still remains the default search engine for Safari, Apple's desktop and mobile web browser).[15] Apple has been dabbling with an in-house advertising exchange using the iAds platform for app developers since 2010. Whether the company decides to take the high road and find additional leverage in staying above the fray of the digital advertising and user data collection game is yet to be seen (see Figure 4.7).

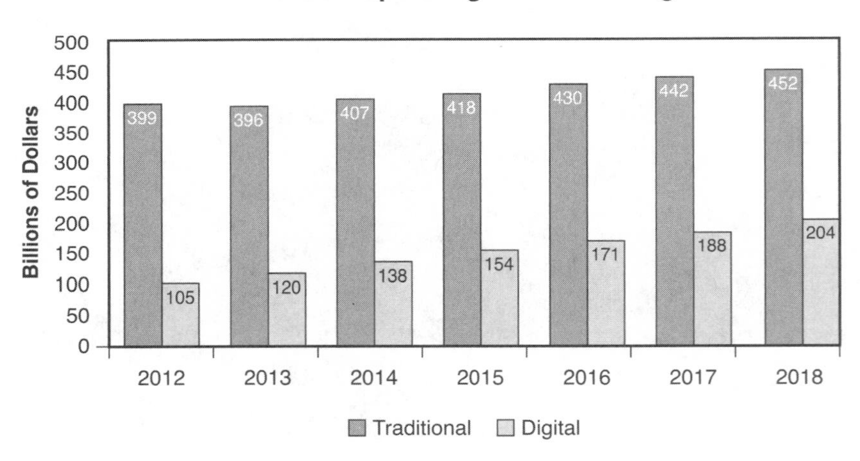

Figure 4.7 The Steady Growth of Digital Advertising
Data Source: eMarketer

But the lure of digital advertising is strong. According to a report from the Internet Advertising Bureau and PwC, Internet advertising surpassed cable television advertising in 2012 and topped spending on broadcast TV in the United States in 2013 (see Figure 4.8). Most of this growth is coming from the huge drive into mobile advertising, which in the United States more than doubled from $3.4bn in 2012 to $7.1bn in 2013.[16] Global mobile advertising, according to Gartner, is set to leap from $18 billion in 2014 to nearly $42 billion in just three years. In the United Kingdom, mobile advertising revenues are already greater than print and radio advertising revenues, and according to eMarketer, by 2016 mobile will overtake television to become the single largest advertising channel in the United Kingdom.[17]

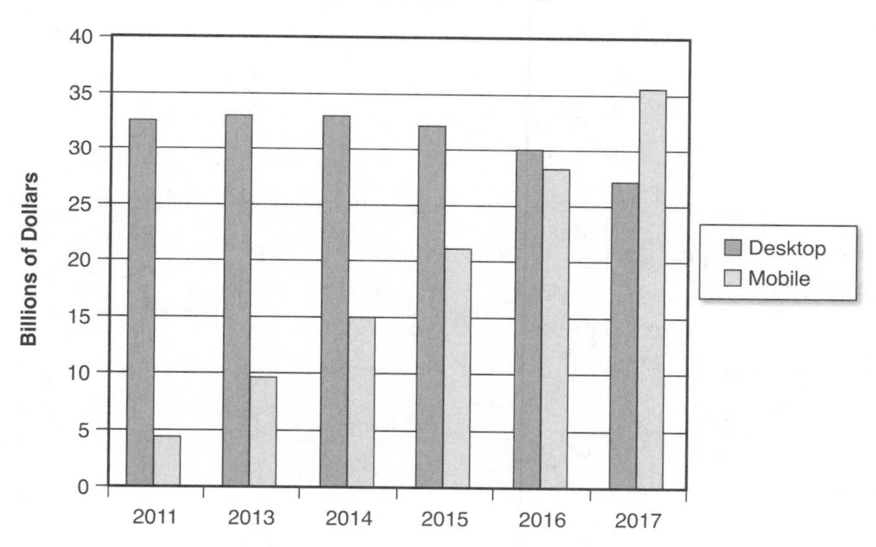

Figure 4.8 Digital Advertising Moves Away from the Desktop Computer

Data Source: eMarketer

Apps and Ads Everywhere

As we've seen, possibly the most remarkable effect of the mobile phone revolution has been a dramatic shift from PCs to smartphones and tablets as the primary interface between the public and the Internet. Around the world, users are turning to their smartphones to search the Internet, buy products online, watch YouTube or stream live or on-demand TV programs and films, and play games and music. These users want to use those same devices to control programs through their TV screen at home (if they even have a TV now), or while traveling to work, or in shops, airplanes, or trains. They also want to be able to use them as mobile wallets, as a safe and dependable alternative to credit cards and cash. And they want to be able to access work applications—documents, presentations, spreadsheets—while out of the office. Users want those same things, or variations of those things, in New York, Shanghai, Paris, and Lagos. In short, the new consumer expects Internet access through mobile devices, anywhere, anytime. As a result, everyone from individual software entrepreneurs to global Internet tech companies, hardware manufacturers, and Madison Avenue advertising firms, are all trying to get a piece of the mobile pie.

But to make money at the levels necessary to fund this type of expansion, and to satisfy the expectations of investors, requires the Internet tech companies to pull in advertising revenue—by the billions. To do that, they need to make digital advertising to customers easy and profitable. In short, they need to fulfill their side of the Faustian bargain to collect and use (or resell) vast amounts of customer data.

5

From Social Media to Digital Advertising Markets and Exchanges

Key Chapter Points

- As digital advertising shifts from PCs to mobile devices, electronic advertising markets and exchanges are proliferating.
- Real-time bidding (RTB) provides high-frequency online auctions for matching digital ads with targeted viewers.
- Both Facebook and Twitter capitalized on their large pools of user data and plunged into the electronic ad marketplace through strategic purchases.

To appreciate how Big Data is affecting this mobile device marketplace, it's necessary to appreciate how digital advertising evolved, because it is the application of Big Data principles and tools that allows millions of targeted users and millions of customized ads to be brought together onto a user's smartphone, which in turn funds the availability of the networks, hardware, and software that make the devices useful in the first place. In short, targeted adverting is a good part of what Big Data in the consumer context is all about.

The Evolution of Electronic Advertising

In the recent past, when a digital ad appeared, it was pretty much a blunt instrument, much the same in content and placement strategy as a print ad; with little targeting and no data captured on the potential customer's reaction. Usually it took the form of a banner ad placed on a web site where it was assumed that the subject area might seem attractive to a potential customer. Advertisers weren't able to target individuals, because they didn't have the personal user profile data that now exists, nor did they have any accurate way of tracking whether the ads were effective—or, for that matter, the reasons behind why they were or weren't.

Today things are different; tracking technology, and the acceptance of tracking technology, has come a long way in just the past few years. Now when a user visits a web site—*The New York Times*, Dictionary.com, Weather Underground—and particularly any web site that has a Twitter, Facebook, or Google+ button available to click on, he or she can be sure that those groups and often hundreds of other tracking groups are actively monitoring their visit. That tracking is usually anonymous, but if the user also has an account with any of those groups, or if the user views those web sites while logged on through Facebook or Google platforms, the user's web activities will be monitored and matched against his user ID, or device ID, which allows the companies that the user has registered with to record all the web sites he visits and all activities (pauses, clicks, page visits, scrolling, and so on) that occur while the user is online.

One of the reasons why mobile advertising has expanded so rapidly is the emergence of digital advertising markets and exchanges, because these platforms allow digital advertisements to be delivered instantly to a targeted user when the user visits a web site. This happens through sophisticated electronic matching systems known as real-time bidding (RTB). There are a growing number of these electronic advertising exchanges, auctions, and networks, the largest of which, like Millennial Media, InMobi, or AdMob (owned by Google), have databases that contain millions of user profiles and distribute many millions of ads matched against those profiles every hour. Although the technology is sophisticated, the idea is simple: Every time a user accesses a web site or opens an app, he or she creates an ad request, which is then sent to various RTB exchanges so that advertisers can bid in real-time for the opportunity to place a targeted ad on that page. And all this happens in a fraction of a second.

The Basics of Real-Time Bidding

By 2017, about one-third of digital advertising will involve high-frequency, computerized trading and matching of ads through a process known as *real-time bidding (RTB)*. Sometimes known as *programmatic instantaneous auctions* because they are determined by preset parameters and computer algorithms, RTB allows buyers of digital advertising to bid (automatically, through computers) for ads that are held in an Ad Exchange's inventory through an electronic auctioning process. The Ad Exchange functions much like an electronic stock market, using real-time software that conducts an auction in the milliseconds a web page takes to load. Publishers (who own web sites and are usually selling multiple spaces for ads on that site) may use *supply side platforms (SSPs)* to help them manage and sell their web site space during the auction process. Advertisers (who are buying space, known as *inventory*, on sites) use *demand side platforms (DSPs)* to set the buying parameters for their ads and to monitor how well those ads perform (are clicked on by device owners/viewers). These digital ads can come from a huge collection of ads available from ad networks, and these DSP technologies are capable of determining the value of an impression in real time (less than 100 milliseconds) and bidding on a space with a selected ad based on what is known about a viewer's history. Payment is calculated by the number of *impressions* (with an impression, or an "eyeball" being the number of times an ad is seen). With RTB, each time a web site opens, the site's ad spaces are filled with ads targeted for the viewer through a near-instantaneous auction that ensures that each impression is sold for the highest possible price. This type of real-time time bidding is making headway against the *static auction*, where publishers sell bundles of impressions (typically 1,000 at a time) directly to ad networks.

Not content to stop there, the more sophisticated systems today also track the same user on multiple platforms and multiple devices—so they follow the user from Google to Twitter to Facebook, and from the user's mobile to their PC and to their e-reader. This is the Holy Grail of digital advertising, because this type of multichannel monitoring greatly increases the level of information granularity that keeps pouring in, 24 hours a day, to Big Data profile databases.

So what does digital advertising have to do with social media or instant messaging?

The answer is, much more than we realized, because with the purchase of WhatsApp and the announcement of the Facebook Audience Network (FAN), Facebook made a giant leap forward toward combining this type of real-time bidding with its vast inventory of user profiles. Even more surprising, and a reflection of the growing rivalry between them, with the purchase of MoPub, Twitter is moving quickly down the same path. In terms of Big Data and our personal data, that rivalry, and their recent moves, may turn out to be very important.

The Social Media and Messaging Rivalry for Digital Advertising Revenue

It may seem curious that competition among the search engine groups (Google, Yahoo!) and online retailers (Apple, Amazon) would come in the form of the third revolutionary Consumer Internet trend: mobile messaging and social media. But nothing illustrates the powerful nature of Big Data on the personal data side more than the rise of Facebook and Twitter. Together, the two groups have become a phenomenon in themselves, making about $60 billion each year just selling advertising space on their sites.[1] And their early success wasn't just with individual users. With an average outlay of almost $19 million a year for social media and related marketing, some 70% of Fortune 500 companies have a Facebook page (and 77% have a Twitter account).[2] That places these two companies at the heart of users' daily lives, both at work and at home.

In 2013, Facebook celebrated its tenth anniversary. Its origins are recounted in the film "The Social Network"—how the company began at Harvard as a site for sharing gossip and student details, realized through the ambition and acrimony of Mark Zuckerberg and his erstwhile classmates. Today Facebook has more than 1.2 billion users worldwide, many of them from an older generation who may never before have bothered to log onto the Internet, but who find themselves slavishly addicted to their Facebook page. It is truly an all-ages phenomenon.

Like the search engines and online retailers, Facebook also sees its future success as dependent upon being able to capture massive amounts of personal data through a variety of sources, feeding the display ads that go out to its billion (plus) users and producing advertising revenues worth an estimated $23 billion by 2017.[3] Facebook is now the world's second largest digital advertising platform, still behind Google, but having overtaken Yahoo! in 2014.[4]

Again, as part of the Faustian bargain, while Facebook users are thinking about shared photos and messaging, Facebook executives are thinking about Big Data—that is, collecting personal data and selling mobile advertising. And to get people all over the world to voluntarily give them that personal data, what better than a site that is easy, helpful, and enjoyable: an inviting wall for posting and sharing photos, thoughts, likes, and dislikes; and a way of communicating (either through messaging or e-mail). Add to that other tantalizing offerings such as forums and blogs, music sharing, instant messaging, and voice-over Internet Protocol (VoIP). Do all that right, and people by the hundreds of millions will gladly tell you all about themselves and give you access to their personal messages.

What Is VoIP?

VoIP, or *Voice over Internet Protocol,* is the technology that allows analog audio (phone calls) to be converted into digital data and carried over the Internet. Sometimes called IP telephony, the technology means that phone calls can be made (free, in the same way that e-mails are free) over the Internet data network, rather than through the telephone company's network. Skype is a well-known example.

This "social media" approach made Facebook uniquely rich in personal customer information, because unlike search engines or online stores, Facebook invites a much more intimate level of data: photos, categories of interest, likes and dislikes, friends, and influencers. As early as 2011, Facebook's Timeline offering invited users to provide a full chronicle of their life in photos, addresses, and memorabilia. It was a masterpiece in data collection. For inducing people to voluntarily give up their personal data, Facebook still is unrivaled.

But how to hold on to these users in a highly competitive world? With a market valuation of $175 billion, and as the first to think up the idea of social media, Facebook had it good for a long time, but maintaining that lead through pure social networking may not be all that easy.

Facebook's first challenge is straightforward competition. Once the business model became obvious, competitors rushed to emulate it with social media platforms of their own. Google came out with Buzz in 2010, which struggled and was replaced by GooglePlus. Microsoft came out with Yammer. Salesforce came out with Chatter. There was also Meme and Tibbr and SocialCast. Alibaba created a similar system in China. Naver has emerged strongly in South Korea. And then there are the "secret" social networks, where users can find greater anonymity: Truth, YikYak, Secret, or Whisper, which, despite their exclusivity, still openly admit that they track their users.[5] Large companies like DHL, PwC, and Vodaphone created their own more specialized and focused social media platforms.

Facebook is also challenged by the fact that social media as an offering has begun to mature—and possibly grow a bit stale. For several years, the company has feared that as its user base grows older, these adults will be less interested in the attractions of social media. Those fears were confirmed in a 2013 survey that found that one-third of users said that they would be using Facebook less in five years.[6] That means that Facebook needs a way to retain its current 1.2 billion users, to appeal to adults throughout all phases of their lives, and to capture the hearts and minds of upcoming teenagers in the future. These teenagers want to be heard and to communicate in a simple way, and to be able to exchange small video clips and photos. And that, these days, means mobile messaging.

Instant messaging is an area that has exploded because it provides a less expensive and easier alternative for young users on mobile phones. Even so, it is still estimated to be worth more than $300 billion a year.[7] More to the point, Big Data experts like Facebook, Naver, and Alibaba know that if they don't "own" the online messaging market, they risk ceding the broader social media and network market to those who do. After all, most messaging groups already offer some level of photo and video sharing. Twitter and Snapchat pretty much provide the Facebook platform in a small package. Chat apps like Kik, WhatsApp, Line, and GroupMe are biting at their heels, threatening to create a separate Internet just for messaging. The last thing Facebook wants is to go the way of Myspace or Friendster.

Mobile Messaging

SMS, or *short message service*, is what we usually just call *texting*. These text messages are limited to 160 characters and can be completed over the fixed line telephone networks, over the Internet, or through mobile networks. Most commonly, SMS is used these days to describe mobile-to-mobile texting, which is done through the mobile phone network's service.

MMS stands for *multimedia messaging service*, which is like SMS, but also allows the user to send attachments to the message (photos, audio, video, and so on).

OTT, or *over-the-top* content, describes the wide variety of audio or video media that today is delivered over the Internet to laptops, game consoles, Smart TVs, or mobile devices from a third-party (Hulu, Netflix, myTV, WhereverTV, and so on), leaving the Internet service provider (ISP) to provide these third parties with a "free ride" to deliver competing content over its network service. Similarly, *OTT messaging* describes instant messaging services provided over the Internet by a third party (such as WhatsApp, WeChat, iMessage, LINE, and so on) usually through applications on mobile devices (which means users can avoid paying mobile network operator fees).

It's true that messaging, chat apps, and microblogs are not the money spinners that a full-fledged social media offering is because they don't have the richness to gather substantial amounts of personal data. But these groups are still highly attractive to Big Data companies, because they attract the young, entice users to constantly monitor their phone, have photo and video capabilities that can support advertising, and provide access to a lot of data for message monitoring and social media "scraping."

But possibly the most difficult challenge Facebook faced until now is the shift from PC to mobile. With its rich and layered web site, Facebook was a core platform designed to work on a PC with a large screen and a keyboard—not with mobile users on a bus or in the park.

But we now live in a mobile device economy where the interface has to be just larger than the palm of your hand. That calls for different tactics.

Aware of the key functionality needed to dominate the mobile advertising market—ties to mobile devices, content and entertainment apps, payment systems, and copious amounts of user data—Facebook moved quickly to build mobile apps compatible with both the iOS and Android operating systems. It made an unsuccessful $3 billion run on Snapchat, and in 2012 bought Instagram, built for mobile users, for $1 billion, bringing Facebook 200 million more users worldwide.[8] It also secured an additional 450 million users (with an estimated million more joining each day) with WhatsApp, for $19 billion, giving them the capability of servicing nearly as many messages as now flow over all the world's mobile texting systems combined.[9] The move allowed Facebook to make huge inroads into mobile communications and advertising: It secured the attractive core focus of photo sharing with Instagram, acquired a strong market in instant messaging through WhatsApp, and provided millions of users with a mobile device e-mail equivalent of Google's Gmail, on which Facebook can base its e-mail and personal message monitoring as a basis for expanding mobile advertising.

These strategic buys place Facebook in a more dominant role in global communications than any traditional cable or satellite Internet providers. In fact, if the company pulls it off over the next few years, the approach may make conventional telecom and cable giants like Comcast and Verizon seem almost parochial. With WhatsApp, Facebook can offer low-cost, simple, fast messaging and virtually free phone calls to nearly half a billion current users worldwide—over a data network owned by Facebook that rides free on the very cables supplied by the traditional telecoms groups.

Some estimate that this online messaging platform, including VoIP, could potentially pull nearly $400 billion worth of revenues away from the conventional telecoms sector by 2018.[10] Much more powerful than Skype, Facebook could in five years be the international phone company for the world, making it the global Internet gatekeeper and putting it at the heart of the Big Data-industrial complex.

Facebook is also beginning to dominate the customer messaging and advertising market among small businesses (a group long dominated by Google) by offering small and medium-sized enterprises (SMEs) a simple, easy communication platform—and, once again, by allowing these small companies to tap into Facebook's massive database of customer data. Facebook now offers SMEs the opportunity to upload their customer contact files to Facebook and to advertise directly on their existing customers' (and their customers' friends') Facebook pages. That allows small companies to customize ads to their local clients and contacts, and also contributes to Facebook's ever-growing database of customer profiles (see Figure 5.1).

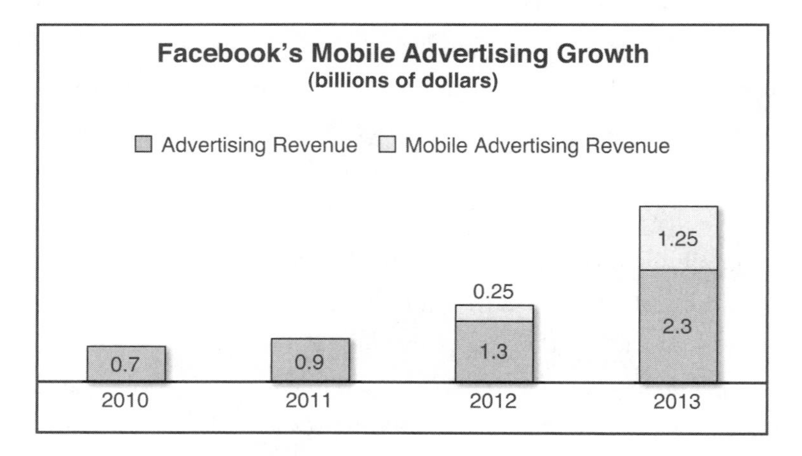

Figure 5.1 Paying Off: Facebook's Rising Advertising Revenues
Data Sources: Bloomberg

Perhaps even more than Google, Facebook's business model was based on a two-phase proposition: first, subsist on investor money for a few years while expanding its user base and collecting as much personal and aggregated user data as possible. Second, become a highly-paid conduit between advertisers and those users.

Now comes the pay-off, and it's working. Facebook is now second only to Google in the US digital advertising market, the global digital advertising market, and the global mobile advertising market.[11] And that global mobile market is where Facebook sees the real opportunity: Every day more than 750 million people worldwide (nearly 80% of Facebook users) log onto their Facebook (or Facebook-owned) services through their mobile devices. And with worldwide ad spending growing at a rate of 90% a year, that means that in the first quarter of 2014 alone, Facebook's global ad revenue reached $1.33 billion—just from advertising on mobile devices.[12] The company has pulled together a combination of deep data analytics, large data sets, and a variety of data sources—the perfect Big Data combination.

But the Facebook site itself can only support so much advertising before it becomes overwhelming to users. So what to do with all that time-sensitive, deeply personal user data if Facebook has reached capacity for advertising on its own site?

The answer is to go into the digital advertising sales business.

For several years, Facebook has been toying with the idea of a mobile ad network that would allow it to leverage its huge data sets with a broader group of advertisers, without cluttering up and diminishing the appeal of its own Facebook site with too many ads. By late 2013, they began experimenting with the idea of allowing advertisers and app developers to tap into Facebook's rich pool of users' personal data to develop advertising through apps not directly associated with Facebook itself—in short, Facebook wanted to sell its users' data on a digital advertising marketplace. The company knew it had a real advantage over other mobile ad markets (such as InMobi and AdMob, for example), which have more limited, often only "inferred" data about users. Even Millennial Media, the largest digital advertising unified audience platform, which boasts more than 440 million mobile users worldwide and an audience database of 131 million profiles (bought from more than 20 third-party data providers), seems limited in comparison.[13] Facebook has personal client data on 1.2

billion people around the world that has been uniquely authenticated directly by the users themselves on everything from their tastes in clothes, music, and film, to employment and personal history.

On the other hand, as valuable as that user data is, there could be a real drawback to releasing it in other than anonymized or aggregated form to external groups—something far less profitable on the digital ad market than more personalized profiles. Not only would Facebook dilute its own market by releasing such detailed personal data, but there is a good chance that it might see a user revolt as customers realized the data they willingly gave to Facebook, and most likely was to some degree protected by Facebook's privacy tools and rules, was now being sold on to anyone who would pay for it.

What Is Frequency Capping?

Hoping to avoid "banner burnout," in digital advertising *frequency capping* is used to restrict (cap) the number of times a particular advertisement is shown to a user. This is done by dropping a unique ID cookie on the viewer's computer to monitor the "impressions" or number of times (or sometimes, the length of time) that a particular advertisement has appeared. It may be a welcome relief to the annoyed viewer not to have to see a repeating ad, but the cookies themselves can be (and often are) used not only to count the number of times that a user views an ad, but to then track the viewer's ongoing Internet activity until the user cleanses the browser.

The solution Facebook came up with was a win-win for both sides; it simply reversed the flow of data. Instead of selling user data to advertisers, Facebook simply directs advertising to users. This arrangement allows Facebook to provide the advertisers with live "targets" based on Facebook's personal profile data, but at the same time allows Facebook to retain control of the actual targeting process, and most importantly, its own user data. Clients send their customized ads to Facebook, which then forwards those ads to the appropriate users on both the users' Facebook page and, taking advantage of mobile apps, on many hundreds of non-Facebook advertising opportunities/sites.

To this end, in 2014 Facebook announced the Facebook Audience Network (FAN), which provides that service directly to app developers and advertisers as a one-stop-shop mobile advertising platform, so that they can "re-target" users based on the personal and behavioral information that those users have given to Facebook over the years.

FAN means that Facebook maintains ownership and confidentiality of users' personal data, while at the same time satisfying clients by placing well-targeted ads. The investment community loves it because it reassured investors of their initial endorsement of Facebook as a Big Data money maker. Application developers love it because it helps them earn advertising profits, and advertisers love it because they can target their ads more effectively. And the advertisers themselves can use FAN's Big Data analytical tools to assess their progress by tracking specific sales-related activities to specific ads for specific clients. It is Consumer Big Data at its most effective.

What Is Re-Targeting?

Re-targeting (sometimes called *behavioral remarketing*) is a way of monitoring an online user's Internet buying interests and then, if the user doesn't buy a product, advertising that product, or similar products, on other web sites that the user accesses as he or she continues their Internet activities. Again, the tracking and monitoring mechanism requires a tracker cookie to be dropped on a viewer's computer when they first access a web site. If no purchase is made, the cookie continues to follow the user through other sites, and for those companies enrolled in the same ad network, displays ads for the previously viewed brand or product on each website the user visits. Re-targeting can be particularly frustrating around Christmas, when everyone else in the family can infer what presents have been considered by monitoring the banner ads that appear on the family computer.

But Facebook is not alone in moving toward this new role as a customer data intermediary and digital advertising hub.

Valued at $25 billion at the time of its IPO in November 2013, Twitter is another surprise of the Big Data era. It has become one of the most valuable companies in the world, even though it has few physical assets, has never made a profit, and is only making around $500 million in revenue. Investors are willing to bet, though, that the company will come out ahead in the race to capitalize on user data.[14] One of the ways that Twitter intends to do that is through the purchase of MoPub Marketplace, the mobile advertising exchange that Twitter bought in 2013. The MoPub Marketplace monitors more than one billion unique mobile devices through Android and iOS applications all over the world, for a total of nearly 130 billion electronic advertising requests each year. That's a lot of ad requests.[15] In 2014, 80 percent of Twitter's ad revenue came from mobile, which explains why in 2014 they announced the purchase, for around $100 million, of TapCommerce, a platform that allows for retargeting advertising on mobile devices.[16]

But Twitter has never had the Big Data searching or analytics power of a Google, an Amazon or a Facebook, and to provide the user profiles from its own data, it had to buy Gnip, a Big Data analytics firm (see Chapter 9, "Big Data Technologies") to help sort through its trillions of Tweets looking for meaningful commercial trends. And although posting Tweets of 140 characters (even if there are more than 500 million of them from around the world every day)[17] hardly compares with the intimate and comprehensive profiles Facebook has access to, Twitter has been successful in providing a mobile advertising platform with enormous scale, combining the three key features of Big Data: large data sets, a variety of sources, and sophisticated analytics.

Microsoft, too, has moved toward digital advertising, paying $6.3 billion for the online advertising group aQuantive in 2007. But Microsoft has its roots in software, and without any real mechanism for vacuuming-up user data, it had little leverage among the pure-play ad exchanges. They took an ignominious $6.2 billion write-down on the company just five years later in 2012. And the great irony is that aQuantive was purchased from Microsoft by Facebook in 2013 for a small, undisclosed sum, and added to the social media giant's growing set of digital advertising exchange offerings.[18]

Still, Microsoft's instinct might have been right, even if their timing was wrong. The problem is, for all its talents and success, Microsoft is a software developer and not really a Big Data player. It has never really sought to collect personal data, has no real platform (other than Bing) for leveraging digital advertising, and has few of the required elements yet that Google, Facebook, or Amazon have built or purchased to dominate the Internet gateways. But with the 2014 purchase of Nokia's device business and the formation of Microsoft Mobile, the once irrepressible software giant has signaled a strategic change in direction away from just software and toward a transformation into a mobile devices and services company. That may not be as easy as just buying its way in with mobile hardware though, because to make that transition, Microsoft needs not only to fight the urge to focus on its still lucrative Windows software market, but also to summon both the brains and the stomach to get into the middle of Big Data collection and digital advertising.

6

The Global Battle for the Consumer Internet

Key Chapter Points

- By every measure (computers, Internet use, mobile and smartphone sales, and so on), the global Consumer Internet is expanding rapidly.
- US and European companies persist in maintaining a presence in China, despite what is known as "The Great Firewall of China."
- Chinese Internet tech companies are equally interested in competing in US and EU markets.
- This global competition, although occasionally fractious, may be enhancing innovation and growth in the Big Data technology market.

Before we leave the Consumer Internet, it is important to realize that although we tend to think of all this happening in the United States and Western Europe, the same trends are occurring worldwide. If the US Defense Department was responsible for the Internet and Silicon Valley was the first to exploit it, that exclusivity is waning. And despite their early advantage, Western Internet companies are finding that politics, competition, and the NSA are beginning to make their efforts to expand overseas more difficult, just at the point where the opportunity is at its greatest.

The Global Internet Explosion

The expansion of Big Data and the digital economy globally can be measured in various ways, and one of those ways is to look at the number of computers per capita around the world. Computers have become part of commerce, industry, and personal life nearly everywhere, and more than almost any other commodity, they are international in their manufacture and sale (see Figure 6.1). Apple, HP, Lenovo, Dell, Acer, Toshiba, IBM, and Fujitsu all are manufactured and sold internationally. And as the take-up of computing has expanded, the relative size of the US and Western European market has decreased, making emerging markets the obvious target for growth. This trend is obvious if we look back again to the early 1990s when nearly half of all computers were in America. By 2000, that number was down to just over a third. And with an international growth rate double of that in the United States, by 2015 the United States may have as little as 15% of the global inventory of computers.[1]

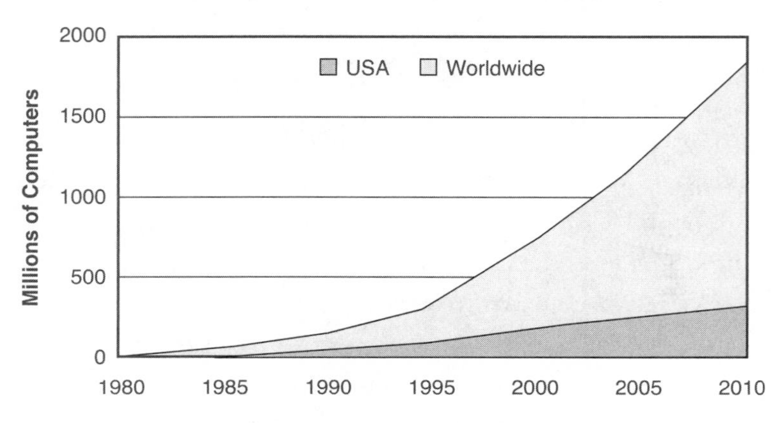

Figure 6.1 Thirty Years of Computer Growth

Data Source: eTForecasts

Internet figures themselves are equally revealing, because they too, indicate that the highest growth areas are in developing countries (see Figure 6.2).

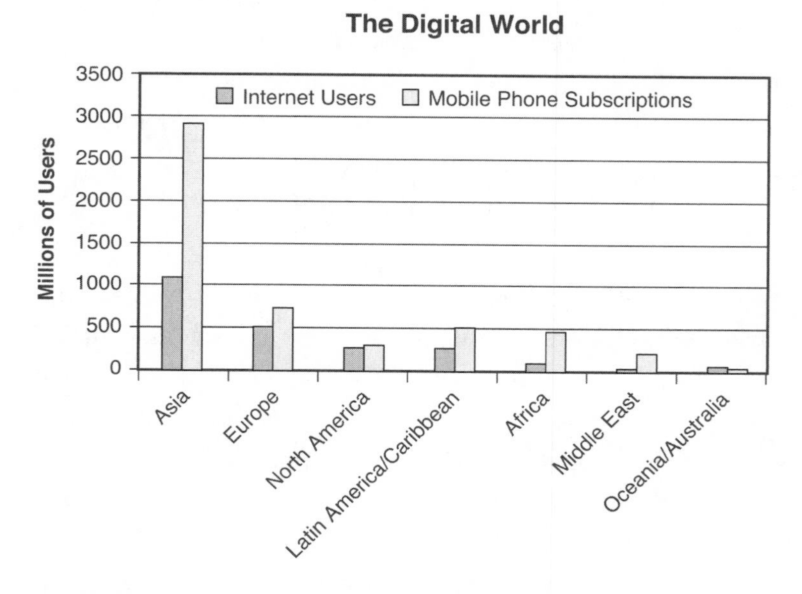

Figure 6.2 Worldwide Internet and Mobile Phone Usage
Data Sources: Internet World Stats and eMarketer

This pattern of growth is equally true with smartphones and mobile devices, which revolutionized telecommunications and messaging, allowing inexpensive, universal communication through phone calls, texting, and e-mails. More affordable than a PC, low-cost mobile devices are invaluable not only for developed economies but especially for users in less-developed nations, who only a decade ago, struggled with poor landline infrastructures and often had almost no access to a telephone at all. A uniquely democratizing technology, the cell phone has become omnipresent, among rich and poor, found in town and country, with young and old, all around the world.

Among mobile operating systems, as we've seen, Google's Android, with its ties to Samsung, is particularly popular globally, and in a reflection of the growing importance of the emerging economies, it is estimated that by 2017, more than 75% of Android's sales will come from emerging markets.[2]

In fact, with more than 400 million viewers already, China has a much larger market for online streaming video and television than the United States and has also been building a superfast 4G superstructure throughout the nation. Based in Guangdong, Huawei, the largest telecommunications equipment maker in the world, is already working on next generation 5G technology, promising speeds up to 100 times faster than the current 4G framework by 2018.[3]

Competition is particularly strong when it comes to social media and messaging. South Korea's Naver, originally a group within Samsung, has a multipurpose Internet site that includes games, online shopping, video, and e-books, as well as a search engine that has fended off Google, retaining nearly 80% of the South Korean market. In 2010, Naver also bought KakaoTalk, which provides photo cataloging and a wide variety of virtual goods from games to e-books and brings an additional 60 million users (sending an estimated 3.5 billion messages every day).[4] Line, in Japan, promotes itself as the "Facebook of Asia." WeChat, owned by China's Tencent, is strong not only in China but also in expanding markets such as Mexico and India."[5] The list goes on.

Not all these emerging-country Internet tech companies are as reliant on digital advertising as their equivalents in the United States. Most rely more on sales of virtual goods like games and apps and, puzzling to many in the West, continue to do a brisk trade in the highly popular cartoons and cute animal emoticons—known in Asian markets as "stickers"—which are purchased almost like a stamp to be included when sending e-mails. When combined, these groups account for hundreds of millions of users worldwide, and with their own version of Big Data and Internet technologies, they also provide a growing level of competition to the traditional Western internet tech groups.

In fact, China has overtaken the United States both in terms of the sale of smartphones and in e-commerce, and will soon become the world's largest m-commerce arena, as many millions of Chinese move directly from no phone to mobile phone, omitting the traditional landline. In 2013, 81% of Chinese Internet users accessed the Internet using a mobile device, and online sales in China are expected to expand from $370 billion in 2014 to $670 by 2018.[6] And just like American, European, Japanese, and South Korean companies, Chinese Internet giants are setting their sights on cashing in on the global smartphone revolution.

East Meets West

Relations between all these competitors and countries are not always cordial, and every nation still retains its champions. But as with the Western Internet tech companies, there is increasing competition between those national champions themselves.

Since YouTube is banned in China, Tudou, owned by Youku, the Chinese equivalent, has targeted younger viewers with streaming content from around the world, and its viewership has grown from 100 million in 2012 to 300 million in just one year.[7] This rapidly growing viewership—and the advertising and sticker revenues that come with it—has not gone unnoticed by China's other large Internet and media conglomerates. In a mirror image of the struggle for control of the Internet going on in America, Sohu, a subsidiary of Baidu, the largest search engine in China with a market share of nearly 70%, and Tencent, the hugely successful social networking and gaming conglomerate, are both vying for China's massive viewership with programming that provides younger users with an alternative to state-controlled television. Tencent recently bought WeChat, a competitor with Twitter, which has more than 600 million users, and 100 million of those are outside China.[8] In fact, although it's not a perfect comparison,

Tencent, with its combined social networking and gaming revenue, is larger and more profitable than Facebook; in 2013 reporting $2.5bn in profits (on $9.9bn revenue) against $1.5bn in profits (on $7.9bn revenue) for Facebook.[9]

Chinese corporate protectionism, political censorship, and the complexity of the Chinese language has meant that the Western Internet giants—Google, Facebook, Amazon, and Twitter—have only been able to compete in a limited way within Chinese markets over the past decade. But in many ways, ironically, that resulted in a sort of hybrid vigor in which potential global rivals to the Western Internet giants have arisen with different systems and approaches. Ultimately, this may be a valuable thing in terms of innovation.

The Great Firewall of China

Since forming the State Internet Information Office in 2011, the government of the People's Republic of China has strengthened its Internet censorship capabilities in what is often called "the Great Firewall of China." The main purpose of the censorship is to restrict the availability of Internet sites that are thought likely to contribute to social or political instability, and the Chinese government has from time to time banned or blocked access to many of the prominent Western search engines, social networking sites, content providers, and Internet communications tools, including Google, Yahoo!, Facebook, YouTube, Twitter, Amazon Japan, Netflix, Wikipedia, and even the *New York Times*.

Still, despite restrictions and firewalls, western companies are determined to maintain a foothold in China. As a testament to the power of the Internet, although officially banned there, GlobalWeb Index's Social Platforms Report suggests that there were more active Twitter users in China in 2012 (35.5 million) than were actively tweeting in the United States (23 million). In fact, by 2015, despite the ban, almost one-third of Twitter users are expected to be in Asia (compared with 24% in the US and 17% in the EU). India and Indonesia are both poised to overtake the United Kingdom (see Figure 6.3) to become the third and fourth largest Twitter populations, respectively, this year.[10]

Similarly, although also officially blocked there, China has become Facebook's largest market even though it only manages to maintain 6% market share. Even Google, after withdrawing in 2010 over censorship issues, was back by 2012, reflecting its concern at missing out on the opportunity in a nation with more than twice the number of Internet users as the United States. Google is now the third largest search engine in China after Baidu and Soso.[11]

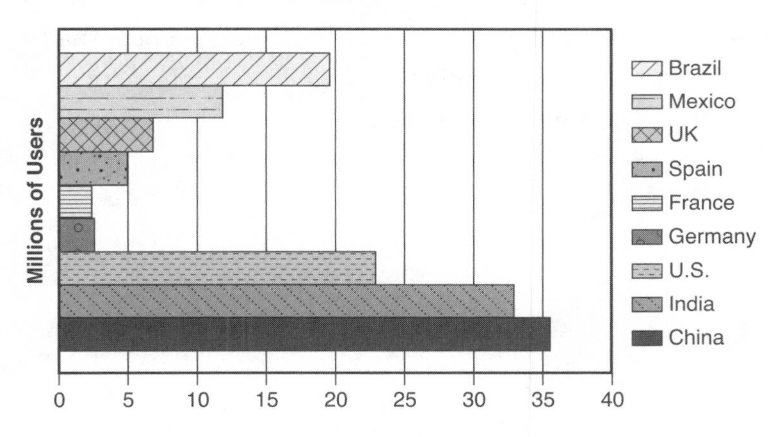

Figure 6.3 The Growth of Twitter Around the World
Data Source: eMarketer

There is every indication that this global integration and competition will continue, as US and European firms compete with Japanese, South Korean, Indian, and Chinese firms—all for an ever-expanding global market. In fact, in terms of global users, after Facebook and Google+, Chinese firms already make up three of the top five largest social networking groups—with Qzone (owned by Tencent) coming in third with nearly 20% of all global users.[12]

More remarkably, the Chinese government, realizing the potential for global reach, lifted its long-running ban on initial public offering (IPO) listings for Chinese companies—an extraordinary thing for what is still ostensibly a communist (anti-capitalist) regime. Groups like Alibaba, China's e-commerce equivalent of Amazon, already account for around 80% of all e-commerce in China. Alibaba, in turn, is partly owned (a 22% to 24% stake) by Yahoo! and has spent more than $200 million on a stake in Tango, an American messaging app, to boost its value in preparation for an IPO in New York in September 2014.

And Alibaba isn't the only Chinese group that wants to be listed on the Nasdaq. Sina Weibo, the Chinese equivalent of Twitter, announced its intention to file as an IPO, and both Tencent, the massive social networking and gaming group, and Baidu, China's search engine and Internet portal, are buying up other companies worldwide in preparation for a future clash of titans.[13]

7

The Industrial Internet and the Internet of Things

Key Chapter Points

- Self-sensing and performance-reporting machinery are creating efficiencies throughout the global supply chain in what is becoming known as the Industrial Internet.
- These "smart parts" will also be central to the monitoring and control aspects of the Internet of Things in our houses, our cars, and even in the clothes we wear in the future.
- The Internet tech companies intend to be the leaders in providing the coordinating software that ties together all this digital data.
- The combined Industrial Internet and Internet of Things will produce huge amounts of mostly structured data, but that data will be revealing about how users live their lives.

Although the Consumer Internet is certainly the largest contributor to the explosion of digital data occurring around the world today, there is a corollary of this Big Data movement occurring in the industrial workplace, where "make-and-move" companies are increasingly employing self-sensing and self-reporting networked devices and machinery performance sensors at the system, component, and part level. In what is called the *Industrial Internet*, these new data-gathering technologies are beginning to fulfill the long-held promise of mechatronics (the combination of mechanical and electrical engineering, computing, and communications) to produce efficiency and productivity improvements throughout global supply chains. This machine-produced digital data is an important part of the Big Data Big Bang.

Smart Parts and the Industrial Internet

The idea of self-sensing and performance-reporting machines has been a goal of modern manufacturing for years, but only recently has industry been able to turn to the Internet and Big Data storage and analytics to capitalize on the potential of these intelligent components. And by intelligent, I mean virtually any type of component or system that can identify and report on itself in a digital format. That can mean anything from a performance-monitoring computer to an on-off-registering valve in a remote pipeline.

Today these intelligent components can monitor and report on their status (temperature, pressure, rotational speed, vibration, fill levels, and so on), and convey that data instantly from machine-to-machine to make necessary performance or safety corrections, and to convey a real-time performance report to expert technicians anywhere in the world. The same digital communication system (which may include satellite, GPS, and Wi-Fi connected to mobile devices) can also be used to alter those components and systems remotely (to adjust the temperature, to close a valve, or to place an order for repair or new parts).

This type of self-sensing technology and the communication possibilities afforded by the Internet have the potential to revolutionize supply chains, especially if that digital data (and as these components may be reporting at intervals of many times every second, there is a huge amount of digital data being produced) can be captured, stored, and analyzed for diagnostics, pattern recognition, and even reliability and failure predictions.

It is not only self-reporting machinery that is revolutionizing the Industrial Internet. Scanning and tracking technologies promise to greatly improve on the amount of data that accompanies a product from production through consumption. Since 1974 and early days of modern computing, product identity has been tied to the Universal Product Code (UPC), a barcode limited to basic information (product identification and pricing), which had to be read directly with an optical scanner. But today's radio-frequency identification tags (RFID) have the capacity for sophisticated sensing and reporting technologies at the item level, not only relaying information about the product or container itself, but also about where that product has been and when it was there (tracking), the temperature and humidity of the environment in route (quality assurance), and whether the product was tampered with or opened (safety and security).

These RFID tags can then be read using Near Field Communication (NFC), or be monitored remotely via Wi-Fi and the Internet by the company or the customer from almost anywhere in the world. And as the power of these RFID tags has increased, their cost has dropped dramatically—by 80% since 2010. A typical RFID tag may cost as little as 10 cents today.[1]

Near Field Communication (NFC)

Near field communication (NFC) is a set of standards for short-range radio transmission using electromagnetic radio technologies that can be used with smartphones and other mobile devices to exchange data with NFC-supported devices or chips (sometimes also called *stickers* or *tags*). A user's identification information is held on the SIM card of the user's mobile phone, and by tapping or swiping the smartphone against an NFC sticker or device, the user can invoke a growing number of apps—from mobile payment systems, to purchasing tickets or updating store loyalty program information. NFC technologies are already supported by Android devices, Microsoft and Blackberry smartphones, and will probably become integral to Apple's "iWallet" in its upcoming iPhones.

The market for RFID technologies and supporting services is growing as technologies and standards evolve, and IDTechEx Research estimates that the RFID marketplace will be worth $23.4 billion by 2020.[2] All these new self-monitoring and reporting devices produce huge amounts of digital data, something that is predicted to explode by a factor of 15 by 2020.[3]

These new Industrial Internet technologies are proving to be revolutionary in several areas:

- **Supply Chain Optimization:** Smart parts (intelligent, self-monitoring, and reporting components) are already taking control over much of the manufacturing and production process, as machine robotics coordinate with Enterprise Resource Planning (ERP) systems (see Chapter 9, "Big Data Technologies") for just-in-time ordering, quality assessment, and manufacturing or assembly, using finely calibrated tools and sensors to make automatic adjustments for variances in materials, temperature, or humidity. Sensors can scan RFID tags in a large warehouse setting, instantly creating an inventory for hundreds of thousands of items, and then make merchandise adjustments, or deal with shortages or overstocked items by coordinating inventory across manufacturing sites, and with often many thousands of suppliers connected via the Internet. Even vending machines can value-price (adjust their price according to their environment: higher prices for cold drinks on a hot day, for example) and provide real-time data on how much money they are making, or alert a local delivery driver if they are approaching a low stock situation or sensing a part failure.

Possibly most revolutionary of all, the combined technologies of RFID, self-reporting components, and GPS tracking, provide an extraordinary new level of supply chain visibility throughout the logistics process. A good example of the efficiencies that come from this type of visibility can be seen in a company like UPS, which can capture more than 200 data points on each of its 10,000 trucks in the United States: monitoring fuel use, speed, direction (forward or reverse), RPM, oil pressure, and even whether the driver is wearing a seat belt. All that data can be broken down by region, fleet, truck, or driver performance. This level of Big Data monitoring and analysis quickly leads to improvements in lower maintenance costs, better fuel efficiency, a reduced rate of emissions, better customer service, and improved driver safety.[4] It also creates a lot of digital data (though much of it is structured) to be stored and analyzed.

- **Computer/Condition-Based Maintenance:** Intelligent sensors and components can also be used to monitor any related mechanical equipment throughout the entire supply chain process—gathering real-time performance data on everything from jet aircraft to the engines of delivery vans, and manufacturing line equipment to vending machines. Temperature, vibration, rotation speed, pressure, and many other measurable variables not only reveal output and performance levels, but importantly, can be used to assess the reliability of components. Next to fuel costs, fleet maintenance is one of the highest costs that transportation and logistics groups have to grapple with. Big Data analytics helps to correlate data based on component usage, maintenance, and failure rates, setting up a platform for preventive maintenance that not only allows the company's engineers to predict the likelihood that a part is about to fail, but also allows the company to avoid the downtime and expense of scheduled maintenance regimes that force them to replace perfectly functioning parts.

> This type of CBM can be data heavy: A five-hour flight for a single jet engine, for example, can generate as much as a terabyte of data.[5] McLaren's Formula 1 cars can carry some 200 sensors that transmit real-time data at the astounding rate of 3TB per race.[6] Multiply that across entire fleets of aircraft, boats, trains, trucks, and cars, as well as nuclear and electricity power generation plants, the power grid, and increasingly throughout the manufacturing process of companies worldwide, and we're talking about a lot of digital data. All that has to be captured and stored (and then backed up) and analyzed: a perfect opportunity for applying the more sophisticated analytics of Big Data.

The Industrial Internet's use of Big Data isn't limited just to make-and-move companies. Opportunities exist to use this type of Big Data-set analysis in a variety of industries. The financial markets, of course, already use Big Data analytics for trading. Banks are adopting it for risk modeling and fraud detection. And as groups like Google, Amazon, Facebook, Alibaba, and others move into the online payment systems, mobile devices will be tied back to cloud-based platforms, providing the gateway to financial accounting and tracking services traditionally provided by banks and credit card companies. As the population continues to age, in America and around the world, Big Data analytics will become increasingly important in the health care arena, used to track patient records from multiple sources between hospitals, clinics, and physicians, collecting outcomes from treatment regimes that will be linked together and analyzed for successes and failures. Farmers, too, are increasingly combining data collected from sophisticated farm machinery and in-field sensory networks, which help them to make better decisions on planting, fertilizing, watering, and harvesting. Self-driving tractors map out a field efficiently using GPS-based software. Like self-driving cars, the technology for self-propelled farm equipment, programmed and controlled by a mobile phone, is only a few years away. Importantly, in terms of Big Data, large agricultural groups like Monsanto and DuPont already collect huge data sets based on input from these farm-based sensors to advise on seed types or fertilizers (and, as with the gathering of personal data on the Consumer Internet side, usually also using that data to advertise or sell their products or services to the farmers).[7]

This combination of mechatronics, intelligent systems, and improved data storage and analytics is occurring in nearly every sector of the economy, in some areas promoting significant improvements in productivity by eliminating duplication and inefficiencies and reducing energy usage and resources. When combined with robotics, miniaturization, and growing success with artificial intelligence, it will eventually revolutionize the supply chain.

In fact, 2014 marked the first year when more digital data was generated by machines than humans, a remarkable milestone. The number of connected electronic devices is set to explode to between 30 and 50 billion by 2020.[8] In time, there may be billions of these smart devices, communicating, commanding, even reasoning together, all linked in enormous networks over the Internet that Gartner recently estimated could involve up to $4 trillion of related hardware and software spending worldwide.[9]

But those sorts of numbers don't reflect just an expansion of the Industrial Internet; smart parts and self-sensing and reporting components can easily be transferred into our homes and personal lives, where the realms of business and consumers intersect. That arena is what Kenneth Ashton from MIT's Auto-ID Center (the group that created the standard for RFID and similar sensors) first called the Internet of Things (IoT) as far back as 1999—a world where digital data is produced by machines, transferred by machines, and read and responded to by machines, without the need for any human-to-human data transfer.

The Internet of Things

Capitalizing on these same intelligent technologies is a burgeoning area of Big Data activity that encompasses much of everything else that makes up our economy and everyday lives. The confluence of consumer and industrial Big Data, and arguably the area where Big Data will bring the greatest benefit to society (in terms of better health care, safety, prosperity, and convenience), the Internet of Things includes important aspects of everyday life—financial services, pharmaceuticals, health care—as well as the myriad of new monitoring and electronic management systems for cars, homes, and even for our bodies.

The Home

The most obvious use for monitoring or controlling data in the home (apart from the TV) is utilities. But there is nothing particularly revolutionary about being able to monitor energy and water usage; utility providers have been predicting usage patterns and probable outages, or on the consumer side, providing performance-based rates or rewards, for some time. Although they understand already how much energy we use and could probably infer from the rise and fall of energy usage when customers are at home or go to bed (or for that matter when they get up and shower or even do laundry), utility companies have not traditionally been interested in understanding their consumers' lives in any depth.

Recently, though, the powerful Internet tech companies have showed up at the door, and they are *very interested* in knowing exactly what individuals are doing. With a bundled set of services combining aspects of the Consumer Internet (telecoms and media, smartphones, apps, and m-commerce) with the Industrial Internet (self-monitoring and reporting sensors, machine-to-machine networking), companies like Google, Amazon, and Facebook are championing an Internet of

Things that will provide a wide variety of home services, from streaming TV to temperature control, alarm systems to smart refrigerators and networked kitchens. And they want all that activity to be channeled through their mobile devices, running their operating systems, and tied into their application hubs with the data stored on their cloud services platforms.

The variety of applications that can be included in this type of networked house is limited only by the self-sensing components that can be invented and controlled through a home's Wi-Fi network: smart toilets, washers, light bulbs, refrigerators, and even self-monitoring containers that will alert users by text if they are low on milk or eggs. Eventually, these systems will be able to notify repairmen when they are broken, and even unlock the doors for them (with the owner's validation through the mobile device) when they arrive.

Estimates as to the extent of the level of connectivity vary, but many believe that by 2020, most homes will have as many as 200 devices linked to the Internet.[10] Intel says that nearly 3.8 billion devices are already connected but estimates that number will jump to 30 billion in the next five years. Cisco sets the number of machine-to-machine (M2M) connections even higher at 50 billion by 2020 and suggests that this Internet of Things ecosystem could add as much as $14.4 trillion in combined revenues and efficiencies to the global economy. They've even developed a real-time online Connections Counter that gives estimates of the rate at which these connections are happening.[11]

But the Internet of Things isn't just about the componentry; the technology to make a self-monitoring and reporting system on a microchip is already widely available, and microprocessors have been embedded in household appliances—from alarm clocks to microwaves, dishwashers, and security systems—for many years. And although groups like Cisco (and other Internet networking infrastructure, server, and assorted hardware companies) stand to do very well with the huge expansion of digital data being captured through the

IoT, the bounty for them comes from selling more of the type of product that they already make, rather than moving into the development of new monitoring technologies themselves.

What will bring all this to life, and what has been missing so far, is the control software to coordinate all the data from various components and appliances around the house in one, easy-to-use system. And chances are that type of coordinating platform won't fall to the traditional IT or component manufacturing firms like IBM, GE, Intel, or Cisco. Those coordinating/operating systems will be provided by groups like Google, Apple, and Amazon. And coordination and data-crunching on this scale will not be locally based. Any successful operating system for the IoT will need to provide the basic elements of the Consumer Internet: smartphones, killer aps, and cloud-based software and services. With the application being accessed through a user's smartphone, that coordinating system will reside in the cloud, which means that data from the home will need to be sent, stored, and interpreted before being bounced back to the user's mobile device. That means that all the data being collected in the home—what is bought, how often, how many calories are eaten, how much energy is used, whether a product is old or faulty and needs replacement—will be shared with the cloud system owner, adding more data to ever-growing personal profiles, which can in turn be used to point advertisers, products, and services toward that user.

These operating systems will not only be able to collect data so that it can be used for targeted advertising. They'll also need to be able to manage the actual devices themselves. It is this layer of software—a control system that can connect to and manage a wide variety of components and appliances seamlessly and dependably (unlocking our front doors to hackers or setting our house on fire by turning on an empty microwave is not going to go down well with homeowners)—that so far has been missing.

Who will step forward to provide that operating system?

Only a handful of companies have the wherewithal and expertise to capitalize on smartphones, Big Data, cloud computing, and sophisticated analytic software in this way, and, again, we find ourselves back with the usual suspects. Samsung, with its ties to electronics and appliances, announced a smart-home platform that allows homeowners to monitor everything from washing machines to kitchen appliances from a mobile app. It has the advantage of being a sophisticated electronics designer that also manufacturers refrigerators, TVs, and washing machines, and are also the maker of a best-selling global brand of smartphones (and soon to come, smartwatches) running on the globally popular Android operating system. Google, of course, moved into Internet-based home security space with the Web-based thermostats and alarms that came with its purchase of Nest Technologies for $3.2 billion in 2014. They followed this with the purchase of Dropcam, a company that makes sophisticated, motion-sensitive home security cameras.

Apple announced its new plan for the smart home, which will be an integrated, iPhone-based platform for monitoring and controlling lights, household appliances, and security systems. It wants to be able to link all that to Apple's online payment service and the expanded sale of smart home products both through its online App store and through its popular retail stores, which already sell Nest products, self-reporting light bulbs, and the Dropcam cameras. The retail stores give Apple a significant advantage over the other contenders (none of which have bricks-and-mortar stores), because they will be able to also capitalize on selling specialty IoT-enabled appliances and components on the retail floor, as well as through its Smart TV and online TV shopping platform. And the very fact that Apple has committed to the IoT will surely drive app developers, component makers, and appliance manufacturers like GE and Whirlpool to accelerate their release of smart home products that tie into the Apple platform.

Microsoft has been making versions of its Windows Embedded suite for devices as varied as navigation systems and in-car computerized entertainment, to real-time point-of-sale and manufacturing systems, for more than a decade. But recently it made significant inroads into specific IoT services leveraging its Azure cloud-based platform. Known as the Intelligent Systems Service (ISS), the platform provides the software for managing machine-generated data from a wide variety of devices and sensors, regardless of their make or operating system. The cloud-based ISS also provides users with Big Data analytics for querying and analyzing the data over the Internet. Anticipating what it calls *ambient intelligence* (intelligent M2M interplay working on behalf of humans), the ISS offering suggests that Microsoft wants to be the integrating operating system for the IoT in the future. The ISS offering complements the Analytics Platform System (APS), which provides both SQL and Hadoop (see Chapter 9) technologies to companies over the Web in what Microsoft calls "Big Data in a box." And Microsoft is looking at buying or building various devices itself, from wearables (watches and glasses) to home-automation systems.

Possibly best positioned of all to take advantage of the IoT, Amazon has a variety of offerings that provide an interface and Big Data platform for large amounts of machine-generated data. Anticipating the need for a platform that can capture and manage a broad variety of digital data from many types of sensors and intelligent devices, its Kinesis offering from Amazon Web Services (AWS) provides a variety of Big Data services to companies through the cloud. Even more than Apple, Amazon can see a future as the home shopping service for millions of households, building on its AmazonFresh platform for home grocery shopping and delivery with Amazon Dash, the voice recognition and grocery shopping tool that allows users to scan or speak the name of a product to put it in their home shopping cart and then use their recently announced Amazon Fire smartphone (for ease-of-use, also tied into Amazon's Fire TV technology) to pay for the groceries and schedule delivery.

Whoever controls all that data, however, will need to garner trust, because possibly the greatest potential drawback to this type of connected house is security: Not only will that company need to assure users that the personal data being gleaned from households is going to be kept private, but it will need to ensure that the connected-home's systems won't be hacked into or infected with a virus. Owning the coordinating platform for the IoT may be lucrative, but it isn't necessarily going to be easy.

The Car

Most new cars today already boast a prodigious number of microprocessors and sensors that collect data on everything from engine and electrical system performance to location and driving patterns. When combined with GPS navigation, traffic condition data, and car-to-car recognition and avoidance, these new intelligent-car technologies promise to set loose a new torrent of digital data production and collection.

With some 50 different computer systems in the average car, these extraordinary levels of digital data output are no longer just the domain of Formula 1. A Mercedes-Benz S-Class saloon, for instance, already comes equipped with a stereo camera that generates some 300 gigabytes of data every hour.[12] Audi's 2014 A3 Sedan features integrated GPS, social media, an app hub, and high-definition video streaming for up to eight separate channels in the car, and Audi is working on Wi-Fi systems that will communicate directly with other cars, toll gates, and parking garages. The company says it will be investing some $17 billion on these types of Big Data technologies through 2016. Altogether, in 2013 automakers collected some 480 terabytes of data on their cars, a figure expected to skyrocket to 11.1 petabytes by 2020 (that's nearly 350 megabytes per second worldwide).

Not just service and maintenance-related data is being produced. The Ptolemus Consulting Group estimates that by 2020, there will be

100 million cars on the road being actively monitored by third parties interested in how the cars are being driven.[13] In fact, black boxes—like those on airplanes—are now common on US manufactured cars and may soon become mandatory. The European Union is already considering requiring cars to have an automatic GPS-locating 911-type of notification service called e-Call, along with a SIM card that automatically activates when the car is involved in an accident and allows drivers to acknowledge whether they need medical assistance. This race toward Big Data in the automotive industry has been so exuberant that it has prompted VW's CEO recently to caution the industry against allowing cars to become "data monsters."

Car insurers, too, are pushing for more data on driving habits. Already more than 5 million cars are tracked by insurance companies with systems that detect excessive speed or aggressive driving, so that drivers can be penalized or rewarded accordingly. Progressive Insurance, for example, gives discounts for drivers that sign up to have their car monitored for good-practice speed and braking in what it calls the Snapshot program, which monitors for the time of day or night the car is driven, the miles clocked, and speed and braking patterns. The company already admits to having collected more than a trillion seconds of driving data from 1.6 million customers. In Europe and the United Kingdom, insurance companies already use GPS and a car's "black box" data to analyze fault in car accidents.[14] More accepted in the United Kingdom, today only 2% of car insurance companies in the United States offer this type of product, but that number is projected to grow by up to 15% over the next three years.[15]

And then, of course, there is the connected, self-driving car. It is estimated that there will be more than 150 million connected cars on the road worldwide by 2020, and Booze & Company estimates that the market for these self-driving cars is expected to reach $113bn by then.[16] Google announced that it will manufacture its own self-driving cars to be on the road by 2017, and every major manufacturer from Volvo to Ford is working on some type of computer-driven vehicles.

Mobileye, a company that manufactures artificial vision image processing for collision avoidance systems, recently raised $400 million to create a platform for these self-driving cars.

But the data required for a driverless car—navigation, collision sensors, computing software—can run to a gigabyte a second. In a country dependent on cars (Americans drive an average of 600 hours each year), the output from the United States alone would equal about 2 petabytes of data for every car, each year. That's a lot of digital data for someone to generate and store.[17]

As with the connected home, security is going to be an issue. With driverless cars, not only do we need to trust in a machine that we don't have any control over, but we also need to be confident that the car's systems themselves are secure. It seems an unlikely scenario, but the potential for taking over a car's control remotely was made real in 2013 when a collaborative experiment conducted between Twitter and IOActive found that it was possible to hack directly into a Toyota Prius, disabling the steering and brakes.[18]

The Human Body: Wearables and Health-Monitoring Devices in the Home

This proliferation of sensors also means a new market is growing around *wearables*—wristbands, watches, shoes, shirts, belts, and even underwear, with built-in digital monitoring and computing capacity. In fact, we are already well within the realm of Dick Tracy's two-way wristwatch, capable of providing the user with everything from video to location data, personal identification, and online data search. Driven by the same evolutionary computing and communicating force that moved us from desktops to laptops and then to mobile phones, this process of consolidation and miniaturization is simply continuing to take us down to the level of a wristwatch or a pair of eyeglasses. These miniaturized technology bundles have the advantage of convenience and the ability to provide real-time, hands-free information while the user is on the move, but the disadvantage of reaching a level of miniaturization that can make entering data difficult. That's why developers are moving toward voice recognition, iris-control, or tilt-of-the-head technologies and tying the devices back to the user's smartphone.

Interest in wearables comes from a variety of companies that range from the traditional watch manufacturers to sports groups like Nike, and all types of ideas and devices spring up on a weekly basis. One of the best known, and more contentious, of the new wearable devices is Google's Glass technology. Eyeglasses boasting smartphone-level technology based on a microprocessor and with an LCD screen set in the upper portion of the glasses' lens, Google Glass also provides a camera and video, as well as a small but growing array of apps. This same glasses-based technology can monitor your eyes and your blinking activity to warn you if you are falling asleep. And, more controversially, using facial recognition or cell-phone ID and other methods, the technology can provide the user with Internet search and other capabilities that potentially identify (and tell them all about) the person they are about to meet at a party or even on the street.

Although some of the new technologies are single-focus area devices equipped with a SIM card that connects to the mobile Internet, as with music, search, GPS, and other once stand-alone activity monitors such as odometers, all these wearable technologies in the future will generally be tied into a single, integrated, and all-encompassing operating system through the user's smartphone. It is likely, and certainly the goal of those producing these bundled wearable technologies, that as they move toward an integrated set of offerings, life-logging, or whole-life monitoring, complete with video, location, and records of who we meet and speak with, may all become a part of the data-obsessed life of the future.

As the population globally continues to age and at the same time live longer, one key growth area for the wearables market will be personal health. The process is well under way with sport and fitness, where it was fairly easy to make devices to monitor individual exercise and activity levels. But a broader opportunity exists to adapt these technologies so that they can provide detailed and constant monitoring for well-being and health in what has become known as *lifelogging*. Using a vast array of technologies available from arm bands, watches, and T-shirts that can track pulse, blood pressure, or heartbeat, we are now in a position of making available technologies that monitor everything from sleep to the calories eaten and expended, including bras or belts that automatically alert us of weight gain and loss. There are already a range of "smart toilets" that record hydration and vitamin levels.

Many see particular promise in smart clothes, which may in a few years feature standard, low-cost beacons that allow parents to track and monitor their children. In fact, the idea that humans can become mobile transmitters is now gaining ground; it's possible, according to French researchers, that there may be a market for using the sensors and devices embedded in our clothing in the future as routers for local Wi-Fi nodes. In this way, humans would essentially become a transmitter for a connected network, not just tapping into a node, but actually being part of that node.[19]

This level of monitoring sounds futuristic, but it's already here and has been for some time. A good example is the British Olympic cycling team, where the high-technology racing bikes were equipped with sensors on the pedals and tires that not only collected data on speed but also on the pressure levels of every push of the pedal by an athlete. That data was collected for every practice run and every race for months and was integrated with other data—on heart rate, blood pressure, weight, breathing, and sleep levels—monitored with devices worn by the athletes themselves. But they didn't stop there. They also used wearable monitoring devices to record the world around them—air temperature, humidity, air quality. They even analyzed the social media of the individual athletes to detect emotional changes.[20] Apple and Samsung are both actively working to accommodate these types of technologies in their mobile devices, and Google even hired Art Levinson, Apple's Chairman and the former CEO of Genetech, to work on Calico, its health venture.[21]

Whether that level of lifestyle monitoring will ever catch on among the public at large is uncertain, and curiously, this type of data may be a minefield for groups like Google, which also might want to use or even pass on that very personal data in some form to advertisers or other third parties. Personal health and medical data is one of the few areas strictly addressed in American law, and although fitness devices are much less regulated, the overlap in definition and data is not always clear-cut. Similarly, clandestine photos taken from Google Glasses or even video-recording people who the user is looking at (and who may not be aware that they are being videoed) may be going too far, even for a society that has become accustomed to a high level of personal data exchange.

It is still early days, and there is a lot of skepticism about the demand for these types of devices, but both device manufacturers and app developers see the wearables market as big business. Current sales for wearables show the market to be worth around $2 billion today, increasing to $8 billion by 2018.[22]

The Sky: Drone Technology

Drones are not the sort of thing that are generally thought of as consumer-friendly, but apart from monitoring a person's movements and then firing a missile, the technology can have many beneficial uses, from environmental modelling to search and rescue and crop monitoring. Google has been interested in this area for some time. They bought Titan Aerospace, a company that manufactures solar-powered drones, to augment its ongoing Project Loon, which also involves, among other things, high-altitude balloons. Facebook has similar plans for the future, and according to the *Financial Times*, has hired specialist engineers in free space optics from NASA's Jet

Propulsion Laboratory as part of Facebook's Connectivity Lab program, confirming that Facebook is investing in the development of drones, satellites, and lasers as part of a futuristic platform that involves firing communications lasers between satellites and drones. As part of that effort, Facebook bought Ascenta, another drone manufacturer, for $20 million in 2014.

The companies may plan on working in all those areas, but it is most likely that they are (as Google suggests) simply looking for ways to amplify and relay Internet signals and local Wi-Fi to areas of intensive broadband use or to rural areas where Internet signals are patchy or nonexistent. Although Google is having some success with its Google Wired program in various metropolitan areas around the United States, it has learned from those efforts that installing conventional infrastructure (burying fiber-optical cable), especially in built-up areas or in other countries, is problematic. To be able to expand its user base and extend its sphere of influence in the future, high-capacity Internet access is crucial, and it may well be that drones, balloons, or Google-owned satellites will all be needed and accepted as part of Google's global expansion.

Amazon, too, announced in 2013 that it was developing an aerial drone program. They even suggested that the drones might be used within the next five years to actually deliver parcels to the doorstep. Although the explanation was dismissed as an exaggeration for Christmas season publicity, the idea is not so far-fetched; whatever a drone's delivery capabilities, the most likely purpose of Amazon's program is something similar to Google and Facebook—to provide an auxiliary and private infrastructure that can extend Amazon's control over the Internet.[23]

Protocols and Standards

If multiple brands and technologies—from kitchen appliance manufacturers to thermostats, cars to data-processing bras—are to provide users with a single whole-life view of their world, the industry must agree on ways to allow for data coordination, consolidation, and comparison across different technology types and platforms. That has not traditionally been something that competing innovators have been good at—think of BetaMax versus VHS, or iOS and Windows.

Perhaps surprisingly, to some extent that type of cooperation is already taking place, brought together by the necessities of the existing mobile phone and app market. Anticipating the need to attach the growing number of devices coming online, in 2012 the Internet Protocol Version 6 (IPV6) was introduced, which made available a schema for assigning individual components and even individual parts—in fact an object of any size that was capable of producing an electrical ID, or being flagged through an RFID-type identifying technology—with a distinct, digital identity. This means that in the Internet of Things, all the things (even, conceivably down to the atomic level) can be assigned a unique digital identifier that makes it universally recognizable.

It also means that product-specific data—warranty information, performance data, maintenance records, sell-by dates, and so on—can all be associated directly with the object digitally, using either embedding technologies or a simple RFID smart tag. This, in turn, allows for identification, validation, and data reading of almost any object using a smartphone and NFC-type scanning technologies. Known as *identity management*, this type of data tagging is an important first step to being able to allow machine-to-machine recognition and communication on a network. This is potentially revolutionary, because it puts the "smart" in smart parts and can be used to attach and update data to an object—about its outside surroundings, its location, its price, the sender and receiver, or even videos on proper installation—as it moves through the supply chain.[24]

Apple was quick to take advantage of the protocol. It has developed a new type of low-energy emitting identifying technology called iBeacons that capitalizes on Bluetooth Low Energy technology and is being built into most Apple products. This means that an iPhone user (or at least their device) will be instantly recognizable to other users, including the Apple store staff. It also means that the iPhone can be used to swipe objects using NFC technologies and not only read any attached information about that object but order it instantly—and that data will be confirmed and recorded electronically. This is an important part of the automatic replenishment and payment systems that Apple is developing for its online store and its TV-based online services.[25]

Similarly, a consortium of industrial powerhouses, including General Electric, Intel, IBM, Cisco, and AT&T, announced in the spring of 2014 the formation of the Industrial Internet Consortium, a technology standards group that will work toward developing compatible engineering, communication, and data exchange standards for sensors and computing systems in major industrial industries such as refineries and manufacturing. The White House and other US government agencies have endorsed and supported the formation of the (all-American) standards group, no doubt aware that these founding members will have a huge influence over the development of Industrial Internet standards worldwide.[26]

Breaking and Entering

There is potentially huge money for companies that can provide a powerful interface for all these data; McKinsey recently estimated that by 2025, the Internet of Things would generate between $5 and $7 trillion dollars every year.[27] But simply because the industry giants recognize the need to exchange data between systems doesn't mean that the IoT is suddenly going to spring to life. There are any number of serious technical and security hurdles to overcome.

As mentioned earlier, manufacturers of household appliances may not be particularly adept at blocking malware from taking over the refrigerator or the home's air conditioner, and hackers could potentially turn on or off everything from ovens to toasters in a fully-wired Internet of Things household. This type of security breach could disrupt not only households but the entire electrical grid. What happens when Google self-driving cars collide? Who is responsible when an Internet-based heart monitoring system fails (or, as when the fears of former Vice-President Dick Cheney are realized and a malicious outsider manages to hijack someone's Internet-monitored and controlled pacemaker)?

Even putting these security issues aside, whoever becomes the gatekeeper(s) to the Internet of Things will have to work for it, because tying all these components and systems together will not be simple. First, there is the actual operational management of the various systems and components themselves. Users want to be able to actively manage their various devices over the Internet, and they will expect a reliable system that has the ability to control, check, troubleshoot (and even repair) a house and garage-full of connected components. To allow users to do that, the platform integrator will need to provide a coordinating software system capable of managing everything from machine data identification to power outages.

Who will have the capabilities to provide this all-encompassing platform?

Obviously, controlling hardware and software that you own is easier, and that may be the reason why Google is moving into hardware and devices—from robotics to Nest—so that it can begin to take command of the physical (as well as logical) componentry that they eventually will propose to manage. That may come more naturally to Google, since this type of coordination is essentially what it does for the Internet itself, where they coordinates access to web sites instead of thermostats or alarm systems. Google can also use the same customer data/digital advertising business model that has served it so well (so profitably) over the Internet during the last decade. They even tipped their hand somewhat in 2014 by admitting in a letter to the SEC that in the future, Google "could be serving ads and other content on refrigerators, car dashboards, thermostats, glasses, and watches, to name just a few possibilities."[28] Although it later clarified the statement to say that these were possibilities and not necessarily Google's product roadmap, the implication was clear. There is even talk of Google being able to offer "enhanced campaigns" that will maintain a consistent marketing campaign across the user's multiple home devices, car, and mobile phones.[29]

Certainly Facebook also sees itself fulfilling that coordinating role: providing a single log-on through a Facebook page via a mobile device would give the user all the apps, analytics, and communications necessary to manage home and car and to maintain whole-life data. And as we've seen, both Amazon and Apple want to help coordinate a wired home (wired directly to their online stores).

But to be the single interface for this level of personal data in whole-life monitoring (from house security settings to fitness data) involves a level of customer intimacy that goes even beyond the relationship users have with social media. Customers may feel wary about allowing this level of monitoring (particularly if it is all held in storage on a vendor's cloud-based system) without stronger assurances that personal data will be held in confidence. That puts the Internet tech companies that aspire to control the Internet gateways to this personal data in a difficult position. They know well that this type of deeply personal data—detailed monitoring of every aspect of their users' day-to-day lives—is a potential gold mine for them. And if they genuinely believe what they say about highly personalized marketing being good for the user, then they will be hesitant to abrogate their hard-fought right to collect, analyze, characterize, and sell that personal data to advertisers and other interested parties.

8

The Data Collectors

Key Chapter Points

- As the amount of consumer-related data has grown, several groups of companies have begun to specialize in collecting, aggregating, and selling that data for profit, including the following:
    - The Internet tech companies
    - Credit reporting agencies
    - Retailers
    - Smaller online data tracking groups
- These companies all use cookies or other tracking technologies to follow a user through online activities.
- Online customer data is being combined with business customer data in an amalgamation process known as *data onboarding*.

So far we've focused on why the Big Data phenomenon is happening and on the sources and quantity of digital data being produced on the commercial Internet and also in the burgeoning Industrial Internet and the Internet of Things. But recalling our definition of Big Data—collecting large amounts of digitized data from a variety of sources and applying sophisticated analytics—we now turn to the flip side of the Big Data phenomenon and look at who is collecting all that data and what they are doing with it.

The Wellsprings of Consumer Data Collection

Large data computing has many uses. As we have seen, it can be a valuable tool in analyzing large data sets for epidemiology or gene research. It has been used for many years in financial services and banking, crunching market data on a real-time basis. These are specialty groups working with mostly structured data and sophisticated networks of servers dedicated to analytics. For the most part (with some exceptions), they are not looking for information in the wide variety of unstructured, often personal data that can be found across the Internet in social media or through online activity monitoring. And although often cited as good examples of Big Data, for the most part, these industries are talking about *more* computing, even *better* computing, using more data. But they're not really talking about Big Data.

In fact, most companies interested in collecting Big Data these days are not trying to solve complex scientific or health-related problems, nor trying to sample real-time commodity prices. The vertical industries where that level of number crunching is integral to their success—genetics, financial services, insurance, or engineering—are not what's causing the explosion of new data-related technologies or the intense interest among investors that we've been talking about so far. Let's be honest. Despite the advocation for its unique value in more specialized fields of science, engineering, and economics, when people talk about Big Data these days, we can be pretty certain that they're talking about applying those principles—and a good deal of money and technology—to one thing: specifically, *to the collection and analysis of personal data.*

The reason that companies want to collect and analyze personal data—mostly, but not exclusively, to support digital advertising—is a relatively new phenomenon. Until recently advertising took the form of mailed flyers, newspapers, and TV and radio ads, which for the most part were designed to appeal to a generic audience. The inducement was usually price; sales and coupons were used as a loss leader to draw customers into the store. Anything more sophisticated than that (such as product differentiation and brand recognition) was left to the Madison Avenue advertisers—and was pursued through packaging, jingles, slogans, and broader national campaigns. Despite surveys and focus-group testing, in fact there was no way for companies to understand, other than at a generic level, which pieces of advertising worked and which didn't. Even if an advertiser could know how to make its product appealing to a 35-year-old environmentally aware divorced woman with an advanced degree in humanities and three or more children who commuted more than 20 miles from her home and liked organic foods, there was no way to identify who that woman was, or any mechanism for getting an advertisement to her in a format tailored to her interests.

The idea of being able to direct customized advertising toward a potential customer at an individual level was simply not considered. And this is where Big Data comes in. It is not where the Big Data phenomenon started (science and engineering), and it may not be the area where Big Data can do most to help humanity. But this is where majority opinion believes it can make the most money for the most people, and so this is where the technological and economic dynamism is currently focused.

To understand the extent to which personal data is being captured, we need to look at four groups. The Internet tech companies are there, to be sure, but they are not alone. They have competition and synergies with three other important groups: data brokers, retailers, and small data trackers.

Credit Agencies, Data Brokers, and Information Resellers

Although the infrastructure for gathering personal data over the Internet is fairly recent, in fact, one group of companies has been collecting large amounts of personal data on individuals for a long time: the credit agencies.

Many people have still never heard of Equifax, TransUnion, Experian, FICO, or Acxiom; if they have, it is probably from checking their credit scores when applying for a credit card or a loan or mortgage. Authorized by Congress in 1970 under the Fair Credit Reporting Act (FCRA), these consumer reporting agencies are regulated by the Federal Trade Commission (FTC), and their original mandate was public service: to collect data on citizens to give a disinterested, third-party rating of an individual's creditworthiness.

These credit reporting agencies (CRAs) were obliged by Congress to collect data on an individual's identity, income, spending habits, check-writing history, criminal activity, and credit records, with the goal of preventing financial fraud by validating information on applications for credit cards, mortgages, insurance, and so on. For nearly 45 years, CRAs have been collecting data on almost everyone in America: their identity (age, sex, race), employment, income and spending, major purchases, creditworthiness, criminal activity, marriages, divorce settlements, and courthouse appearances. This data was intended to be kept private—only to be made available to authorized financial groups—and to be subject to scrutiny and correction by the individual consumer. That is still the case.

But there was a loophole; the FTC data privacy requirements only applied to transactions that fell under the Fair Credit Reporting Act, which means that, as long as they were not involved with an FCRA information request, these credit agencies were potentially free to sell all the data they had collected to almost anyone. The more entrepreneurial of these companies quickly realized that there was a lot of money to be made if they augmented their databases with information on individuals from other sources and then sold this information to advertisers, retailers, or collection agencies in non-FCRA-related transactions. In many ways, these CRAs were the precursor of the modern personal data collection frenzy that surrounds Big Data, and the model for groups like Google or Facebook, who were able to extend personally-linked data collection to the Internet and digital advertising.

Soon these CRAs began to vacuum up data on individuals from every possible source—retailers, public records, credit card companies, banks—anywhere they could get it. They bought whole databases of purchasing data from retailers' loyalty card programs. Recognizing the market for medical information (for insurance companies, elderly care services, and product manufacturers), they specifically sought out medically related information for individuals—their illnesses, doctors, treatment regimes, and what they purchased from drug stores or pharmacies. They found out what charities people gave to, what newspapers, books, magazines, and journal subscriptions they were buying. And as the world discovered the Internet and e-commerce expanded, the consumer reporting agencies began to buy information directly from online retailers, search engines, and a myriad of new Internet data trackers that began to populate the Web.

The CRAs (sometimes also known as data brokers or data aggregators) now have extensive dossiers on millions of individuals: on our jobs, what we earn, what we spend, what we buy, where we live, what cars we drive, and our political party affiliation. And although the confidentiality of credit scores and medical records is still protected by law, these data aggregators have expanded their services to include selling on individual profiles—usually categorizing individuals into a socioeconomic group that captures in a single phrase our life with a cruel honesty: from "savvy singles" to "rural and barely making it," or "ethnic second city strugglers" to "credit-crunched city families."[1]

Shortly after the millennium, I facilitated a strategic executive workshop with the executive team of one of these agencies, a modest organization in modest accommodations, and was surprised when they explained that they already knew everything about me down to my eye color. I scoffed, but they proved it was true (they collect eye color from our driver's license). Even then they were compiling personal folders on millions of families and individuals, not only in the United States but around the world, with a strategic vision to move from being bureaucratic credit agencies to the powerful database marketers that they are today. They are now among the leaders in an estimated $150 billion industry in the United States, known as database marketing. It is big business and big money.

A CRA like Acxiom, for example, based in Conway, Arkansas, made profits of $77.26 million in 2013.[2] With its 23,000 computer servers, Acxiom completes more than 50 trillion data transactions each year, constantly updating profiles consisting of around 1,500 data points for each of more than 500 million individuals worldwide. Reported to have the largest commercial consumer information database in the world, they score and file all these individuals using its PersonicX classification system, which assigns consumers to one of 70 socioeconomic "clusters." 190 million of those individuals are in the United States. Clients can buy this data on individuals or households outright to add to their own marketing databases, or Acxiom will maintain the customer databases for them (as they do for 47 Fortune 500 companies).[3]

FICO (formerly Fair Isaac Corp.), headquartered in Minneapolis but active in more than 90 countries, is another of these large CRAs. FICO reported revenues of more than $600 million in 2013. True to its roots, it is still one of the most powerful credit agencies, but the company has built a Hadoop-based "analytic cloud," and in 2013 bought Karmasphere's Big Data analytics software to provide cloud-based Hadoop analytics capabilities to other companies; in FICO's words, to "accelerate the democratization and wide-scale adoption of

Big Data analytics by organizations of all sizes and across all industries." Along with Experian (the second largest CRA, with revenues of nearly $4 billion) and TransUnion (the third largest at $1 billion), these four companies not only control most of the credit rating business in the United States, but they maintain far more digital data on individuals than even the NSA.[4]

But not all data aggregators come from credit bureau origins. Many others—Thomson Reuters' Westlaw, Infogroup, LexisNexis—have origins in paper-based or computerized directories of the past. Others specialize in collecting data from specific sources. Datalogix, for example, collects information from store loyalty cards, tracking personal purchases against more than 1,400 brands.[5] Moneysupermarket.com, the UK's biggest price comparison web site, collects data on the 15 million cars and 14 million houses of nearly a third of the UK population (21 million customers). It is expected to generate £10 million from selling trend data to insurance companies in 2014.[6] Credit card companies, too, have been collecting socioeconomic data on their customers for decades.

And, of course, there are myriad smaller, often less reputable data brokers, using search and data recognition tools to collect digital data on individuals and selling that information on. Like their giant CRA counterparts, these new data aggregators adopted new Big Data technologies and tapped into the multitude of data sources now available to them to set up their own specialty offerings: For a fee, cross-matching an individual's name, addresses, Social Security number, cell phone number, and relationships, and then revealing everything in their life that they might want to forget—from criminal history to bankruptcies, divorces to civil suits. All that information, accurate or not, is available for a price on the Internet.

One area of rapid growth is employment analysis, where companies like Evolv help clients to analyze potential employee skills and work experience in part by looking at how those individuals use social media (they claim, for instance, that individuals with two social media accounts perform at higher levels than those with fewer or more accounts). Their sales grew 150% from 2012-2013.[7] Finland's Joberate uses similar social media scanning of some 6,000 online "channels" to identify when potential employees are unhappy with their work or are looking for a job (they also sell the software to HR staff so that they can monitor their own employees' social media activity).[8]

Unfortunately, applying Big Data analytics and a little indifference to personal privacy and law, these third parties can also infer whether individuals have diabetes, are pregnant, or have been raped, which has caused many civil liberties groups to press for more stringent regulations on this type of data exchange. It's a worrying development, because few controls are in place to prevent misuse of personal data once it is openly available on the Internet. In testimony before the US Senate in 2013, senators were told that data brokers would "sell any information about any person, regardless of sensitivity, for 7.9 cents a name."[9] This is an area of growing concern, and something we cover in more detail in Chapter 11, "Living in a Big Data World."

Internet Technology Companies

Chances are the first time you heard the phrase Big Data, it somehow involved a search engine—probably Google or Yahoo!. And that was probably because these search engines were the first to gain notoriety for tracking our Internet activity; capturing IP addresses, and logging all searches and web site visits. This tracking was necessary, they explained, to provide the frequency and relevancy logic that would make their search engines effective and was also the basis for their advertising revenues, which were earned for charging sponsored company links for the prized top page positions (the highest-paying advertisers highlighted in blue to identify them as paid prioritizations) on search results.

This combined search, memory, and advertising logic was all tied to something known as a *cookie*—small pieces of computer code named initially because they resembled a message-containing fortune cookie—which is embedded automatically in the user's computer the millisecond the user accesses the search engine. Most search engines "drop" cookies, as do most browsers, and those browsers owned by search engines (that is, Google Chrome, Microsoft's Internet Explorer) tend to be configured to work together in a way that collects the most information from the user as possible. Part of the attraction of browser cookies is that they could provide for users a history of their web site visits—so that it is always possible to click back to revisit previous sites or return to them whenever the user wants. As e-commerce expanded, these cookies became even more important in terms of user convenience, because they allowed online shoppers to remember what items they browsed and what they saved in their shopping carts.

Privacy advocates made a small amount of noise when the nature of cookies became understood in the late 1990s (the first cookies actually began with Netscape Navigator in 1994), and we began to realize that search engines could use these same cookies to identify the user by IP address and to some extent monitor web searches and track an individual's online activity—what search terms were used, what web sites were visited. But the search engines, and particularly Google, brushed the criticisms aside, assuring the public that the data wasn't personally identifiable (a cookie only registered IP addresses) and was collected anonymously in the aggregate—it didn't relate to our names—so not much was made of it. Besides, we were told, the cookies could be removed, or "cleansed," simply by shutting down our browser.

Since those early days, Google, Yahoo!, and latterly Microsoft's Bing, have emerged as the most powerful of these all-purpose English-language search engines, although as we've seen, other nations have developed similar search powerhouses such as China's Baidu,

Japan's goo, or South Korea's Naver. A huge number of area-specific search engines also have cropped up all over the world (for searches on everything from news to jobs, medicine to games). And although some earlier search innovators—AOL, Dogpile, Lycos, Excite—continue as less well-known combined search, news, and advertising portals, others like NorthernLight or Infoseek didn't have the Big Data technologies or the focus on collecting customer data necessary to sustain them through the early, low-yield days of search advertising. Almost all these search engines use cookie tracking to monitor search terms, with the notable exception of DuckDuckGo, a relative newcomer to the search engine market, which has built its growing reputation by swimming against the current and exploiting the fact that they don't track the user's searches.

Understanding Cookies

Cookies are small data files that are "dropped" onto a computer each time the user accesses a web site, assigning the user a unique identifier that includes the user's IP address, the time, the browser being used, and the user's approximate location. These cookies are used to follow and record activity while on the web site, or to store login information, passwords, or credit card information, so that it is available the next time the user wants to use the web site's service. Cookies are kept in a file in the user's browser directory and usually remain on the computer until the user clears the browser or purges the cookies through some type of software. If the cookies remain on the computer, each time the user returns to the web site the browser sends the cookie back to the web site's server, which retrieves the records from the user's last visit to the site and adds any new activity, thereby building up a profile against a given IP address.

HTTP or browser cookies are sometimes known as *first-party cookies*, because they come from the actual web site the user is visiting. A *third-party cookie*, sometimes called a *persistent cookie*, is a file dropped on a user's computer (usually, but not exclusively) by advertising placement companies that are present on popular sites.

Third-party cookies track a user's online activity as the user continues to visit other sites (usually on other sites where the company has a matching web bug or provides similar advertising). Third-party tracking cookies continue to collect and store data on the user's online activities across multiple sites and are called persistent because it is possible for them to continue to track a user for years, sometimes even if the user switches or upgrades their browser or even changes Internet service providers. Whenever the user's IP address is recognized in the future on any of the sites represented by that ad placement company, the cookie will be matched against that profile and a targeted ad will be delivered to the user.

Whenever a user registers or provides personally identifiable information to a web site, though, their identity can be matched against those persistent cookies, which means that once one company or web site knows the user's real identity, other participating companies can potentially synchronize cookies to assign personally identifiable information data to that profile. Privacy settings on most modern browsers provide for blocking of third-party tracking cookies but usually need to be activated by the user.

In their privacy policy, Google explains how data is recorded from a generic DoubleClick cookie. It looks like this:

time: 06/Aug/2008 12:01:32

ad_placement_id: 105

ad_id: 1003

userid: 0000000000000001

client_ip: 123.45.67.89

referral_url: "http://youtube.com/categories"

This tells DoubleClick the time and date you saw an advertisement. It also shows:

userid: The unique ID number the cookie has given your browser.

ad_id: The unique ID of the ad.

ad_placement_id: The ID of where the ad was seen on the site.

referral_url: What page you were on when you saw the ad.

The vast majority of the other search engines around the world use these cookies to track a user's "traffic" patterns on web sites and to monitor the user's reaction to ads that they post, usually on the search page or the site's main portal. Google, for example, bought DoubleClick in 2008 and uses the software on its own sites, as well as making it available to web site publishers (so that they can track ad traffic levels on their own web sites) and advertisers (who use it to monitor traffic against their ads over multiple sites). Using DoubleClick allows these groups to track the IP address of the user (anonymous except for ZIP code) against an ad, recording the time and date when the advertisement was seen, and where the ad was on the publisher's web site. Google also runs a service called AdSense, an advertising network, which encourages publishers to pool the information they have gleaned from their tracking to look for broader trends. Similarly, Google Analytics is a tool that allows web site publishers to monitor which users (again, identified only by an IP address giving location) visit their web site, and what they look at while they are there. As long as a user is accessing a web site, or clicking on an advertisement anonymously through a web browser, these tools only collect trend-level data on search terms, web site visits, and advertising interest, based on traditional cookie-tracking technology and a user's anonymous IP address.

However, the days of the judicious search engine may be numbered, as Internet-based companies of all stripes, but particularly these powerful search engines, have started to pursue strategies that allow them to collect more personally identifiable data on their users. More and more, a caveat appears in their Terms of Use that explains that they claim the right to identify and collect personally identifiable data on a user's activity (matched not just against an anonymous IP address, but tracked against an actual name or address) if the user has *voluntarily disclosed* that information. And the simplest, and most effective way, of securing that voluntary disclosure is through membership registration, because the act of "signing in" not only acknowledges that the search company has the right to collect personal data; it also sets cookies on the user's browser and assigns a unique ID for the user that allows the search engine to collect and compile all search activity and e-mail data against that personal profile. That's true for Apple's iCloud, Facebook, Gmail, the Chrome browser, the Google+ network, or for any other service site requiring a login.

E-Readers

Cloud-based digital library services are at the forefront of digital tracking. Nearly one in five adults in the United States use e-readers to download books and journals, and groups like Amazon, Barnes & Noble, Copia, and Kobo all collect data from their e-readers, including (at a minimum) the age and gender of readers, what they are reading, how many hours they spend with each title, how fast they read various chapters or sections, and how far the reader gets if they don't finish. This data is then sold to publishers, but there is little agreement on how a reader's data can be shared, or with whom, and usually no way for the user to opt out of the monitoring process.

Can They Keep Track of Searches for Books?			
Google Books	**Amazon Kindle**	**Barnes & Noble Nook**	**Kobo**
Yes Logs all search data with IP address. Will also associate searches with user's Google Account if logged in. Will not associate searches with user's account if not logged in.	**Yes/Unclear** Logs data on products viewed and/or searched for on the device, and associates info with Amazon account. Searching the Inside Book feature requires login to Amazon account. It is unknown whether searches for books done at locations other than Amazon are also reported back to Amazon, but the Privacy Policy does not exclude this possibility.	**Yes/Unclear** The privacy policy indicates that searches made on the Nook are probably not recorded, but B&N generally logs data on searches made and pages viewed on B&N web site. B&N does not disclose whether it associates book searches with a user's account if logged in. It is unknown whether searches for books done at locations other than B&N are also reported back, but the Privacy Policy does not exclude this possibility.	**Yes** Kobo seems to have the capability to keep track of book searches because it indicates that it shares those searches with third parties.

E-Reader Privacy Chart, 2012 Edition by the Electronic Frontier Foundation, https://www.eff.org/pages/reader-privacy-chart-2012.

Users of Google's free e-mail service, Gmail, for example, provide Google with basic personal information (including their formerly anonymous IP address, which is easily derived during registration). They also acknowledge that Google has the right to scan their online activity, ostensibly for security purposes (to identify spam and malware), but of course, this process also allows Google to analyze all incoming and outgoing e-mails, as well as any e-mails stored on Google's servers, for keywords and sentiment analysis. And although Gmail users have agreed to all this with the acceptance of Google's Terms of Use, those contacts that are e-mailing Gmail users (and may have no affiliation with Gmail) are also having their e-mails scanned—without their knowledge or consent. This process allows Google access not only to the content of all these e-mails (allowing them to apply automated sentiment scanning to derive affiliations, interests, and so on) but also to the contact information of both Gmail and non-Gmail users (e-mail addresses of the sender and those copied on e-mails). In this way, like the data aggregators discussed earlier, Google and other search engines can build up profiles not only of their own registered users but on millions of other non-affiliated e-mail contacts as well.

Free e-mail is not the only way that Google and other search engines collect personal data. For example, many hundreds of thousands of web site owners use Google Analytics to trace visitors on their sites; Google has access to these data too. Users of Google's Android operating system on their mobile phones have the option to back up their system with Google as a means of transferring their data to another Android phone. Although this makes it easy to set up a user's new phone, Google in the meantime gains access (with full consent of the user) to all the user's e-mails, messages, favorite sites, contact lists, and passwords.[10] Google also receives a wealth of user data from the Google+ social network and from Google TV. And, of course, its own browser, Google Chrome, allows the company to combine the search and browser functions in one, avoiding data privacy provisions that might arise with other browsers like Microsoft's

Internet Explorer or Apple's Safari. Chrome also allows Google to track users on non-search visits (since a user often uses apps these days from a mobile device and don't necessarily need to work through a search engine). They are also the default search engine for browsers like Firefox, which in turn, receives 85% of its income from Google.[11]

Google is not alone in this shift toward collecting personally identifiable data. After losing its number-two slot for US digital advertising in 2013, Yahoo! is pushing for its 800 million users to have Yahoo! e-mail accounts and to register for a Yahoo! ID to use services like its photo-sharing Flickr software.[12] Registration can involve providing information from name, birth date, and gender, to occupation, personal interests and assets, and even Social Security numbers. All this non-anonymous information can be shared, according to Yahoo!'s Terms of Service, with "trusted partners" who "may use your personal information to help Yahoo! communicate with you about offers from Yahoo! and our marketing partners."[13] They also requires registration for their Smart TV platform, which monitors online streaming program selection and then provides users with viewing and commercial recommendations. Yahoo! recently announced that it will anonymize personal data, including page views and clicks on ads, after three months instead of thirteen, while Google still is still holding out for nine months (it always before reserved the right to keep it for 18 to 24 months). Bing retains personal details for six months.[14]

The approach taken by e-commerce mega-retailers like Amazon is similar. Amazon provides users with the same level of search capability for products in their ever-growing inventory as powerful search engines like Google or Yahoo!. They also use cookies during this search process to identify the online shopper's computer, and clickstream tracking technologies to monitor shopping patterns. Less controversially, since those details are integral to the online buying process, Amazon also collects users' personal details and buying preferences. That means that Amazon collects data on what more than 150 million customers look at and buy, whether they went high end or low end with products, and whether they paid extra for standard or express delivery. Amazon also collects similar data from its Kindle Fire tablet and Kindle e-readers, as well as through their Fire smartphones.

In fact, their recently released Fire phone is, according to *ComputerWorld*'s Mike Elgan, "the most effective device ever sold for harvesting the personal data from its owner." The technology behind this monitoring process is again, Amazon's Firefly voice and facial recognition system, in this case activated by a button on the point-and-click remote control, which includes both a microphone and a camera that recognizes whatever it is pointed toward: a book, a song on the radio, a piece of fruit, or a brand name—anything contained in Amazon's database of 100 million objects. All that search data, including GPS coordinates, photos, and audio clips (even video or TV programs playing in the background) will be captured by Amazon, uploaded and cross-matched against the user's personal profile, building up an ever-growing picture of the user's activities, interests, and location throughout the day.[15]

There are differences between search engines and retailers, of course. The search engines use the personal data they collect, in part, to sell to advertisers, while Amazon has traditionally used the personal data it collects to fuel its recommendation engines. Apple is in a similar situation, in that it claims that it is interested only in collecting user data to make it easier for customers to buy Apple products online.

What Is a Recommendation Engine?

Most people probably associate recommendation engines with Amazon or Netflix, but a variety of analytical software offerings are now available to help a wide range of companies from insurance to financial advisors sell to customers based on an analysis of historical activity or purchasing patterns. A logical adjunct to the process of targeted advertising, recommendation analytics allow companies to use the previous purchasing or viewing behavior of a customer, often compared with other customers (known as *collaborative filtering*), to recommend products with similar characteristics (known as *content-based filtering*) to prompt the next purchase. The more sophisticated analytics offerings provide access to a wide variety of unstructured data, including voice recordings from customer service calls, to provide salespeople with sales and marketing strategies for customers on an individualized basis.

That distinction may no longer be valid, though, because in 2013 Amazon announced its own digital advertising network, which directs ads to a wide variety of online sites and mobile users, including Apple smartphones and mobiles and tablets running Google's Android operating system. As we've seen, other Internet powers like Google, Facebook, Microsoft, and Yahoo! all now own digital ad networks and real-time bidding exchanges, which allow advertisers and developers to bid on and buy advertising slots across the Web. That's because online advertising (and especially advertising to the mobile market) right now enjoys a profit margin of between 20% and 30% (compared with around 4% for Amazon's online retail margins). With accurate browsing and purchasing records on millions of customers going back many years, Amazon knows it has possibly the best collection of purchasing-interest customer data in the world—which puts them in a unique position with eager advertisers. If FICO knows your financial history, Google knows what you look at online, and Facebook knows who your friends are and what interests you, Amazon knows what, when, and how often you buy actual products.[16]

Like Google, Amazon has leveraged its massive global technology infrastructure and moved into providing remote Big Data storage and analytics platforms for companies through the cloud. Amazon's Web Service (AWS) provides companies access to Amazon's Elastic MapReduce platform (leveraging its Hadoop framework), which now provides "for rent" Big Data engine and storage for companies and organizations as diverse as Netflix, Dropbox, and even the CIA.[17]

And then, of course, there are social media, where decade-old Facebook has been responsible for a revolution in the collection of customer data. Initially intended for teenagers and college-aged students but quickly adopted by adults, Facebook invites its users to share personal, private, even intimate details of their life with others throughout the digital world. Combining the intimacy of private sharing and the openness of a community, Facebook has been wildly successful in convincing users worldwide to throw caution to the wind when it comes to giving up personal data. The idea behind "friending" was sheer genius, because the process makes it a social competition to link to as many other people as possible—and each of those links tells Facebook something more about the user and the persons in their "social proximity" (an approach also leveraged successfully by groups like LinkedIn, for example).

Facebook has been successful so far at deflecting many of the criticisms over its data collection practices in part by leveraging the personal nature of its service. For example, stressing the need for authentic identity, Facebook in the past wouldn't allow pseudonyms or multiple accounts—the type of common online behavior that, among other things, is used to avoid revealing our real identity but dilutes and undermines the completeness and accuracy of personal data for those trying to monitor us. At one point, Facebook even tried requiring scans of passports or users' driver's licenses. Although this did provide for authenticity, it also meant that each week Facebook was able to upload more than 20 billion preferences, biographies, photos, and almost anything else users were willing to tell about themselves, and associate that data directly with the genuine names (or an anonymized but consistent identifier) of its users.[18] As with Amazon's real sales records, this type of authenticity is invaluable when it comes to selling on data to advertisers.

One of Facebook's most innovative ideas was to devise social plug-ins—the Like, Subscribe, or Send options that Facebook maintains on other web sites. These social plug-ins can be found on thousands of web sites across the Internet and are attractive to other web site publishers because they offer the opportunity of having Facebook users recommend or send their site, video, or blog to other Facebook users. In fact, these social plug-ins are so popular among web site publishers that a recent study by the *Wall Street Journal* found that Facebook cookies and other tracking code could be found in 67% of the top 900 sites they scanned. Google+ also uses them (in the same study found on 30% of sites), and so does Twitter (found on 54% of sites).[19]

What Is a Social Plug-in?

Everyone is familiar with Facebook's "thumbs-up" Like button, but Facebook has many other social plug-ins, all of which, in addition to being convenient for the user and the web site owner, provide Facebook with a rich flow of sentiment and personal data. Facebook plug-ins include the following:

Send: Allows users to send content to friends through a private message, an e-mail, a posting, or on the friend's Facebook page.

Like: Lets users share favorite web pages or content with other users.

Activity Feed: Displays the content and activity that's been occurring on a user's site.

Login button: Provides a gateway for other users to log in to a user's site and displays the profile pictures of friends.

Comments box: Encourages visitors to leave comments on a user's web site, and then forwards those comments to friends and even friends of friends.

Recommendations: Displays the user's personalized recommendations.

Live Stream: Provides users visiting the site with real-time comments and activity monitoring.

Google uses a similar approach; G+ widgets or Google Maps embed code automatically in millions of web sites so that the tracking code loads whenever a viewer enters the site, whether the user uses the Google buttons or not.

These social plug-ins help Facebook too. When a user logs in to his or her Facebook account, a cookie is placed on the browser and matched against a unique personal ID number that identifies the user to Facebook and associates them with a Facebook page. If the user remains logged on to their Facebook account but then searches other sites, Facebook tracks that activity through that logon cookie. And even if a user logs off Facebook, as long as they don't clear their browser, that same logon cookie will notify Facebook of the user's presence on any associated web site (sites that contain a Facebook social plug-in and therefore recognize the user's ID cookie), even if the user never clicks on one of the social plug-in options at all. As we have seen, this is known as a third-party tracker code. That information includes the user's Facebook account ID, IP address, browser type, and web site the user was visiting.

All this is necessary to make the social plug-ins work—to capture and transfer the user's "like" or "share" choices and post those back onto the user's Facebook page and to the pages of other Facebook friends. But, this same process allows Facebook to essentially track the majority of its users throughout their daily web travels.[20]

Of course, Facebook doesn't really need to track users to collect personal data; users have already volunteered all that information anyway. But a user's likes and dislikes all contribute to a personal profile that Facebook (and now others) use when deciding what advertising to send the user. In fact, these likes and dislikes reveal a great deal about a user, as confirmed in a 2013 study by Cambridge University, which explained the extent to which attributes for a user can be inferred using Big Data analytics, citing the fact that Facebook likes "can be used to automatically and accurately predict a range of highly sensitive personal attributes including sexual orientation, ethnicity, religious and political views, personality traits, intelligence, happiness, use of addictive substances, parental separation, age, and gender."[21]

This technique provides Facebook with a huge amount of valuable web traffic data that adds to its demographic and trend data, again, to be sold to advertisers. And using Facebook's sophisticated Big Data algorithms—the equivalent of an advertisement recommendation engine—means that any user that clicks on a like or an ad itself will be sent similar likes and ads in the future. It's a sophisticated form of machine learning, and each transaction and user reaction builds up a more complex personal history on the user. Even the user's Facebook friends become part of that targeted advertising scenario, with Facebook's systems assuming that if a user thinks a friend would like something, it's pretty likely that the friend would like to see a related ad.

But despite the wealth of information Facebook has already on its users, it augments these user data with information bought from the major data aggregators reviewed previously, including Epsilon, Acxiom, and Datalogix. And the Facebook Audience Network (discussed in Chapter 5, "From Social Media to Digital Advertising Markets and Exchanges") means that advertisers can gain access to much more of these data to use for targeted advertising on non-Facebook sites.[22]

To get into digital advertising, however, Facebook needed a mechanism to point advertisers toward a highly personalized profile without actually releasing personal details. To do that, Facebook created a "pseudo-identity" layer by selling a coded identifier with the user's characteristics attached. Using a system known as *hashing*, Facebook encrypts a user's name and e-mail or log-in address, turning it into a random alphanumeric code. The retailer (Target, CVS, and so on) does the same. Then a third-party (Datalogix, for example) compares the two anonymous strings looking for similar traits (common purchases, interests, potential illnesses, and so on). When there is a match, the retailer knows that there is someone who is potentially interested in its product, and the retailer's is then targeted to the Facebook site of that user.[23]

More controversially, according to an investigation by the *Wall Street Journal*, although Facebook claims that it doesn't give e-mails or personal data away to third parties, Facebook will direct those third-party ads to Facebook users if the third party has already targeted those users and has their e-mail addresses.[24] Either way, if your local car dealership or bakery wants to contact you with a special coupon, you may find it on your Facebook page tomorrow morning.

Big Data and Bricks-and-Mortar Retailers

So we know that the consumer credit bureaus and the Internet technology companies are now collecting massive amounts of personal data on consumers. That's not so surprising, because it is what data aggregators do for a living, and in truth, as we've seen, it is the *raison d'être* and key to the business model for many Internet technology companies. But the practice of personal data collection doesn't stop there: It also extends into our day-to-day activities with many of the department stores and retail services that we interact with each day. Among retailers, the maxim has always been, "know your customer." But until recently, retailers didn't really know their customers at all. Now they are doing everything they can to know them intimately.

It could be argued that the move toward customer profiling began years ago when retailers moved from Green Stamps to loyalty cards as a means of drawing customers into a store by providing discounts for their continued patronage—rewards for buying volume, or sometimes for just being a member. These loyalty cards are usually tied to—or at least appear to be tied to—significant discounts, so there is a real incentive for shoppers to acquiesce. A recent study by Nielsen found that today nearly 85% of shoppers say they are more likely to visit retailers with loyalty programs (and with associated discounts).[25]

But by the early 1990s, retailers began to realize that these loyalty cards had a value beyond simply pulling in customers. For the first time, point-of-sale (POS) systems were becoming important for inventory management, using new barcode systems that recognized product IDs and captured sales data automatically. It didn't take long before enterprising IT groups realized that they could use these POS systems to match up the customer's personal information associated with a loyalty card with all the customer's purchases through stock keeping units (SKUs) captured automatically.

Suddenly retailers knew a lot about their customers' likes and dislikes. They knew who paid in cash or with a credit card. They knew what the customer bought—the types of food they ate, and in what quantities; whether someone bought whole milk or skim; fruit or candy bars. They even knew their customers' dress size and belt girth. And as grocery and general retailers moved into pharmacy sales in the 2000s, they soon learned what prescriptions individuals bought and what doctors wrote those prescriptions—an oncologist, an ophthalmologist, or an obstetrician.

But simply because retailers had these data didn't mean that it was valuable to them; for years retailers collected information on their customers but didn't really know what to do with it all. At best, they could generate coupons for items, or related items, that a customer had bought before to encourage the customer to buy again (for a lower price). The opportunity for getting these coupons in front of shoppers was equally limited. They could mail out Sunday fliers in a newspaper or have them printed off with the customer's receipt at the register. These methods were expensive, unfocused, and laborious for the customers and the retailer's administrative staff alike. And simply paying customers (through discounts) to buy what they were probably going to buy anyway has always been a fairly weak form of advertising.

It was only when companies like Google, Amazon, and Facebook explained to investors that the data they were collecting on users could be leveraged into revenue through targeted electronic advertising that retailers (or, to be more precise, management consultants who then advised retailers) began to appreciate that they had a similar treasure trove of personal customer data at their fingertips. As bricks-and-mortar stores adopted a parallel e-commerce model, retail chains began to tap into this same customer data collection model.

The first retailers to take the plunge in the United States—Barnes & Noble, Walmart, Target, CVS, Kroger—were large and powerful national or global retail chains that had the money, the customer base, and the foresight to invest in the same types of Big Data technologies being refined by the large search engines and their growing nemesis—Amazon.com. Today, customer data collection and profiling is standard practice among every major retail group, processing millions of customer transactions every day from a myriad of customer interactions that range from point-of-sale transactions to credit cards, store cards, coupons, refunds, or visits to the retailer's web site. Walmart, for example, collects consumer data on more than 145 million Americans mostly through its online web site and new store-based technologies for mobile phones. This type of data collection and analysis is now seen as a necessary and core competency for retailers, making them strong rivals to the consumer reporting groups and online tech giants. Walmart's US CEO Bill Simon boasted in September 2013 that "Our ability to pull data together is unmatched."[26]

As with Amazon, retailers have the advantage of being able to capture real buying data on their customers directly from their point-of-sale systems, and mirroring Amazon's recommendation engines, new technologies such as Syngera's Simplate have emerged as interactive POS terminals, retrieving a customer's personal buying profile directly from a retailer's enterprise (ERP—Enterprise Resource Planning or CRM—Customer Relationship Management) system, and then providing to customers at checkout targeted offers based on their profile, the store's inventory, and ongoing promotions.[27] This type of predictive data marketing software is proliferating: Groups like AgilOne, for example, provide retailers with a self-learning system that analyzes customer purchases from their POS records and predicts when customers are likely to be interested in purchasing the product again.[28]

Large retailers are also shifting their Internet and digital advertising focus toward mobile users, taking advantage of a new trend that involves in-store tracking of customers using technologies that include Wi-Fi and closed circuit TV (CCTV)-based monitoring, customer purchasing histories, predictive analytics, and even facial recognition. At its most basic, systems like ShopperTrak can be used simply to count shoppers that enter and exit the store. Its more advanced offering includes an *interior analytics* service that tracks a shopper by Bluetooth or cell phone MAC address as the shopper moves around the store (this data is anonymized but then collated and sold in the aggregate). Euclid, based in California, provides a video and Wi-Fi analytics system that identifies the customer and instantly provides to the retailer's staff data on the customer's last visit and what he or she bought.[29] Web Decisions and nGage Labs have partnered to provide a cloud-enabled, "real-time offer personalization engine" that provides customers with coupons and flexible pricing information on their mobile devices while they are in the store.[30] These customer location tracking services even extend beyond the store walls (*out-store tracking*)—Starbucks is piloting a geolocation pilot with Foursquare, the location-based social networking company in the United Kingdom, to provide ads to potential customers even as they approach their stores. UK's Tesco supermarket uses facial recognition software mounted on cameras at the pumps at their gas stations to tailor ads to potential shoppers before they drive across to their main store.[31]

As both a retailer and an Internet tech giant, Apple is getting into the in-store tracking game with the release of its iBeacons, small pieces of ID emitting code built into smartphones that is the basis of a microlocation smartphone targeting system now used in its US stores. Using these iBeacons, Apple staff can pinpoint a customer's location with much greater accuracy, so that shop clerks can send targeted content to a potential customer's phone when they notice them looking at a specific product or display. They have even developed a version to fit on the Major League Baseball's smartphone app At the Ballpark, which uses the position beacons to direct fans through the stadium and guide them toward concessions with targeted coupons.[32]

The more sophisticated of these systems identify customers entering the store either through the MAC address of their smartphones or, in some cases, through facial recognition systems like those offered by the UK-based Realeyes, which using camera-based software, "analyzes facial cues for responses to online ads, monitors shoppers' so-called happiness levels in stores and their reactions at the register."[33] These systems encourage customers to scan items, compare prices, receive coupons, read reviews, and even check out, using their mobile device. Of course, the retailer is monitoring all that online activity—as well as the shopper's facial expressions—and collecting the data under the user's profile.

What Is a MAC Address?

Every smartphone has a unique 12-character identifier known as a *Media Access Control (MAC)* address, which is permanently linked with the network interface card (NIC) of each particular device. Whenever a smartphone is turned on it sends out query signals in search of a Wi-Fi or Bluetooth network connection displaying that MAC address, and those same signals can be captured by various types of sensors. Similar to an IP address, in that it identifies the device not the specific user, a MAC address is not considered to be personally identifiable information (PII) according to US privacy law, and a wide variety of software is now available that can pick up that signal and use it to identify the device and the location of the user.

With iOS7, Apple phased out its use of the MAC address and the Universal Device ID (UDID) used by app developers and ad networks to identify a device without access to PII. Their smartphones now contain the iBeacons technology described previously.

RetailNext provides one of the most advanced combinations of behavior analytics and in-store tracking systems with its Clutch platform, which uses the retailer's loyalty program data to send promotions on a variety of media (online, mobile, social media) to customers before they set off for the store. Those customers who respond positively to a targeted advertisement are tracked when they enter the store and can be sent an offer for any product they find interesting. The system allows the retailer to monitor what particular items a customer looks at while in the store and then later re-send those customers an offer through another medium. And this is not just a trial system. The Clutch platform can be found in 450 retailers worldwide and has data on more than 40 million consumer accounts. RetailNext systems have more than 65,000 sensors installed in retail stores and monitor the behavior of more than 800 million shoppers a year.[34]

What Is Omni-Channel Retailing?

In its annual report, Macy's says that it has moved so much toward *omni-channel retailing* that it now views various sales channels—bricks-and-mortar, television, mail and catalog, online, mobile—as one. This reflects the move by many retailers away from a multi-channel sales model (using several sales channels, but each separately) to an omni-channel sales model (creating a seamless overlap between all the customer sales opportunities) by capturing and integrating a customer's purchasing interests electronically and responding in a way (online or offline) that ensures the sale.

All this reflects retail's adoption of the same concept of omni-channel retailing being championed by the large Internet technology groups. There are many examples. Kroger, the American grocery chain, announced this year a plan to digitize almost every aspect of its stores with a strategy they call Retail Site Intelligence, which combines wireless networks, mobile devices, point-of-sale systems, and video cameras.[35] Tesco, the large UK supermarket chain, has a program called The Orchard, which invites shoppers to review discounted or free products with friends over their choice of social media. These reviews are then monitored by Tesco, and shoppers who provide extensive (and, presumably, positive) social media reviews are rewarded with more discounts or free products.[36]

And appreciating that more than a third of Walmart.com's online traffic comes from smartphone users,[37] the global giant moved ahead with a formidable Big Data strategy that combines both home Internet and in-store Internet shopping with smartphones. It has already installed its Scan & Go self-checkout systems in a number of stores, which allow users who open the Walmart app on their iPhones and Android devices to scan items, check prices, receive customized coupons, and pay, all using just their mobile phone. The store's Wi-Fi network allows the company not only to track customers as they move about the store, but also to collect the behavioral data that customers provide as they check items, prices, and coupons during their visit. That data, in turn, is stored in Walmart's search engine, Polaris, which combines customer data from the Walmart.com site, relevant postings from the users on social media, and the items that the customer has previously clicked on during online and mobile in-store searches.[38] The analytics behind all this comes in part from Walmart's purchase of Kosmix, a Big Data startup whose software collects a vast array of data (hundreds of millions of entities and relationships) on people, products, and trends by trawling through social media sites. Renamed as @WalmartLabs by the retailer, the system is supported by an index of 60 billion social media documents and uses sentiment analysis and a popular interest monitoring system broken down on a geographical basis. The results are then matched against customer searches and sales trend data from bricks-and-mortar stores to find correlations with customers who can then be presented with targeted advertising on their mobile device.[39]

Walmart's CEO of Global E-commerce, Neil Ashe, explained the company's goals to investors in 2013: "We're building a global technology platform whose goals are as simple, frankly, as they are audacious. We want to know what every product in the world is. We want to know who every person in the world is. And we want to have the ability to connect them together in a transaction."[40]

There is little doubt that these Big Data trends and technologies are becoming a core competency of mainstream retailers, and it won't be long before sales clerks greet customers by name as they enter the store, and have the items they believe that customer will want already collected and bagged. They could already do that in many stores if they didn't think it would frighten the customer.

But all that customer data is just as valuable to other companies and can be sold for considerable profit. The *Wall Street Journal* recently found that in a survey of 70 popular web sites, for those that required a login (name, e-mail address, and other personal details), more than 25% of the time those personal details were passed on to third parties.[41] Walmart admits to sharing customer data with more than 50 third parties.[42] Disney admitted to Propublica in 2013 that it shared customer data among its own companies—ESPN, ABC—as well as others such as Honda, Dannon, or Almay.[43] And as we've seen, Walgreens sold anonymized data on its prescription patients (the drug, the patient's sex, age, state, and the ID of the prescribing doctor) to pharmaceutical companies for $749 million in 2010 (data very valuable to the pharma groups that could then target high-volume or new drug-prescribing physicians with their own marketing efforts).[44] Civil libertarians claim that much of the data being exchanged is either tied directly to a person's name, or if anonymized, could easily be derived (which we'll discuss more in Chapter 11), but since this type of data exchange is done confidentially between companies, it's hard to know to what extent such data are personally attributable.

The Invisible Data Trackers

But retailers, data aggregators, and big Internet tech groups are not the only ones collecting personal data. All this demand to track and capture digital data over the past several years has been the impetus for a flurry of technological activity among groups that provide online tracking and monitoring functions in a way that most people never see and seldom appreciate. In fact, whenever a user visits a popular web page, in the first fraction of a second, his or her computer is deluged with a variety of computer code from sometimes as many as several hundred groups that want to monitor user activity on that site—and if they can—to latch onto the user electronically and continue to follow their web activity on other sites as he or she progresses through the day. As invisible as these stealthy data trackers are, this is not a trivial thing.

A recent *Wall Street Journal* investigation used a test computer to visit the 50 most popular American web sites (which, interestingly, account for nearly 40% of the web pages viewed by Americans). They found that simply from visiting these sites more than 2,224 items of computer code from 131 different companies were loaded onto their computer. That broke down to an average of 64 tracking technologies poised surreptitiously on each of the top web sites, waiting to pounce on site visitors. Twelve sites had more than 100 monitoring companies "dropping" code. A single visit to Dictionary.com resulted in 223 files being downloaded onto the test computer. Only Wikipedia, which doesn't advertise, had none.[45] A similar 2013 study by *The New York Times* identified 105 different tracking technologies that accumulated on its test computer in a 36-hour period of web surfing.[46] In 2013, researchers at AT&T Labs and Worcester Polytechnic Institute identified tracking technology on 80% of 1,000 popular sites.[47]

That means that each time a user accesses a popular site (*The New York Times*, Target's online store, *The Huffington Post*, Wunderground, and so on), the site's server logs the request (on server logs) and captures basic information such as the user's IP address, the date and time, what pages were looked at, for how long, and if possible, what sites preceded and followed the visit. Apart from those server logs, the site owners and many other third-party trackers will also be dropping cookies and web beacons on the visitor's computer to track activity on the site. Sometimes known as tracking bugs, these small files of computer code can also be embedded in advertisements themselves, so that the advertiser can monitor when and how often their ad is being viewed.

Most of these companies and site publishers claim that they never sell personally identifiable data, but as users are increasingly choosing software and techniques for disabling cookies, even that level of relative anonymity may soon pass. This, combined with the fact that much (if not most) of the mobile activity takes place from within an app (that is, not a browser), means that browser cookie tracking technology is no longer as useful for the mobile market as it was for PCs. This trend is forcing companies like Google to consider an upgrade to the old-fashioned cookie, and they are reportedly working on a replacement for third-party cookies, which would be similar to Apple's iBeacon and would create the foundation for a "persistent identifier" that would not only carry data but be much more resilient than the antiquated browser tracking cookie, which can be disabled or disappears whenever a browser is cleansed.[48]

The large number of tracking companies can be explained in part because the process for getting the appropriate digital ad to the web visitor involves a myriad of intermediary companies, many with overlapping functions. These include groups such as Metamarkets, used by the FT.com site, which serves as a "business intelligence platform for publishers," analyzing ad inventory, evaluating and consulting on ad placement, and advising the FT on their likely audience. Or TruMeasure, which helps to assess how well the purchased advertisements are performing (based on unique visits, time on site, page views, and actual follow-on sales through phone or e-mail). Or a company like Adometry, which works with 70 advertisers from various industries to provide attribution—that is, the proper credit—for online ads.[49] Each of these groups wants to place its tracking code on your computer whenever you visit one of those popular sites.

The Evolution of Tracking Technologies

Although cookies usually work in a similar way on mobile browsers, most mobile users will also access the Internet through apps, which will vary in the way that they utilize cookie tracking technologies. Typically, mobile apps use a technology called "webview" to present website or ad content to the user, and cookies are stored within this webview technology much in the same way that they are on a browser. But because app developers use a wide variety of technologies and techniques in app development, the information derived from those webview cookies may not be easily combined with data pulled from browsers or other apps. This shift toward mobile apps and the emergence of new cookie blocking technologies, has bolstered the development of new and more effective ways to track users on both PCs and mobile devices. Some of the more innovative methods include the following:

A MAC address and/or Universal Device ID (UDID), which cannot be turned off by the user.

HTML5: Using the local storage feature of HTML5 (the Internet's core technology markup language) to hide tracking cookies so that they are undetectable.

Browser fingerprints: A growing field that uses analytical tools to analyze a wide variety of user activity characteristics (including cross-matching fonts, operating systems, location, and even typing speed) to make a record of a user's digital "fingerprint" matched against a user ID. Google's "preference IDs" (PrefIDs) use a similar approach: They drop these PrefID cookies on a computer in order to ensure that the user's preferences (font, language, filter settings, number of search results, and so on) are retained. Those same settings, however, when matched against other telltale Internet activity characteristics and location, can provide Google, or third-party advertisers, with a potential user match in their profiling efforts.

This type of digital fingerprinting is unerasable and practically invisible and can be used to track users across various devices. And because they are not cookie-tracking technologies, they may not be subject to current data privacy laws.

Registration and log-in: And, of course, the most effective method for identifying a user may simply be to require them to register first, and then to log-in each time they use an app or a service.

What data are they monitoring? Let's look at what Adnxs.com, a digital advertising exchange that supports advertising platforms like Google's DoubleClick, is capturing. According to its web site, the information that may be tracked from a browser includes the following:

- A unique identifier (so a browser can be recognized when it appears on another web site using AppNexus's services)

- What ads the browser has seen
- What page the browser was on when it saw the ad
- When the browser saw the ad
- Whether the ad has been clicked
- What type of pages the browser has visited (to build an idea of what content might be used)
- IP address (to infer location)[50]

Just a few years ago, that level of tracking would have been inconceivable, but now is fairly common. Today, tracker technologies can not only follow the targeted users, but they can even follow the piece of advertising itself, recording every user who looked at it and their reaction to the specific characteristics of that customized ad (increasing knowledge about the targeted user and the effectiveness of the ad at the same time).

What Is Web Scraping?

Web scraping (often also known as *web harvesting*, *crawling*, or *cutting*) is the computerized search for information from web pages. Web scraping often targets social media groups such as Twitter, LinkedIn, Facebook, or Instagram, and over the past several years, a myriad of companies have appeared that search the Web for user-generated content (UGC), particularly contact details, résumés, e-mail addresses, or a user's comments on discussion boards, blogs, or online chatrooms. Using the same type of crawling technology developed for search engines, but usually targeting specific web sites, these programs search for key words or sentiment data using software "robots" that simulate human search but are anonymous and difficult to detect.

Although the privacy settings and terms of use of social media sites often are designed to deter this type of computerized spying, scraping companies often enter sites illicitly by using fake profiles and a variety of tools (spiders, robots, harvesting bots, and so on).

In fact, so much money is involved in this type of digital monitoring of ad viewing, and so many tracking companies are monitoring users' ad views, that it was only a question of time before things got out of hand. Fraudsters are already creating software to mimic the behavior of online viewers to artificially boost the hit rate of ads. The *Financial Times* reported that in 2013, a Mercedes-Benz online advertising campaign was the victim of this type of tracker fraud: In an investigation, it was found that of 350,000 ad impressions brokered in a three-week period, 57% of these ads were "viewed" by computer programs instead of humans.[51]

Adding Customer Profiles from Company Enterprise Systems

As we saw in earlier chapters, one of the most important trends in data collection is occurring in the Industrial Internet, and an integral part of that Big Data movement is the expansion of CRM and other ERP modules, which collect and aggregate a company's customers' data. These are the non-retail stores—our phone and ISP services, water, insurance, charities, or financial advisors. All these organizations collect and maintain customer details captured in some way in their enterprise systems, and all these organizations can potentially sell that customer data to data aggregators, Facebook, advertisers, or anyone else who wants to buy it.

And now data coordinating companies like ClearStory Data are even beginning to combine personal online customer data collected on the Internet with the customer's offline data that resides in the CRM systems of companies around the world. Known as *data onboarding* (or sometimes *CRM re-targeting*), this integration of online and offline customer information, and particularly the ability to capitalize on CRM customer data through online advertising channels, is something that the large data aggregators and high-tech Internet companies have been working on for some time.

Data onboarding not only allows companies to be more effective in placing online ads (offline-to-online marketing), but also provides companies with access to additional customer profile data being collected from online tracking. And, of course, it is a two-way exchange, with the large aggregators, as well as the Internet Tech giants, augmenting their own customer profiles with customer data currently locked up in the CRM systems of many thousands of companies.

This data onboarding movement is potentially revolutionary, because it marks the amalgamation of hundreds of thousands of offline and online customer databases. That's why Marin Software recently announced an alliance with Google to provide support for its remarketing lists for search ads (RLSA). The need to better understand the effectiveness of advertising channels (mobile, online, e-mail, and offline) is why Google purchased the marketing analytics group Adometry, and why AOL recently bought Convertro (also an online attribution firm) for $100 million.[52] It is also why Oracle has bought BlueKai, and why Acxiom has paid $310 million for LiveRamp, a company that helps to compare data between these many marketing applications and coordinate multichannel marketing campaigns. The deal brings Acxiom potential access to the CRM systems of more than 200 top-tier companies and access to a partner in LiveRamp, which is at the center of coordinating online advertising activities with around 100 marketing applications (including BlueKai).[53] According to Acxiom, together they have access to more than 7,000 customers and partners around the world, and more to the point, direct access to some form of advertising contact with 99% of the population in the United States.[54]

The Big Data Collection Universe

So we know that personal data is being collected by both retail stores and non-retail entities like utility companies. It is also captured from online searches, purchases, or web site visits by both high-tech companies and many hundreds of smaller monitoring technologies. And all that data is being sought out and collected by data aggregators—often former consumer credit reporting agencies—that maintain profiles of many million individuals worldwide. Below is a short survey of the kind of data that falls under the heading of the Big Data Collection Universe today:

Internet-originating digital data sources:

- Online shopping and sales (product catalogs and web sites)
- Uploaded films, videos, images, and music
- Online advertising
- News, journals, articles, blogs, white papers, scanned literature
- Internet searches and web traffic
- Social media (sentiment data)
- Web visits (log files and clickstream data)
- Employment sites and web-based employment postings
- Broadband-based home and mobile streaming media
- Output from smart components, performance monitoring, and computer-based maintenance (CBM)
- Soft grid applications
- IoT applications from cars to sports watches, thermostats, washing machines, and refrigerators
  - Online purchases
  - Articles read
  - Internet searches
    - Favorite sites
    - Scraping of social media
    - Sentiment analysis and online customer reviews
    - Credit reports

- Text captured from credit applications
- Recorded account opening interviews
- Call center and customer service notes
- Social media chatter and other customer market research

Non-Internet originating digital data sources:

- Cell phones
- GPS
- Credit cards
- "Back Office" business functional software: ERP, CRM, Office and Security Employee and payroll, insurance, accounts in and out, and buyer relations and agreements
- Line-function monitoring (power generation, telephones, production lines, and so on)
- Financial services: Low-latency data and algorithmic trading
- Supply chain management: Sensors and intelligent reporting systems
- Make and move logistics, tracking, and performance systems
- Business-to-business ordering and payment tracking
- Store discount cards, warranty cards, and so on
- Bank, mortgage, and other financial transactions
- CCTV cameras and surveillance

Other offline social, financial, and behavioral data:

- Credit card transactions and balances
- Financial records/auto and other loans
- Store preference/supermarket savings cards
- Brand preference/product warranty cards
- Mortgage and property records

- US Census records
- Motor vehicle data
- Magazine and catalog subscriptions
- Responses to surveys
- Sweepstakes and contest entries
- Church attendance and tithing
- Contributions to political parties
- Criminal records
- Health-related data
- Hobbies, lifestyle data
- Income and socioeconomic status

Mobile, smartphone, and apps:

- Geographical data
- GPS
- Cell phone records
- Social media locators
- Toll booths (EzPass)
- Zip codes on store purchases
- Phone and mobile communications
- Twitter
- Location[55]

But all this digital data collection and utilization is only possible if companies have access to the tools and technologies that support this level of Big Data manipulation: tools that can capture digital data accurately and reliably from a wide variety of offline and online sources, store and retrieve that data efficiently and inexpensively, and analyze that data to extract meaningful patterns and conclusions. Let's have a look now at those Big Data tools and technologies.

9

Big Data Technologies

Key Chapter Points

- Big Data management technologies have their origins in the concepts that originated with enterprise resource planning (ERP) and other enterprise business systems.
- Big Data analysis capabilities evolved from Google and Yahoo!'s use of massive parallel processing and Hadoop/MapReduce technologies.
- Because traditional relational database management systems don't work well with unstructured data, new non-relational databases have emerged.
- These new technologies can produce significant cost savings and provide unique analysis but are not intended for business-critical data.
- These Big Data technologies are increasingly available to users to buy or to access through the cloud.

Previous chapters give a sense of the scale and variety of digital data being produced and collected and of the many parties involved in efforts to monetize Big Data in the digital economy. But to store, retrieve, and analyze the types and volume of data involved—everything from video and text messages, to online sentiment analysis of likes and dislikes posted on a Facebook page—requires technologies different from the traditional relational database and business intelligence tools that dominate the conventional IT world.

Most of these new technologies have their origins in the companies that spearheaded the Big Data economy in the first place—in particular, the search engines Google and Yahoo! and the online retailer Amazon—because these companies first developed the search engines, software frameworks, and storage platforms necessary to allow millions of users to access many more millions of web sites and products over the Internet. As we've seen, these Big Data companies and the technologies that they developed are quickly becoming a parallel IT infrastructure to rival the one created by the likes of IBM, Oracle, and SAP over the last 30 years of technological growth.

There are some important differences, however. As influential as Google and Amazon are, they can never control and contain the technology itself in the way that IBM, Oracle, or Microsoft once did. The Big Data technologies they developed have become much more democratized, in part because they are available stand-alone, or for rent, through the cloud (although both Amazon and Google are huge players in cloud-based storage) for much less money than has been traditionally spent on mainframe or relational database systems. It is also because many of the technologies are based on open-source frameworks and standards. And although to some extent groups like Google and Amazon still exert tremendous influence on Internet and data management policy, the advantage of this process of technological democratization (and an easily accessible data storage facility like the cloud) is that any organization, of any size, anywhere, can participate in the Big Data world in some way.

Data Basics

Capturing and organizing numbers is what early computing and tabulation was all about; after all, computers had their origins in computation, and the genius of Hollerith's punch card was that all data could be reduced to 1s or 0s. Traditional database technology has, for that reason, been set up to capture, compare, or calculate based on numeric (and alpha/numeric) data and is usually organized for retrieval in tables that allow for (comparatively) easy search and analysis.

Although it accounts for only around 15% of all digital data being created currently, this type of structured data remains important because it works best with traditional computing and enterprise systems—ERP, CRM, SCM—and the powerful relational databases and spreadsheets that still hold and display most corporate data today. *Structured data* simply means that the data can be organized to fit into a model that specifically defines how the data is stored and retrieved. That usually involves a set of tables that define what categories of data will be stored (names, addresses, medical record numbers, payment dates, social security numbers, and so on) and what type of data they will be (numeric, currency, alphabetic). The data model also usually sets strict rules for data consistency, such as limiting the number of characters or using only numbers or lowercase lettering. This approach to data storage and retrieval is the basis for relational databases and spreadsheet data management tools that have been used for nearly 50 years—and that is reflected in both the way that most of these technologies function (the logic of columns and rows) and in their limitations. As long as the data used are accurate and adhere to these preset rules, relational database systems are extraordinarily powerful and dependable, because the logic of the relationship between all the data fields is clearly understood, and the rules governing those relationships are—with some level of flexibility—set.

The vast majority of business transaction data conforms to the requirements of structured data, including product descriptions, company and customer names, addresses, credit card information, and even logistics data such as GPS output, or operational data produced by sensors or monitoring components. All these are structured data.

But much of the data we've been talking about in the first chapters of this book is data for which words like *accurate* or *consistent* really don't apply—data that come in the form of photos or voice, from e-mails or Internet searches, or from YouTube videos or comments over Twitter or Facebook. Around 85% to 90% of data that exist today—and about 99% of data that will be created in the future—are this type of *unstructured data*, and this is not the sort of data that can easily be captured and placed in traditional row-and-column-based relational database tables.

Steve Hamby, the chief technology officer of Orbis Technologies, makes a nice analogy when he describes the difference between structured conventional and unstructured Big Data systems requirements. Think of the traditional relational database approach as a kitchen drawer, he suggests, containing cutlery; all the knives, forks, and spoons in an appropriately molded plastic tray, every utensil in its place. Then think of Big Data as not one but many thousands of junk drawers, overflowing with every conceivable type of article—old combs, photos, doorknobs, old letters, broken sunglasses, and so on. Trying to do an inventory, or simply to even find something, in the many hundreds of junk drawers, requires a different approach.[1] In the same way, collecting, storing, and analyzing data from such a variety of diverse sources and different formats is much more difficult than reaching conclusions based on structured data.

In fact, not only is it more difficult to store and retrieve, and more voluminous, but as a rule, unstructured data contain comparatively little readily useful information (you might say that on the whole, it is data heavy and information light). There is some possibly valuable information that can be extracted from social plug-ins, online searches, and Facebook photos, but it is never going to be as information rich, or as easy to interpret with certainty as the preselected and verifiable structured data in conventional relational database models. After all, just because there is a lot of it, doesn't always mean it is particularly helpful in terms of providing insight. Much of it is simply worthless. And this combination of variety, complexity, and variability means usefully analyzing this type of unstructured data with conventional business intelligence tools is simply impossible.

A lot of data also falls in-between the two categories: known as *semistructured data*, this type of data has some organizational attributes of both—metadata, for example, which contains an identifying keyword, tag, or e-mail address, lends structure to a search (author, date, subject, and so on) but makes no attempt to analyze the unstructured content of the e-mail's text or attached photo or the video data. Similarly, Twitter Tweets and some other forms of social media messaging (where the message metadata title is essentially the same thing as the content) qualify as good examples of semistructured data. Over the years, as companies have saved more and more of their e-mails, photos, graphics, pdfs, customer phone recordings, and so on, this metadata has been the primary method for organizing and locating this type of data, and that is why in part markup languages such as XML have become important over the years, because they can be used to help manage this type of semistructured data (although any complex analysis of the unstructured data contained under the metadata filings is still impossible without new Big Data tools).

ERP and Big Data

As we saw in earlier chapters, despite all the focus on the Big Data aspects of the consumer Internet, making use of digitized data is relatively new to the average private individual. Before the Internet and mobile phones, information technology was far from entertaining and almost exclusively the domain of business. Hollerith cards, production reports, accounts, sales records—these were the core activities of Information Technology within business processes, supported by mainframes, distributed computing, networked PCs, Windows, and Excel spreadsheets.

Today, most businesses, from service-related industries like insurance companies to manufacturing and distribution conglomerates, are dependent on enterprise systems packed with a powerful complement of integrated applications that collect, organize, store, analyze, and report on a myriad of data produced throughout the supply chain—from design through production and into advertising, sales, and customer service. In fact, arguably, one of the most important formative events in the Big Data Big Bang was when Oracle, SAP, JD Edwards, PeopleSoft, and others began to develop a suite of modules for business software that integrated the key functions of business: accounting and finance, payroll, human resources, production planning, inventory management, and logistics. These enterprise resource planning (ERP) systems drove the collection and analysis of data in ways that had never before been possible, gathering and storing digital data using common database management systems that allowed a variety of departments from around the company—and indeed from around the nation or world—to access that data seamlessly, extracting information relevant to their needs. To organize and understand that data, these ERP systems soon either built-in or integrated with new, increasingly powerful business intelligence software applications that could query the data stored in a relational database for key information.

By the mid-1990s, as companies began to develop intranets and corporate portals, it soon became apparent that the Internet itself could be adapted as a suitable framework for data transfer—not only internally between a company's own employees—but also externally for online ordering, product catalogs, customer service, and marketing and advertising. As groups like SAP and Oracle began to provide Software-as-a-Service (SaaS) options for e-commerce and B2B (company-to-supplier) transactions, soon the Internet became the shared neural network for the core business functions of many thousands of companies. That meant that much of data management moved from the back-office mainframe to the Internet, and the Internet quickly became the primary interface between themselves and the outside world. This process also meant that data management had become a vital differentiator in most companies' success.

That close tie between ERP systems and the Internet was important when e-commerce really began to develop and retailers began to use the Internet as the front end of their order processing system. Groups like Amazon.com, which in the late 1990s began to expand from online book sales into the full-service online global retailer it is today (curiously enough, using veteran data and software architects from Walmart's inventory management team),[2] realized that coordination between online orders and fulfillment was going to be the key to success. As most major bricks-and-mortar retailers began to create online store interfaces, other services, from banking to travel to online dating appeared, all supported by online payment systems that tied into the major banks and credit cards. This was no longer back-office administration; these were front-office functions necessary to the survival of the company.

Appreciating this shift, by the late 1990s ERP systems had moved away from just supplying administrative functions and incorporated important online data management capabilities in a variety of integrated e-business systems, to the point that in 2000 Gartner declared an ERP renaissance (ERP II) and correctly predicted that these enterprise systems and their web-based software would provide the data management backbone for modern business and pave the way for an Internet-based economy. For all their foresight, though, neither Gartner, nor any of the rest of us, could envision at that time the future explosion of digital data that was looming on the consumer side of the equation.

In fact, these ERP systems were also preparing the way for the Big Data Big Bang, because the combined effect of the business world shifting its enterprise systems and distributed PC computing to the Internet in the 1990s was probably more important for the early expansion of the Internet and the Big Data phenomenon than AOL or AltaVista, or any of the other early search engines on the consumer side of the equation.

ERP also introduced several key principles and features of Big Data to modern computing. For example, a crucial element of ERP software platforms is performance measurement—the capability of the system to use data to quantify the efficiency and effectiveness of business activities. The systems also introduced the idea that, whenever possible, data should be collected only once at the source and then be stored centrally so that it can be accessed for analysis by all who need it. ERP architects also insisted that company systems should be standardized and interoperable so that data could be shared among the variety of functions throughout the business at the same time, helping to break down the silos of information that existed with departmental (as opposed to enterprise) systems (see Figure 9.1). And finally, they advanced the idea that large data sets could be analyzed through an emerging set of data analysis tools that became known as business intelligence.

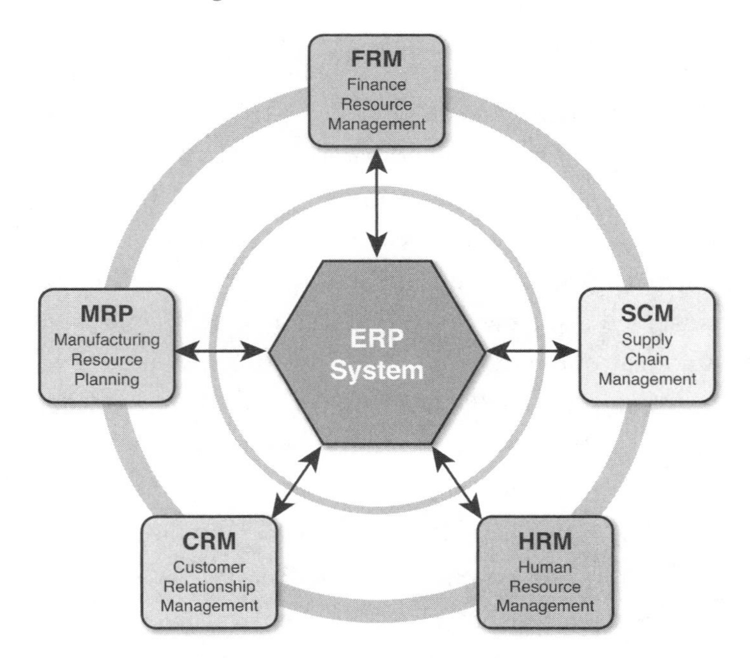

Figure 9.1 Key Modules of an Enterprise System[3]

There is a significant difference, however, between the current set of business intelligence and analytic tools designed for relatively small and structured data sets and the power of the Big Data technologies now available for analyzing massive data sets made up of a wide variety of data (which comes from both inside and outside the company). Enterprise systems—Manufacturing Resource Planning (MRP), Customer Relationship Management (CRM), Supply Chain Management (SCM)-type systems—have always had the capacity for business intelligence and analytics. It is not a clear-cut distinction, but generally while ERP systems help organizations to know *what happened* in the past, conventional business intelligence and analytics help companies to understand *why something happened* in the past, and Big Data analytics (if used effectively) help a company to predict *what will happen* in the future (see Figure 9.2).

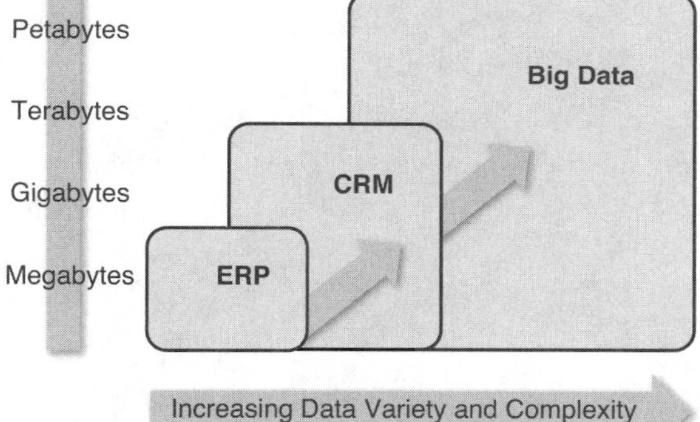

Figure 9.2 Big Data Has Its Origins in ERP and CRM
Derived from a diagram by Teradata[4]

That's why, when dealing with Big Data, enterprise systems and their supporting relational database frameworks have their limitations. In the first place, as large as the transaction data sets can be for an enterprise, the data quantities are dwarfed by the multi-structured data sets being captured and distributed through cloud computing systems and analyzed by Big Data-type technologies. That is, in part, because the transaction data that these ERP systems use is (and usually must be) structured, uniform, and clean, so that it can be organized into tables that form the basis of relational database management (RDBM) systems. RDBM systems were not designed to analyze the content of semistructured or unstructured data from social media, e-mail, voice, or video. And although many powerful analytical business intelligence platforms are available, they are mostly focused on activity-based costing for all types of supply chain-related issues—inventory control, production and logistics planning, supplier performance analysis—and so are less suitable for Big Data applications involving customer behavior and sentiment analysis, for instance.

Big Data Social Intelligence and Analytics

Social intelligence is the process for monitoring social media for data on trending likes, dislikes, brand names, and other sentiment data that can help with marketing or product development.

Social analytics are the tools used to analyze that data, often categorized into what users are talking about (Share), what they are saying about those things (Engagement), and how often they are talking about them (Reach).

Nonetheless, as we discuss in Chapter 10, "Doing Business in a Big Data World," for many companies, this traditional framework—ERP systems utilizing structured data analyzed by conventional business intelligence tools—is perfectly adequate for their needs. Which prompts the question: Do most companies really need to move into the Big Data world?

That is for each company to judge, but again, the most common area companies see as justifying investment in a parallel or separate Big Data enterprise framework is customer relationship management

(CRM), because it is the one area where all three Big Data principles (very large data sets, widely varied data, the need for powerful analytics) come into play. That's because in most modern companies, the CRM system and process ideally not only integrate online and bricks-and-mortar marketing, sales, and customer service functions, but in many ways, create an opportunity on a smaller scale for organizations to emulate the Big Data Internet tech giants like Google and Facebook—allowing them not only to monitor their own online systems for customer behavior data, but also to trawl the wider Internet for sentiment data related to their firm or the products or services they are selling. These days, that combination of customer relationship management and social media analytics is often referred to as *Big Data and social intelligence/analytics.* Today, hundreds of companies (Brandwatch, Sysomos, Google Analytics, Hootsuite, MozAnalytics, Salesforce's Marketing Cloud, and so on) offer social media analytics tools, and these may come as part of an ERP system, as a stand-alone system, or be accessed over the Web. Most CRM systems also include social media features that collect phone, e-mail, calendar, and sales report data and combine it with customer or product-related Internet sentiment analysis (as we discussed before), and a variety of groups (Medallia, Clarabridge, Confirmit, RelateIQ, for example) also can help to interpret that social media data and to coordinate a company's customer relationship management data and tactics.

The idea of being able to do this type of social media scraping on a smaller business scale has become so compelling that nearly 70% of executives in a 2013 survey said that they already had or were seriously considering investing in a CRM system in the next 12 months, and many of those specifically because they were interested in taking advantage of the ability to enhance their customer understanding through these types of Internet Big Data tools. And aware of the opportunities and their own limitations on the relational database side, many traditional database and ERP vendors (Oracle, SAP, and so on) have begun to incorporate non-relational technologies into their platforms and offer these as part (or as extensions) of their enterprise framework.[5]

A Parallel Universe

One of the more confusing aspects of Big Data is the myriad of new data management technologies—with names such as NoSQL, Hadoop, and MapReduce—that have emerged in the past few years. One of the key questions for any organization wanting to process large amounts of unstructured data is whether any (or all) of these technologies are appropriate, or whether it would be possible to live comfortably in the world of Big Data and remain with traditional ERP and RDBM systems. Before describing the technologies themselves, it might be helpful to look at the current state of data management in terms of the decades-old rivalry over how best to apply increased computing power to larger-scale data management.

Companies have two broad options (with variations). The first is to use a central processing unit (CPU) that runs some type of the conventional relational database and can be "scaled up" to handle increased data loads or more complex computing. When a company wants to increase processing power, it increases the size of the system (scales vertically) by buying bigger (or multiple) servers. These CPUs are typically tied together by a single operating system and a single memory, and this arrangement is usually known as *symmetric multiprocessing*, or *SMP*. As a rule of thumb, data storage and retrieval is generally more consistent and dependable using this type of concurrent processing and a relational database system, as long as the data is structured and held locally.

The second broad strategy for modern data management involves distributing those storage and retrieval tasks among many small processors, joined together on nodes (or in multiple nodes, known as clusters) within a distributed network. This is the type of distributed arrangement companies use in the cloud (the Internet, of course, being the largest of all distributed systems, made up of many millions of linked processors, servers, and network devices). If a company wants to add more data or processing power, it simply adds more processors or more nodes (scale horizontally). Typically this type of parallel or distributed processing can be cheaper, because it can be done using the combined processing power of inexpensive PCs and servers, but it also requires a coordinating software framework to assign workloads and priorities to the various processors and to partition up a common database that is being constantly bombarded by data requests from multiple machines. Because it involves distributing data over many different processors and across many nodes, however, there can be a risk to the consistency and safety of the data. Where companies run many hundreds or even thousands of processors and nodes, this type of distributed architecture is often called *massively parallel computing* or *MPP*, which in its various forms simply means that these many distributed processors, each running its own operating system and memory, all communicate through a network interconnect software platform that allows them to complete their computational work *in parallel.*

Relational database technologies can be run either centrally or in a distributed network, but either way they usually use some form of the *Structured Query Language (SQL)*, the standard programming language for communicating with relational databases, which uses statements (for example, "Create," "Update," "Delete," and so on) to store or retrieve data from a database. SQL works very well with standardized tables filled with structured data but typically does not handle unstructured data well. It is associated mostly with the major established vendors providing relational database management systems like Oracle, IBM, Ingres, Sybase, and Microsoft SQL Server.

But the Internet giants like Google and Yahoo! grew up working in a world of distributed, parallel computing and storage, where they needed to provide the results of search and analysis of enormous amounts of unstructured data to users all over the world. For that reason, Google, Yahoo!, Amazon, and other Internet giants moved away from SQL and RDBM systems and developed instead a *non-relational approach* (using technologies such as NoSQL and Hadoop/MapReduce), which not only gave the impetus for the stellar growth of the Internet, but provided a way of combining massive parallel computing with the ability to store and retrieve unstructured data—technologies that became the basis for the Big Data Big Bang.

Over the past few years, there has been a third broad approach to database management that involves *data warehouse appliances*, which takes advantage of MPP and open database connectivity and also has interfaces for Java or various business intelligence tools. A data warehouse appliance combines "bundled" or pre-integrated hardware and software and provides for easy add-on scalability with plug-and-play modules. Appliances have been popular since groups like Netezza (since 2010 owned by IBM) brought out the idea of an easy but more flexible all-in-one database offering. Today all the major vendors—Microsoft (DATAAllegro), Oracle (Exadata), HP (Vertica), Teradata, SAP (Sybase), EMC (Greenplum)—offer these types of data warehouse appliances or cloud-based appliance access.

What Is NoSQL?

NoSQL is a database that gets its name from the fact that it is *not only* SQL, because where SQL has *predefined schema* that works well with the structured data tables in a relational database, NoSQL is a database that has a *dynamic schema* (or in some versions, almost no schema at all) that was created to work with large amounts of unstructured data. In fact, the name is a bit misleading, in that SQL is a standard programming language, and NoSQL is neither a standard nor a programming language; it is a non-relational database. In many ways, it would be more appropriate to call it NoRDMS.

NoSQL databases generally have four characteristics: they are non-relational, they are based on distributed computing, they are open-source (so have been written based on code openly available for developers), and they are horizontally scalable (so can be expanded in size by adding hardware to the nodes or distributed network). These days they are often referred to as cloud databases or even Big Data databases, and there are several different types (key-value store, column store, document, graph, and so on), each of which provides some variation on storing, retrieving, and managing unstructured and semi-structured data (they actually work well with structured data but are generally not considered as fast or as accurate when compared directly with RDBM systems and structured data). The Internet giants like Google (which has its proprietary version called BigTable), Amazon (DynamoDB), Twitter, and Facebook all use NoSQL databases as the framework for their vast and growing data centers, and probably more than 150 versions of NoSQL databases are now available from a wide variety of vendors, including MongoDB, Apache Cassandra, Apache HBase, Hadoop (HBase), Couchbase, and so on. Even Oracle, the largest provider of relational database technologies, is getting into the arena with its Oracle NoSQL offering.

What Is Hadoop?

When most IT people these days think of managing Big Data—massive amounts of a wide variety of unstructured data—they probably think about Hadoop. This strange-sounding software framework (named by Doug Cutting, one of the creators of Hadoop, for his son's toy elephant) has risen from relative obscurity just a few years ago to become so popular that in 2013, a survey found that at least half of the Global 2000 companies had experimented with it. For many, it is their first foray into the world of unstructured, Big Data analysis. Needless to say, the Internet technology companies that helped to build

Hadoop, like Google and Yahoo!, are among its biggest users (it had its origins in Google's MapReduce and Google File System [GFS]). Yahoo has a 50,000 node Hadoop network; Facebook boasts a much smaller 10,000 nodes. In fact, Gartner listed around 1,000 Hadoop systems already up-and-running, from technology powerhouses like Amazon and IBM to companies as varied in their data processing needs as the *New York Times*, Epsilon, and Land O'Lakes.[6]

So what is Hadoop? If NoSQL is the non-relational database architecture, Hadoop is the software framework that enables and coordinates this type of massive parallel processing, by allowing developers to quickly and easily write applications for processing huge amounts of data stored on large clusters of computers in-parallel. It was developed under the Apache Software License, which means that it is open-source, so developers can use, modify, and distribute their own versions of the software however they want.

The Hadoop software framework has several parts: a Distributed File System, common libraries and utilities, a resource management platform (Yarn) that can be used for scheduling resources across a large number of clusters and nodes, and something known as a MapReduce program. Loosely named for two programming functions (mapping refers to recognizing similar data characteristics and organizing them accordingly, and reducing is the process for summarizing the results), the MapReduce program takes large amounts of unstructured data and breaks it down into smaller, separately processed batches. These batches can then be read by clusters of computer nodes, which then re-aggregate the data according to sophisticated algorithms that sort for correlations that would not always be apparent to a human analyst. The MapReduce program began with the proprietary search technologies developed by Google but has since evolved into a popular open-source implementation through collaborative work of the Apache Group, the community of software developers that produce free, open-source software under the Apache License.[7]

Many advantages are cited by companies adopting these Hadoop-based data management platforms. Hadoop was designed for a parallel environment, so it doesn't require sophisticated CPUs or memory technologies, just common hard drives, a network card, and any normal commodity server tied into the network will provide basic functionality. Based on Java code, Hadoop can process many hundreds of petabytes of data on inexpensive, commodity servers and disks, which means that it gives companies a lot of bang for their buck. Since it is open-source, the software code itself is free (or still relatively inexpensive, if managed through a customized software offering), and if you need to add more data, you simply add more clusters—the framework manages the storage and retrieval. And because the data can be stored and retrieved in its natural state, the normally huge data management cost associated with finding, cleaning, and organizing the data (extracting, transforming, and loading operations) is all but eliminated.

The framework is not always fast, but many estimates set its cost, based on terabytes stored, to be from 20% to 40% of the equivalent storage and retrieval costs for an RDBMS (which is much more limited in both size and variety of unstructured data it can manage). One good example of the differences in cost: Neustar, an advertising firm, published the results of an in-house cost study comparing the cost of processing and storing data in Hadoop versus its conventional RDBM system and found that storing just 1% of its enterprise data for 60 days in a conventional data warehouse cost an average of $100,000 per terabyte, while storing 100% of that data for a full year in Hadoop cost only $900 per terabyte.[8] This is the sort of potential cost difference—without even taking into account the value of Hadoop's capacity to manage unstructured data—that is making company IT and finance executives sit up and take notice (see Figure 9.3).

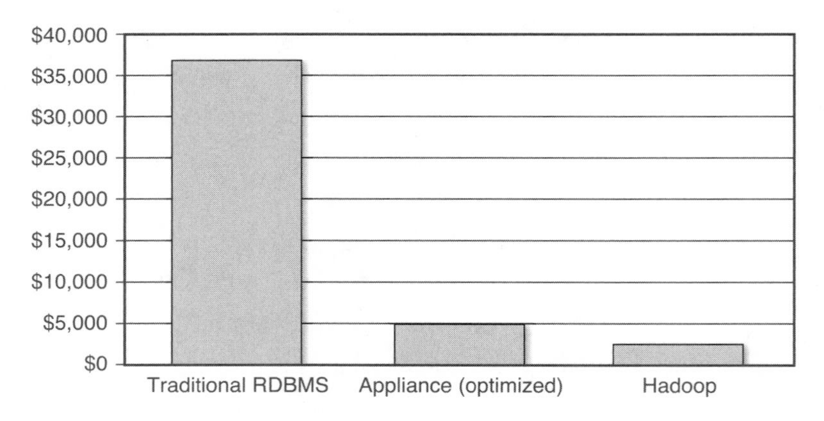

Figure 9.3 Comparing the Cost of Database Platforms

Source: NewVantage Partners[9]

But it is not just cost of processing that matters when it comes to Big Data. In fact, the Hadoop/NoSQL framework's capability to handle huge volumes of data probably has less to do with the technology's success than its method of search and interrogation, which allows companies to look at raw, unstructured data in a way that a typical relational database running conventional business intelligence software can't.

Still, this approach to data management is not problem-free. Hadoop is designed to assess large pools of structured and unstructured data but is essentially a batch processing system and is not particularly efficient when it comes to real-time queries (which means it tends to be used for nonbusiness critical analysis such as long-term marketing or sales trends). As a read-only system, once the data is pulled up, users cannot modify it in any way, which limits the amount of speculative work that can be done on ad hoc queries, and because it is Java-based, the technologies often don't run well with SQL. As an open-source framework, it is relatively low-level, so the programmer has to often write custom programs to perform even simple tasks, and writing MapReduce jobs to query Hadoop is time-consuming and requires specialist skills. That means that companies using the approach need programmers who understand how to use it, and there still aren't that many skilled Hadoop programmers who can write in Java and are experienced with NoSQL databases. Beyond the actual technical issues, it also requires data scientists who are able to develop the algorithms and interpret the results (see the sidebar "Correlation Versus Causation"). When looking for relationships and correlations ("a needle in a haystack") that are not obvious to the mortal man, these searches often produce results that are misleading or simply weird, so it still requires humans skilled in statistics to avoid mistaking correlation with causation (just because there is an apparent relationship doesn't necessarily indicate that that relationship is not random chance, or that the one caused the other). That's why data scientists and analysts with statistical skills are in high demand and can now command high wages.

As the popularity and utility of the framework grows, huge amounts of money and effort are being focused on resolving these types of issues by a growing army of startups and upstarts around the world, and the number of Hadoop providers is growing quickly: Cloudera, Hortonworks (started by members from Yahoo!'s original Hadoop team), IBM, Karmasphere, Intel, Teradata, Pivotal, MapR, Microsoft, Amazon's AWS, and many others all provide variations of this quickly evolving framework to commercial companies either through software or through the cloud.[10]

Some companies are trying to combine the attributes of the new with the old, making it possible to use SQL with Hadoop in a distributed environment. Cloudera's Impala uses an SQL query engine that runs natively in Apache Hadoop and is designed for massively parallel processing (MPP). So does Pivotal's Hawq. The Apache Hadoop group produced HiveQL, which uses Hive Query Language (HQL) statements that are much like those found in SQL and make it easier to query the data stored in Hadoop. Apache Spark, which is similarly open-source, works better with Java and SQL, and boasts of running programs up to 100x faster than Hadoop MapReduce in memory, or 10x faster on disk.[11] Microsoft has an Analytics Platform System (APS) that combines Hadoop and SQL, and Microsoft is also working with Hortonworks to offer Hadoop on its cloud platform (Windows Azure) and to integrate Hadoop with its SQL business intelligence applications in a single platform that Microsoft calls "big data in a box."[12] Informatica has a no-code development environment called Vibe (Virtual data machine) that combines both Hadoop and non-Hadoop platforms so that the two can be fully integrated as a single data process and warehouse offering.[13] All these mark an important move toward pulling the technology into the mainstream.[14]

Others, like Oracle and SAP, are pushing from the traditional side toward NoSQL and Hadoop. Oracle Big Data SQL extends Oracle SQL to Hadoop and NoSQL. SAP's HANA now supports SQL on Hadoop. Teradata announced that its Aster Data nCluster now provides an SQL-MapReduce framework on a distributed, MPP architecture.[15] Google has its cloud-based Big Query product, which allows companies to analyze large data sets for prices as low as $5 per terabyte, using various SQL-related query interfaces to access Google's massive Hadoop-based computing power.[16] In fact, every week it seems there is another announcement in this continuing convergence (mixing the programming ease of SQL with the various advantages of Hadoop, MapReduce, and NoSQL technologies running in a massive parallel processing environment).

Aware of the interest in Hadoop by companies large and small, many vendors now supply data warehouse appliances for Hadoop, including IBM's PureData system, Oracle's Big Data Appliance, HP's AppSystem for Apache Hadoop, Teradata's Aster Analytics Appliance, and EMC/Greenplum's Data Computing Appliance. These offerings allow the buyer a pre-integrated package for Hadoop computing if they don't have the expertise or the wherewithal to buy and run nodes themselves. Of course, that bundle comes at a premium, and these Big Data appliances can be relatively costly when compared with self-managed nodes.

Others have devised a non-relational approach of their own. LexisNexis developed its own open-source HPCC (high performance computing cluster) platform. Amazon's Kinesis, billed as an alternative to Hadoop, is its open-sourced, cloud-accessed option. Splunk provides a stand-alone set of products for Big Data search, retrieval, and analysis on both structured and unstructured data, and allows companies to look at everything from clickstream data to site visits and navigation results. The company uses its own SearchProcessing Language (SPL), which had its origins in a combination of UNIX and SQL, and was specifically created to manage machine-generated data. Splunk is especially strong in log analysis but has growing competition from groups like Graylog2, which is based on Java and will likely eventually fall into the Hadoop camp. Other open-source, distributed Big Data frameworks like Elasticsearch and Solr allow companies to complete complex (for example, full-text) data searches (see Figure 9.4).[17]

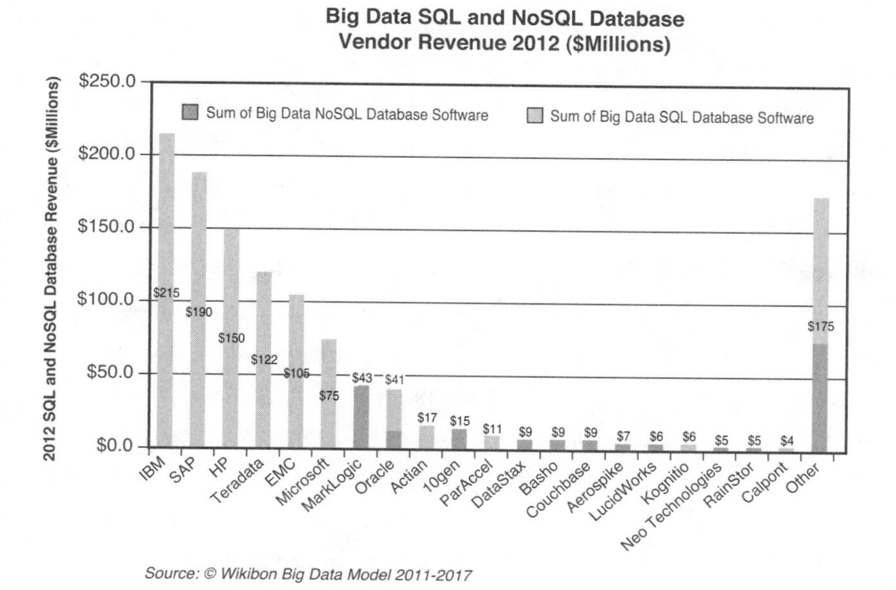

Figure 9.4 The Big Data Database Market[18]

Among all these platforms and frameworks is collaboration and competition, overlap and incompatibility, all mixed up in a scramble by hundreds of vendors anxious to align themselves with the winning technology of the future. But despite this innovative chaos, industry analysts mostly agree that it is only a matter of time before these various permutations of Big Data database management converge (although I suspect there will in fact be more specialization, with companies continuing to choose different approaches and platforms depending on the nature and level of the data they are dealing with), and the best we can hope for in the next few years would be an acceptable level of seamless integration.

All the Data, All the Time

The greatest value of these next-generation database technologies lies not just in storing a much broader variety of data at a cheaper rate. Whatever the relative pros and cons of these various frameworks and products, the most important effect of these technologies is that enterprises no longer have to throw away data.[19] This is revolutionary, because as anyone who has worked with traditional relational database systems knows, when IT costs begin to expand, companies turn to data triage, prioritizing data according to how staff (usually central IT and finance) perceive its value. Despite the key principles of ERP, which call for enterprise-wide data sharing, departmental budgets and perceptions of the relative value of data often leave companies with data collection bias, with the Accounting department making the assumption that, when push comes to shove, its data is much more valuable to collect and keep than something as esoteric as customer click-through data from the company's online catalog. Now all that data—from whatever source and in whatever format—can be retained and then later accessed by anyone in the company.

The result of this "keep everything" approach is that companies are now capturing data of all types in huge quantities, and all that data need to be stored. That type of data policy would normally be disastrously expensive if a company had to own and maintain the IT infrastructure to support it. This combined demand for data organization, analysis, and storage has given rise to what is perhaps the single most important technological development in the Big Data Big Bang—the Cloud.

Correlation Versus Causation

The theories behind Big Data rest in large part upon the idea that the mixture of modern analytics technologies can be used to analyze enormous and complete pools of raw data to extract correlations and insight that would normally be beyond the capacity of traditional technologies (or humans) to recognize. The way that these technologies are used is loosely analogous to the two broad approaches to computer programming itself. The first route, known as *imperative programming*, involves telling the computer, step-by-step, *how* it should approach solving a problem. The alternative route, *declarative programming*, requires only telling the computer *what* you would like and allowing the computer to decide how to get it. The imperative approach is highly prescriptive and hypothesis-based and fits well with tools like SQL and relational databases, where the programmer seeks an end result, and the system then produces that result. The declarative approach leans toward the idea of query-free insight and is much more in keeping with JavaScript and the NoSQL, Hadoop/MapReduce approach, where the programmer simply tells the computer to analyze raw data and find a "needle in a haystack" (that is, correlations) and the system does that without step-by-step guidance.

Big Data enthusiasts suggest that the "analyze everything and see what comes up" approach essentially changes the nature of statistics as we know it, because by analyzing enough data, age-old concerns about statistical significance, causation, and correlation are all eliminated. The idea is that with enough data, the numbers speak for themselves.

Is that true? An example, often cited, was the enormous success of Google Flu trends survey, published in *Nature* in 2009, which the company completed by analyzing the search terms being used on Google for indicators about the spread of influenza. The Google researchers had no hypothesis or preconceived notions, they simply asked the Google technology to find a correlation between what people searched for online (using 45 search terms, which, they assumed, would indicate that the searcher had flu symptoms) to predict in near real-time, rates of influenza around the country. The process was acclaimed as inexpensive, fast, and more accurate than even the best predictive models based on data provided by physicians that were normally used by the Center for Disease Control.

Except it wasn't. In 2013, the Google Flue Trends (GFT) program predicted that 10.6% of the United States was suffering from influenza-like illnesses, where later patient data set the figure at 6.1%. The next year, the GFT once again overestimated the levels of flu by nearly 30%.

What happened? Many things. Fear of catching the flu prompted people to search even when they had no symptoms. Multiple searches didn't distinguish between multiple people or just the same person making multiple queries. People searched for symptoms when they were concerned for others, or when they heard about the potential for flu in their area, even when they didn't have symptoms themselves.

But the problem is not explained away just by poor search analysis algorithms. Economists and statisticians pointed out that the problem with the hypothesis-free, total data modeling is that it often confuses correlation with causation. There are several key issues.

As Tim Harford, the Undercover Economist for the *Financial Times* explains, part of the problem is focusing on sampling error and ignoring sampling bias. Huge samples can help to reduce sampling error, but it is still important that the sample population reflects the underlying population being studied. Eliminating sampling bias is not simple, though, because almost no universe of users is completely random if the way the data is collected—through search engines, social media, or for that matter, any technology platform—represents only a subgroup of the total population. Much has been made about analyzing Tweets, for example, for public trends and opinions, but Twitter users may not be representative of the total population. As Harford points out, US Twitter users have been shown to be disproportionately young, urban or suburban, and African American.

But even beyond sampling bias, the problem of false correlation remains. As Nate Silver, the highly-successful predictor of political elections has pointed out, the problem with Big Data analytics comes with trying to separate the signal (meaningful information) from the noise (irrelevant data). In a nutshell, the likelihood of false correlation increases when irrelevant data is added to any meaningful "signal"—the more variables added the more likely correlations will appear to distort that signal, and that error is magnified by the fact that large deviations are usually a result of "noise." Unless the relevance of the data is well understood—something that isn't easy when collecting huge amounts of unstructured data—the underlying mathematical models will produce false correlations.[20] Some good examples can be seen at Tyler Vigen's web site, *Spurious Correlations* (http://www.tylervigen.com), where he has pulled together a number of Big Data output that illustrates the broader point that correlation does not always reflect causation. These include the fact that, having crunched the numbers, he found that the high consumption of margarine matches closely against the number of divorces in Maine, and that the number of people who were electrocuted by power lines correlates remarkably with the marriage rate in Alabama. Even more frightening is the near-perfect correlation rate (0.947) between the per capita consumption of cheese in the United States and number of people who died by becoming entangled in their bed sheets.

The Cloud

In an interesting use of Big Data to analyze the Big Data market, FactSet recently scanned the transcripts of investor presentations and conference calls for more than 5,000 companies for the most prominent topics of discussion. It found that within those companies, Big Data was mentioned in 841 conference calls and investor presentations during 2013, but cloud computing was the most talked about topic, at 1,356 calls and presentations.[21] In reality, it is hard to talk about one without talking about the other.

For the past several years, cloud-based storage has been one of the fastest growing areas in the economy, and according to IDC, the fastest-growing subsegment of the Big Data market.[22] But cloud platforms offer much more than storage. They also provide a myriad of software applications and analytics. Gartner predicts that between 2013 and 2016, some $677 billion will be spent on cloud-based services worldwide.[23] McKinsey claims that 80% of US and Canadian companies are either contemplating or already using cloud-based services.[24]

So what is cloud computing? It is basically the next step in the move toward outsourcing an application delivery over the Internet, allowing companies and individuals to access a shared pool of computing and database resources, including the network, storage, servers, applications, and support services.[25] The cloud, in fact, is simply the Internet itself, which provides access to many millions of networked servers—and the practical effect is that no longer does an individual, or even a Fortune 500 company, need to host applications or store data locally.

There are various ways to gain access to the cloud.

For the individual, there is the *public cloud*, which provides low-end, web-grade access to a wide variety of application services and is used by millions of people worldwide to work collaboratively or to store personal photos, music, videos, or documents with groups such as Apple (iCloud), Dropbox, Google Drive, Amazon's Cloud Drive, or Microsoft's OneDrive. These cloud-based platforms also provide storage, which is particularly valuable for mobile smartphone users who want to work on the go (and access any of their documents, anywhere, anytime) and no longer want to bother with storing data on a personally owned hard drive or backup device.

Medium-sized businesses have access to enterprise-level applications and storage through what is sometimes known as the *private cloud* and are increasingly taking advantage not only of the storage capacity but particularly of dual (enterprise and cloud) applications designed for collaboration over the Web (such as Salesforce.com, Box, Huddle, Google Apps for Business, Dropbox, Office 365, and a myriad of other cloud and enterprise-based software).

Despite a long history of outsourcing, larger enterprises have been a little less receptive to the idea of becoming too dependent on cloud services. They have understandable concerns over security and access, and usually have a significant investment already in IT staff and hardware. Still, many options are available to the modern enterprise. They can choose a *Software-as-a-Service (SaaS) model*, where the cloud platform provides key business applications, or they can go the other way around and choose the *Platform-as-a-Service (PaaS) model*, where the cloud provides just the computing and storage platform (and the company retains control over its own applications which run on that rented platform). Some enterprises (such as the CIA and Netflix) subscribe to a more integrated *Infrastructure-as-a-Service (IaaS) model*, where they essentially rent access to the central computational power and storage capacity of the massive tech groups like Amazon or Google.

In fact, as the cloud matures, many other models are emerging. The *Business-Process-as-a-Service (BPaaS) model* provides cloud-based applications for specific business areas such as payroll, HR, or e-commerce. Supply chain services are also becoming popular, with online access for a full range of offerings from demand planning to inventory optimization. Companies are even increasingly subscribing to the *Security-as-a-Service model (SecaaS)*, where data security is managed by the cloud platform. Cisco even announced that it will spend $1 billion on what it calls an *Intercloud*, which will provide a bridge between these various cloud-based offerings, private and public.[26]

There are obvious advantages to these various forms of cloud outsourcing: speed, cost, scalability, application integration, access to external expertise and state-of-the-art applications. As the cloud has expanded, the cost of both computation and storage has plummeted. There are many examples. The Spanish bank, Bankinter, for example, claims that using Amazon's cloud-based Web Services (AWS), it is now able to run credit risk simulations that used to take 23 hours with its own computers in only 20 minutes.[27] Google's BigQuery offers users the ability to process 100,000 data records per second, the type of fast analysis that is becoming necessary for companies trying to analyze very large data streams.[28] And access to Amazon Cloud services can now provide a user with the computing power of 10,000 servers (at a nominal cost of $4.4 million to own themselves) for a rental fee of about $90 an hour.[29]

These innovative new storage and retrieval offerings, combined with the drive for companies to capture all their data, all the time, has also breathed new life into what was a struggling analytics and BI marketplace, because even though a company has captured and stored all its digital data, it still needs to be able to extract that data and interpret it in ways that can produce something worthwhile. These cloud-based analytics services allow any size company to analyze more data (larger data sets) over a longer period of time and to look for correlations and "signals"—the beginning of a sales trend, interest in a particular digital ad—that were impossible to find using the traditional relational DB type technologies of the past. Because these analytical tools have been developed specifically for search and interpretation of unstructured data, it opens the gate for companies of every ilk to begin to combine their own enterprise customer data with customer data gleaned from social media, messaging, e-commerce, and search activities.

That is why the evolution of the Big Data movement has become so intertwined with the cloud: especially if a platform can combine all those key Big Data features (a NoSQL/Hadoop framework with massive parallel computing and storage capacity obtained through distributed nodes of low-cost computers, and analytics and business intelligence tools to interpret that data).

The importance of this growth area is reflected in the market success of companies supporting Hadoop platforms in the cloud. Cloudera, for example, a startup that combines Hadoop technologies and cloud computing services, was valued at $4.1 billion and raised $900 million in venture capital in anticipation of its IPO. This was, in part, because Intel, which had been working on its own Hadoop cloud platform, decided to merge its efforts with Cloudera's solution, buying 18% of the company instead (Intel believes that Cloudera will be running on servers with Intel chips around the world). The same week, Hortonworks, another Hadoop-based cloud solution provider, raised $100 million from BlackRock and Passport Capital,[30] on top of the original $23 million provided by Yahoo!.[31] MapR, one of the important Hadoop-based cloud platforms, raised $110 million, much of that from Google Capital.[32]

There is a similar level of activity on the cloud-based storage front. Groups such as Actifio (which recently raised $100 million in financing) or EMC, the data storage powerhouse, are winning over large corporate customers.[33] And then there are the software companies that help companies to manage and understand all that stored data such as WANdisco or Fusionex, which have (both) partnered with the leading open-source software providers Hortonworks and Cloudera. The number of vendors that provide a combined mining and analytics service is expected to triple over the next couple of years, and the market is expected to exceed $4.5 billion in 2014.[34]

And, then there are the traditional giants—IBM, Oracle, SAP, Teradata—facing the Innovator's Dilemma—aware of the evolution toward the cloud yet equally wary of its effect on their traditional, on-premises, highly configured hardware and software platforms. It's not just license revenue; the hardware vendors know that one of the big selling points of the cloud-based Hadoop-like technologies is that they run on low-cost Original Equipment Manufacturers (OEM) servers, which means that traditional hardware companies see their dominance threatened in terms of both market share and price. For a while, it seemed that these giants were simply paying lip service to Big Data and analytics over the cloud, but increasingly, they seem to be bowing to the inevitable and creating parallel offerings that support that move to the cloud. Hewlett-Packard's HP Helion program promotes OpenStack, the open source cloud software, and encourages companies to create their own private cloud systems as an alternative to traditional cloud platforms. IBM is spending over a billion dollars on new data centers (hoping to compete with Amazon's AWS public cloud offerings) along with another billion to continue to expand its prowess in ultra-sophisticated "cognitive" computers such as Watson, which focus on extracting answers to questions (as opposed to identifying trends) based on huge data sets.[35] In fact, based on problem-solving criteria and analytics, IBM can in many ways claim to be the leading advocate for Big Data, pulling in $1.3 billion in revenues for what it labeled as Big Data-related products and services in 2012.[36]

Returning to our theme of the democratization of technology, it is important to appreciate that just a few short years ago this type of storage, retrieval, and analytics technology was only really available to a handful of companies around the world—the Internet tech giants where these platforms originated and a few of the largest and most progressive retailers. But the cloud and the emerging availability of Big Data technologies means that almost any company can now incorporate Big Data into its business strategy. It's that Big Data business strategy that we turn to now.

10

Doing Business in a Big Data World

Key Chapter Points

- Surveys show that there are a significant number of Big Data projects underway in a wide variety of industries.
- Big Data projects can be sponsored by a variety of functions within companies but are mostly driven by sales and marketing.
- This new level of data management means that the traditional chief information officer (CIO) position is evolving into other c-level positions, including the chief data technology officer and the chief data marketing officer.
- Company managers contemplating a Big Data project need to take into account various architectural, organizational, and security considerations before deciding on a Big Data project strategy.

In the world of Big Data and the Internet economy, how an organization manages its data can be an important competitive differentiator. No longer just a back office support function for running static reports on internal business processes, for many companies today, enterprise-wide data management is mission-critical. And for a variety of reasons, Big Data is now seen by a majority of companies as integral to that enterprise data management strategy. And as we've seen, nearly 85% of companies say they are engaged in some type of Big Data project.[1]

Yet as powerful as the new technologies we've been looking at are, a shift to multiplatform architectures and storage capabilities that can support advanced Big Data business intelligence and analytics software is not easy or inexpensive. Building a cost-effective approach to Big Data can be fraught with difficulties, because moving from structured to structured/unstructured data collection and analysis involves a different approach to data sourcing and data preparation. It also requires different technologies, additional skills, and a change to processes and organizational culture—and all this when many organizations continue to struggle with current levels of IT complexity, and are finding it difficult to extract promised value from their conventional enterprise systems.

We've already explored how Big Data can be used in various specialty areas, and we've also seen that with the advent of the Industrial Internet many millions of sensors and self-reporting components are now (or will soon be) available throughout a make-and-move company's supply chain. We've seen how nearly every organization, from retailers to charities, is trying to leverage customer data (from a wide variety of sources) so that it can market or advertise to those customers using new digital technologies and particularly the mobile phone. We've also seen that Big Data can mean many things to many people, and that for many company executives, Big Data is simply the equivalent to bigger Information Technology. To understand the difference between a Big Data project and the improvement of traditional IT infrastructure, let's have a look now at what companies see as their major IT priorities in the years ahead.

Big Data Projects

In terms of size of company, as might be expected, the larger organizations are the ones that have moved rapidly into the Big Data arena. A NewVantage Partners survey in 2013 found that nearly a quarter of companies that were taking up Big Data projects employed at least 500 data miners and analysts, and 25% of respondents said that they plan to spend more than $10 million a year on Big Data projects. Some of the larger groups plan to spend more than $100 million annually for the next three years. The average planned Big Data spending for all the respondents was a staggering $14 million per year over the next three years.[2] That's Big Data for big companies (at big cost) and reflects the integral nature of data collection these days to behemoths participating in the survey such as big pharma (AstraZeneca, Johnson & Johnson), financial services (UBS, Freddie Mac, BlackRock), or retailers like CVS/Caremark (see Figure 10.1).

That is not to say that small and medium-sized enterprises (SMEs) are not interested in Big Data projects, but most surveys indicate that small companies are more likely to opt for the prebuilt analytics tools available to them, both off-the-shelf and through the cloud, that are specifically designed for their particular vertical industry—health care, small manufacturing, transportation, and so on—and provide turn-key solutions that don't require huge investments in staff training, project management, or technologies. Whether that approach provides companies with anything near the potential of Big Data in its most powerful manifestation is hard to say. In many ways (and this is something we explore in this chapter), it may well be that most SMEs simply want to expand their current business intelligence and analytics capabilities to include better customer and social media-related data management—a strategy that inclines more toward traditional IT with some CRM add-ons (in the form of a limited integration with NoSQL/Hadoop-like products or cloud-based programs) rather than the wholesale restructuring of their enterprise system.

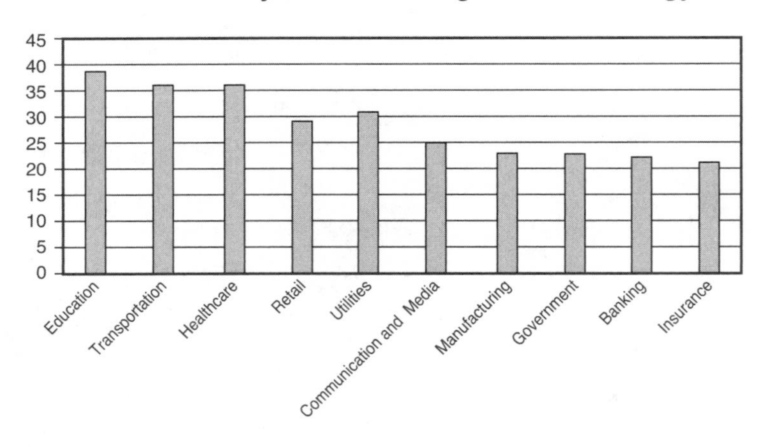

Figure 10.1 Big Data Industry Focus
Data Source: Gartner

To understand what Big Data means to various companies, it helps to look at the types of benefits that companies are looking for in a Big Data project. In the NewVantage survey, companies described a variety of benefits they hope to achieve, from operational efficiency to new product innovations. Interestingly, and probably a reflection of the number of financial services and big pharmaceuticals taking part, 64% of companies responding said they use Big Data for new product development and innovation. Companies also cited reduced risk and higher quality products or as goals. Many of the benefits they sought reflected better decision making capabilities. But when asked to identify the biggest opportunity, more than half returned to the theme of better customer insight, increased sales, and customer loyalty.

Interesting, also, and a reflection of an ongoing frustration with traditional systems, was the fact that so many companies hope to use Big Data projects to overcome data integration and data access issues. One of the most revealing statistics from the NewVantage survey is that more than half the companies that responded said that their main goal with a Big Data project is to be able to access "relevant, accurate, and timely" data. Sixty percent of respondents said that they want to apply Big Data technologies to data that they are already collecting. In short, a Big Data project, they hoped, would help them to overcome the data silos and lack of access to relevant data that still plague so many companies today. More than half companies in the survey said that their current access to "relevant, accurate, and timely data," is less than adequate.[3] A similar survey taken by Avanade found that 43% of all companies said they are dissatisfied with their current tools to filter out irrelevant data, and 46% said they had made poor business decisions because of bad or outdated data.[4]

That means that company managers believe that there is still a lot of untapped value in the data that they are already collecting and reflects the need for better data, alongside more (or more varied) sources of data. It probably also reflects, to some degree, a naïve hope by some companies that moving toward Big Data will help them to overcome many of the problems that they are still experiencing in trying to extract greater value from their (probably badly configured and underutilized) traditional enterprise systems.

Surveys also indicate that of the three Big Data characteristics (large volumes of data, a wide variety of sources, and new search and analytics technologies), many companies are emphasizing variety over volume—hoping to be able to analyze new types of (mostly consumer Internet) data, rather than huge new volumes of structured, transactional data. In fact, according to some analysts, 80% of businesses today are in fact dealing with less than 2TB of data.[5] In short, they're not looking for Big Data—they're looking for different data. But one of the fundamental principles of Big Data is that accuracy and insight come from large data sets; purists might suggest that, although there are a number of small data or "smart data" options available that combine Big Data technologies with smaller data sets, looking through small subsets of different data is really just business-as-usual.

On the other hand, most CIOs know that there is a lot of pressure on them to collect ever-growing amounts of digital data. In a recent survey by Gartner, more than half the CIOs responding said that their organizations were in "real danger" from a "digital tsunami."[6] This is a major concern for many companies today that are unable to optimize the relatively powerful data analytical tools that they currently have simply to analyze the structured data that they already collect. With limited resources and entrenched, often incompatible technologies and information management techniques, many companies still struggle with basic data management issues, and it can be argued that pulling in or analyzing more, or more varied data, can easily lead to data "sprawl." Limited by these types of technological or organizational constraints—or simply so overwhelmed by current data sprawl that they limit themselves to using subsets of data—the value of any Big Data project will be undermined. At the same time, if these companies have problems with basic data integration issues today, Big Data, with its wide variety of sources and different types of data, may only exacerbate those fundamental data management problems.

Who Wants Big Data Projects?

But unlike the past, when senior executives in a company often understood (or cared) very little about what happened in terms of IT, Big Data projects today are driven by a variety of executive sponsors within organizations. It is certainly a topic widely discussed in the "C-Suite" these days, with 85% of projects in the NewVantage survey receiving sponsorship by a C-level executive (or the leader of a line of business).[7] And even more than ERP systems, Big Data seems to affect multiple business lines across the organization.

That may be because most Big Data projects are driven more by marketing or sales than by the tech shop, with the sales teams crying out for better customer data (often through cloud-based applications) and the marketing team hoping to set up and control their own digital marketing campaign, sometimes with their own separate software framework. This seems a natural evolution, given the huge growth in digital marketing and the fact that everything from mobile consumer apps to customer analytics—that is, key applications of Big Data—is driven and used by the Marketing department.[8] It also highlights the growing importance of digital competence within the marketing function. More than 80% of companies with an annual revenue of $500 million now have chief marketing technology officers,[9] and Forrester recently estimated that IT spending by the Marketing department within companies is set to rise two to three times faster than IT spending by the organization as a whole. This puts more pressure on the CIO to provide digital leadership, particularly as nearly a third of marketers in a recent survey admitted that they thought the IT department "hindered success." That's not the sort of reputation CIOs need as we enter this phase of the digital economy.[10] On the other hand, most marketers are not the sort of careful and thorough technicians that guarantee data is backed up or secure. In many ways, the combination of increased technical savvy among employees, the availability of cloud-based applications, and the "data deluge" overwhelming the central data center means that rather than moving toward the data centralization that was at the heart of the ERP generation, many organizations today find a beleaguered CIO trying to contain the spread of IT anarchy (not to mention malware contagion) across the organization.

The growth in chief data officers and chief analytics officers also reflects the growing importance of digital skills within a company's leadership. And of course chief operating officers and chief procurement officers have long advocated the use of process and performance monitoring technologies throughout the supply chain. Much in the way that those skilled in finance made their way to the top in previous generations, increasingly, those data scientists with the analytical, technological, and statistical skills will probably find an easier track to the C-Suite in the future.

All this means that the traditional role of the CIO is evolving rapidly into that of a business data strategist: someone who understands the business of data management well enough to ensure that the company gets the data feeds necessary to make decisions, creates supply chain efficiencies, or markets and sells to customers in the optimum way. And as more and more of a company's infrastructure is managed for them in the cloud, the chief data officer (CDO) may soon displace the CIO in the c-level suite.

Big Data Strategy Considerations

So how does a company decide on a Big Data strategy? There are many routes to strategy development, but several things are worth thinking about before engaging in a Big Data project.

First, it is important to think through at the broadest level, why your company is considering a move toward Big Data. Many companies want to be able to gain insights by capturing more and varied data. Others (nearly 60%) want the ability to do better analysis with the data they already have available. Still other organizations see a move toward Big Data as necessary to preemptively manage issues that may confront the organization in the future, such as building in scalability or better security. It may be a first step to reorganizing both employee and customer data activities around mobile applications, or positioning the organization to better leverage the growing capacity of the cloud.

Whatever the organization's goals, one of the most important first steps to any Big Data strategy project is to understand what data are needed and what data are available. For example, does your organization want to capture multistructured data, sentiment data, or streaming media? Is the company interested in web log and metadata, or does it want to capture data at a more detailed level? Where will that data come from? Will it be captured through company systems, through a third party, or simply be purchased from data brokers? It can be helpful to start the process by reviewing the report requests recently received by IT from the various business units (although even these may only reflect what company users think they can get from IT—not really what they want or need).

Consider also the origins of data your company needs. For example, if you collect customer clickstream or search data from multiple sources, are you certain that that data is your company's to capture or to sell? If so, are there restrictions on its use (or reuse)? How long can your company keep it? Most data sets taken from customer-related web activities are subject to legal controls of some type (data privacy or regulatory compliance, usage rights, and so on) and may require customer consent through a legally vetted Terms of Agreement contract. Even Facebook has to grapple with issues of consumer trust, and it is unlikely that customers will be willing to share information if they believe it could be misused or sold. What should the organization's policies be on data privacy?

Think too about issues of accuracy and completeness (data hygiene) or data latency: When is data considered to be fresh or stale, outdated, inaccurate, or duplicated? Even if the company is hoping to take advantage of large data sets, the more consistent and clean that data is, the more beneficial it will be. Consider whether that data needs to be "handled" in any way—and will it be worth it? Despite the Big Data purists mantra to "collect everything," not all data available to an organization is useful, and capturing large data sets doesn't necessarily mean that all rules of data governance are suspended—a good deal of data available to any organization isn't relevant and serves no business need. An organization needs a policy not just for how to keep data but also for how to get rid of it, and possibly the most pertinent question is "Will capturing and analyzing this data boost our profits?." That calls for a policy of data triage and should involve representatives from business lines across the organization.

Once you understand what data your organization needs, it is important to attempt a first cut at capacity planning and to calculate as accurately as possible how much data, and of what type, will be gathered over the next three to five years. From that, you can begin to consider the implications in terms of cost, storage capacity, and architectural needs.

Finally, consider who in the company needs to see that data and in what format. It is important to identify the users of the data and think about the best way of making it available to them. How do different groups need to see and use (to "visualize") that data; will you need predictive modeling and forecasting tools, or more advanced reporting and analytics tools that can determine things like event correlation, economic modeling, or statistical patterns? Most advanced analytics will require not only data scientists and data analysts to configure the report generators but to interpret and decipher the reports themselves. How can that data be made meaningful to employees across the organization who only know how to use spreadsheet-level technologies? Because this information should be available throughout the organization (often on both PC and mobile devices), consider the types of distribution systems that can provide these advanced analytics to employees at different levels and throughout the different business units.

Architectural Strategy Considerations

One of the most important considerations facing an organization contemplating adapting Big Data technologies is how to acquire new Big Data capabilities at a reasonable cost and with as little disruption to the company as possible. But, as we've seen, the Big Data framework involves capturing huge amounts of unstructured, messy data, and then dispersing it through distributed computing nodes, often through the cloud; a proposition almost in exact opposition to traditional RDBM systems, which collect structured, clean data in orderly tables and manage that data on internal servers. So how can an organization reconcile these two regimes: the clean and the chaotic, the contained and the distributed, the discrete and the enormous, the old and the new?

The biggest concern of most organizations is that their current systems—tied to ERP, CRM, and SCM modules—are already equipped with data warehouses and analytics but are based on traditional in-house storage and retrieval technologies—relational databases, SQL, and so on. These traditional "schema-based" platforms are the backbone and nervous system of most organizations. The data that passes through those systems—accounting and financial data, customer data, product data, performance information—is usually important to the day-to-day functioning of the company, structured (fed into tables and columns developed using a data engineering effort), and, if the company is lucky, stable. Few company leaders want to alter or upset that stability, or worse, endanger the integrity of the systems or the data.

The Big Data environment—cloud computing, NoSQL, Hadoop-like technologies, and advanced analytics—is simply a different world. It can use the structured data that your company already collects, but to get real value from the search, storage, and analytics, you need to augment that structured data with various other types of much less stable, unstructured data. Hadoop and the cloud assume that raw data is mixed together so that it can all be used equally and can all be accessed at the same time. As we have seen, the large enterprise software and relational database companies—Oracle, SAP, and others—understand the situation and have made some progress toward integrating RDBMS/SQL platforms for structured data to accommodate NoSQL/Hadoop-like technologies for unstructured data, but at this point no single, all-encompassing, framework can cover all the data (structured and unstructured) that a company might want to analyze in a single database system.

As we've seen, there is middle ground: Small data (sometimes called "smart data") applications that combine some of the search and data management flexibility of Hadoop-like technologies with cloud-based applications and storage are emerging every day. They have their own value, but even with this approach there are migration costs and subscription fees, and it still often involves extracting and storing data separately from your main databases and enterprise systems, and "dumping" that data into separate, (often) cloud-based storage facilities.

For all these reasons, many organizations are in a quandary about whether the advantages of Big Data search and analytics justify such an infrastructure upheaval and are wondering about the best approach to combining these two different frameworks for their particular organization. There are three broad configuration choices available to them.

Do It Yourself "Build-on" to a Company's Current Enterprise IT Structure

Even if they are not completely satisfied with the current level of data capture and analysis, most companies considering a move toward adopting Big Data technologies already have a well-staffed and relatively modern IT framework based on RDBM systems and conventional data warehousing. Any company already managing a large amount of structured data with enterprise systems and data warehouses is therefore fairly well versed in the day-to-day issues of large-scale data management. It would seem natural for those companies to assume that, as Big Data is the next big thing happening in the evolution of information technology, it would make sense for them to simply build a NoSQL-type/Hadoop type of infrastructure themselves, incorporated directly into their current conventional framework. In fact, ESG, the advisory and IT market research firm, estimates that at the beginning of 2014, more than half of large organizations will have begun this type of do-it-yourself approach.[11] As we've seen, as open-source software, the price of a Hadoop-type framework (free) is attractive, and it is relatively easy, providing the company has employees with the requisite skills, to begin to work up Hadoop applications using in-house data or data stored in the cloud.

There are also various methods of experimenting with Hadoop-type technologies using data that are outside a company's normal operations, through pilot programs or what Paul Barth and Randy Bean on the HBR blog network describe as an "analytical sandbox" in which companies can try their hand at applying Big Data analytics to both structured and unstructured data to see what types of patterns, correlations, or insight they can discover.[12]

But experimenting with some Hadoop/NoSQL applications for the marketing department is a far cry from developing a fully integrated Big Data system capable of capturing, storing, and analyzing large, multistructured, data sets. In fact, successful implementation of enterprise-wide Hadoop frameworks is still relatively uncommon, and mostly the domain of very large and experienced data-intensive companies in the financial services or the pharmaceutical industries. As we have seen, many of those Big Data projects still primarily involve structured data and depend on SQL and relational data models. Large-scale analysis of totally unstructured data, for the most part, still remains in the rarified realm of powerful Internet tech companies like Google, Yahoo!, Facebook, and Amazon, or massive retailers like Walmart.

Because so many Big Data projects are still largely based on structured or semistructured data and relational data models that complement current data management operations, many companies turn to their primary support vendors, like Oracle or SAP, to help them create a bridge between old and new and to incorporate Hadoop-like technologies directly into their existing data management approach. Oracle's Big Data Appliance, for example, asserts that its preconfigured offering, once various costs are taken into account, is nearly 40% less expensive than an equivalent do-it-yourself built system and can be up and running in a third less time.[13]

And, of course, the more fully Big Data technologies are incorporated directly into a company's IT framework, the more complexity and potential for data sprawl grows. Depending on configurations, full-integration into a single, massive data pool (as advocated by Big Data purists) means pulling in unstructured, unclean data to a company's central data reservoir (even if that data is distributed) and potentially sharing it out to be analyzed, copied, and possibly altered by various users throughout the enterprise, often using different configurations of Hadoop or NoSQL written by different programmers for different reasons. Add to that the need to hire expensive Hadoop programmers and data scientists. For traditional RDB managers, that type of approach raises the specter of untold additional data disasters, costs, and rescue work requests to already overwhelmed IT staff.

Let Someone Else Do It in the Cloud

The obvious alternative to the build-it-yourself approach is to effectively rent the key Big Data applications, computation, and storage using a cloud-sourced, Hadoop-like solution, pulling data from your own organization into a common repository held in the cloud and accessed (or potentially even fully administered) by your own data engineers. In this scenario, that cloud-based repository can consist of both structured and unstructured data and can be held entirely separate from the structured day-to-day operational, financial, and transactional company data, which would remain ring-fenced in the company's enterprise and relational database management system. This approach takes a bit of thought and data management at the front end, but once the cloud repository of structured and unstructured data is available, companies can experiment with large data sets and cloud-based Big Data analytical technologies, oblivious to the underlying framework.

The best thing about this approach, apart from the fact that companies don't have to buy and maintain the hardware and software infrastructure, is that it is scalable. Companies can experiment with different types of data from different sources, without a huge up-front capital investment. Projects can be as small (analyzing a handful of products or customers or social media sites) or as complex as a company wants. And, most importantly, a company doesn't have to modify its current systems or run a parallel internal system on their own.

It sounds the perfect solution, but, as always, there are drawbacks. First, even if the rental technologies are really able to cope with hugely varying data, it doesn't mean that the resulting patterns or correlations will mean anything unless a thorough process of data cleansing and triage happens first. Although cloud-based tools have obvious advantages, every company has different data and different analytical requirements, and as we've seen in the past, one-size-fits-all tools are seldom as productive or as easy to use as advertised. And, of course, when the reports come back with distorted findings (and after a futile effort at resolving the technical issues themselves), users from Marketing or Sales will very likely turn to the IT department for help anyway. That essentially means that a good portion of IT staff still needs to be engaged in Big Data management and trained in the tools and data schema preparation that will allow this approach to work. And as noted before, ultimately, using small subsets of data, even when that data is from a variety of sources and is analyzed with Hadoop or NoSQL technologies, is really more conventional business intelligence (with bells and whistles) than it is Big Data.

Cloud-based providers are obviously aware of these issues. They know that to make this model work, cloud-based companies need to make their offering as easy, flexible, and powerful as possible. A good example of this is the recent strategic alliance between Hortonworks and Red Hat (Hortonworks provides the Hadoop and Red Hat provides the cloud-based storage), which they say includes preconfigured, business-friendly, and reusable data models and an emphasis on collaborative customer support.[14]

Running Parallel Database Frameworks

A third configuration involves building a Big Data system separately and in parallel (rather than integrated with) the company's existing production and enterprise systems. In this model, most companies still take advantage of the cloud for data storage but develop and experiment with enterprise-held Big Data applications themselves. This two-state approach allows the company to construct the Big Data framework of the future, while building valuable resources and proprietary knowledge within the company. That provides complete internal control in exchange for the duplication of much of the functionality of the current system and allows for a future migration to a full-fledged Big Data platform that will eventually allow both systems (conventional and Big Data) to merge.

The problem with this approach is that, in many ways, the very nature of a Big Data framework is different from conventional IT. Traditional IT still involves applications, operating systems, software interfaces, hardware, and database management, whereas Big Data involves some database work but is mostly about complex analytics and structuring meaningful reports—something that requires a different set of skills than is found in most IT departments today. Although this side-by-side configuration assumes some level of savings in economy of scale (sharing existing computing power, utilizing current staff, and so on), the reality is those savings may only come at the expense of complicated interfaces between old and new systems that have to be designed and managed.

Big Data Skills Considerations

One of the more important things to think about when contemplating a Big Data project is where to turn for the new skills that will be needed: understanding how to value and collect the sources of data available to the organization, using Hadoop-like technologies to mine and manipulate data, and analyzing and interpreting the output from Big Data analytics tools. These are the skills needed to convert data into meaningful intelligence, and because many of these skills are not readily found in an organization today, it means a company will probably need to hire expensive employees and devise new, dedicated roles.

Big Data Technology Engineers

As we've seen, any initiative will require some in-house Big Data-related language, architecture, and database engineering expertise, and that will come in the rare form of a Hadoop-like technology data engineer who can work with analysts to source and mine the data, create and manage the NoSQL (or possibly SQL)/Hadoop infrastructure, and coax useful information out of the process.

Data Analysts/Data Scientists

Determining what data goes into that Hadoop framework and interpreting the data when it comes out (as opposed to configuring the technology itself), requires a skilled data analyst or data scientist. Usually with a mathematics, statistics, or engineering background, these data analysts are the ones who decide what data can be used from which sources, and apply the statistical structure that allows the Hadoop engineer to create the logical schema for that type of data. They also are needed to structure methods for creating equivalents between the widely varying quantities and data sources being collected and are instrumental in understanding and applying the right analytical tools so that once all that data is crunched, something meaningful and accurate is created. They're called data scientists because they need to have the methodical, hypothesis-based reasoning that allows them to design the statistical models and interpret the algorithms that reveal correlation, patterns, and insight. They also play a key role in soliciting the data needs from various departments around the organization and providing those departments with a way to visualize that information that is most helpful to them. That means these analysts are needed not just centrally within the IT function but within key use areas like marketing, sales, procurement, logistics, inventory, or production, throughout the organization.

Seventy percent of organizations say that they plan to hire people for these types of roles in the next three years, and yet, reflecting the lack of availability and high cost of these skills, nearly 80% of the NewVantage survey respondents said they already find this "challenging" to "extremely difficult."[15] The demand for those skills is reflected in a recent jump in salaries for these technical areas, where the average US tech salary climbed to $87,811 in 2013. According to Dice's 2013-2014 Salary Survey, nine of the top ten highest paying IT salaries were for these Big Data-related skills (see Figure 10.2).[16]

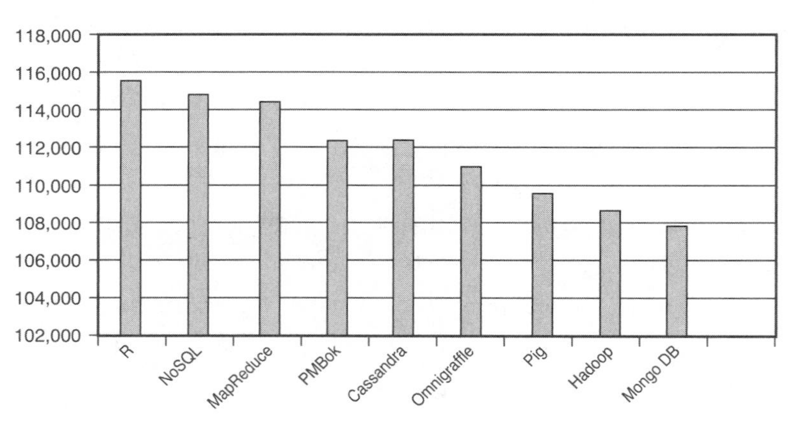

Figure 10.2 Following the Money in the IT Job Market
Data Source: Network World

Given the dire shortage of these skills and the growing demand, it makes sense for organizations interested in Big Data to select current employees for training in these areas, and as an appreciation for the role of Big Data in the future grows, most organizations will probably find a group of volunteers eager to develop these high-paying skills themselves. But that may be easier said than done. Only one-third of companies, according to Gartner, are confident that they can move ahead with a Big Data initiative using their current staff,[17] because not only are their current staff fully engaged, but the rigorous requirements for the role tend to push companies toward hiring graduates with advanced degrees in math, statistics, or engineering that current employees may lack.

Even the largest companies may not be able to cover all the skills needed in a Big Data initiative and so will need to turn to outside consultants or particularly to the services of the technology/tool providers themselves.

Organizational Considerations of Big Data

As we've seen, some 80% of companies responding to the NewVantage survey said that Big Data initiatives involved reaching across multiple business lines or functions (see Figure 10.3).[18] Yet the availability of Big Data applications on the cloud makes unilateral projects at the department level tempting. It is not uncommon for IT departments to complain that business lines have no appreciation of the security or technical issues involved in running Big Data initiatives, and the line functions say that central IT is unfamiliar with business data requirements, dragging their feet on development requests, and not responding to their needs in a new environment.

This central versus distributed authority struggle is an age-old problem, but because much of the new data sought by companies tends to come from unstructured sources—the Web, chat lines, social media—it is now possible for business lines—especially marketing and sales functions—to simply turn to cloud applications independent of the supervision of the central IT department. This means that the traditional centralized control exercised by the CIO and database administrators (who used to *own* the data) is quickly being eroded in favor of a centralized IT help center, or shared-services center, sending out technicians to help keep department-specific initiatives up and running. A recent poll by IDC found that 32% of departments use cloud-based services "in part" and 12% "very comprehensively" without the support of the company's central IT function. That may indicate a new level of departmental independence, but it also reflects their frustrations. Far from IT complaining that the departments had moved unilaterally, in fact, 40% of those department-led initiatives complained that they had received no support from central IT.[19] And this trend is set to continue: According to Gartner, by 2020 nearly 90% of technology spending will originate outside the central IT department.[20]

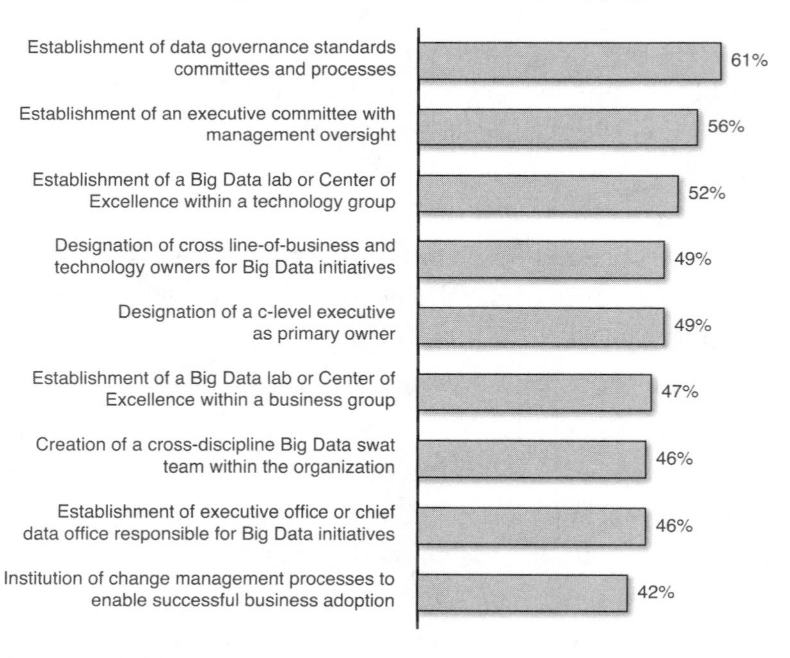

Figure 10.3 Big Data initiatives involved reaching across multiple business lines or functions.

Source: NewVantage Partners Bid Data Executive Survey 2013

To some, this type of decentralized model, where each department or function goes its own way, is welcome freedom and simply reflects the shifting authority from the CIO to the Chief Marketing Technology Officer we explored earlier. To others (particularly to many current CIOs), it is a disaster waiting to happen. Certainly cloud-based applications do promote a more agile use of IT resources, but departmental independence has obvious drawbacks. The lack of central IT control can mean duplication of resources, and a lack of data sharing among silo-focused departments, each with its own set of specialist analysts and its own data collection procedures, can be inefficient and lack strategic continuity. It can also create significant risks to good governance and data security.

Big Data Governance and Security Considerations

It's a good thing that Big Data issues are now in the C-Suite, because collecting and selling customer data, if that is the focus of a Big Data initiative, is a serious thing in terms of governance and privacy. The last thing companies need is department or function heads setting their own standards in terms of collection, use, and security. In fact, a clear and thorough enterprise-wide data charter is essential, as is instilling in employees at all levels the notion of personal responsibility and "stewardship" of customer data.

Venture capitalist Ted Schlein made an interesting observation recently, noting that there are two types of companies: those that have had a data breach and know it, and those that have been breached and don't know it.[21] Hacking has been around nearly as long as computers—and certainly from the time the Internet began to provide access to them—but in the past when computer security breaches occurred, it was seldom publicized by the company being targeted. But now that company databases are filled with all manner of customer data, data security has become integral to customer relations and the company's core business.

We've all heard or read about some of the more spectacular data breaches that have occurred in the past few years. Target, for years boasting of its prowess at collecting customer data, lost 70 million customer details when its point-of-sale system was hacked through one of its vendor's computers. Adobe announced in the summer of 2013 that hackers had successfully broken into its system (possibly even accessing the source code for Photoshop and Acrobat Reader) and stolen the encrypted passwords of 38 million users.[22] Microsoft had its source code hacked as far back as 2004.

Not only are these data breaches harmful to the customers whose data is stolen, but these types of data thefts have a significant effect on the company being breached. In the quarter following the announcement, Target's CIO resigned and the company's income almost halved. That single data breach cost the company more than $61 million.[23] And it's not only large companies being targeted by hackers; the servers of smaller vendors and suppliers are usually less well protected in the first place and have increasingly become the target of e-mail phishing fraud and data theft.

A study completed by McAfee found that of 1,000 small and medium-sized enterprises (SMEs)—everything from dentists, doctors, and lawyers to small, family-owned businesses—90% of those companies had no protection for their customer information. Fewer than one in ten had any security protection for their employees' mobile phones.[24] Not only is customer data (often including contact details and credit card information) vulnerable to these attacks, but these SMEs often provide hackers an easy path through their B2B links into the supply chains (and ultimately the databases) of larger companies (as was the case with Target).

The European Union has become so frustrated with these data breaches and the lack of precautions by companies, that it has proposed sweeping new data protection laws that include provisions where companies could be fined up to 5% of their worldwide revenues for data breaches where they were found to be negligent of taking appropriate security precautions.[25] Cisco estimated that cyber crime was up nearly 15% in 2013 and costs the global economy about $300 billion every year. And there is little doubt that things will only get worse, as hackers stay one step ahead of security and encryption technologies.[26]

Obviously, the more customer data a company collects, and the more it attempts to make that data available to all its employees, anytime they need it, the more exposed they are to financial and reputational damage if (some would say *when*) their systems are breached. And yet, these are exactly the policies and practices at the heart of most Big Data initiatives:

- **Collecting as much data as possible on as many customers as possible:** The idea of collecting everything on everything to apply Big Data analytics also means that your company is responsible for much more in the way of sensitive and personally identifiable (PII) data.
- **Concentrating that data to provide the capabilities for Single Company View (SCV):** The US intelligence services found out to their dismay that SCV has its implications when its "connect-the-dots" policy meant that both Bradley Manning and Edward Snowden could gain access to millions of documents through a single entry point.
- **Making data access available to noncompany employees:** Sharing data with vendors and partners is an inherent part of modern digital supply chain management, and external digital connections form an ever-growing part of a company's IT ecosystem. A third of Starbucks IT projects last year, for example, involved integration with customers, suppliers, or other partners.[27]

- **Allowing departments to collect and store customer data:** Through independent initiatives using cloud-based Software-as-a-Service (SaaS) frameworks.
- **Allowing that data to be input and accessed through mobile devices:** This means not only that employees are transferring work e-mails to their personal phones but are independently signing up for cloud-based storage applications like Dropbox to support their dual work/personal file storage needs (70% of young employees in a recent survey by Fortinet admit using their personal accounts through the cloud for work purposes).[28]
- **Utilizing Hadoop-like technologies through cloud-based applications:** Especially as, if poorly configured, Hadoop may allow malicious applications into the cluster.

All these aspects of Big Data are also aspects of big risk, in that they encourage the concentration of private, often confidential, company and customer data, sharing that data as widely as possible, and the (often) unauthorized (or at least not directly supervised) exchange of that data through personal devices and the cloud (see Figure 10.4).

Of particular concern to CIOs is the trend toward employees accessing company applications and data through their own mobile phones (sometimes called Bring-Your-Own-Device or BYOD). Although convenient for employees, it is quickly becoming a serious problem, as companies find themselves increasingly unable to prevent that data from being forwarded (with no means of tracking it if it is passed on through private e-mails) and equally susceptible to having that company and client data exposed to hackers through mobile-focused malware—which, according to Alcatel-Lucent, rose 20% in 2013.[29] A third of companies now report having lost customer data because of employees using their personal mobile devices.

All this has given rise to new software and management techniques (known as *Mobile Application Management (MAM)*), which

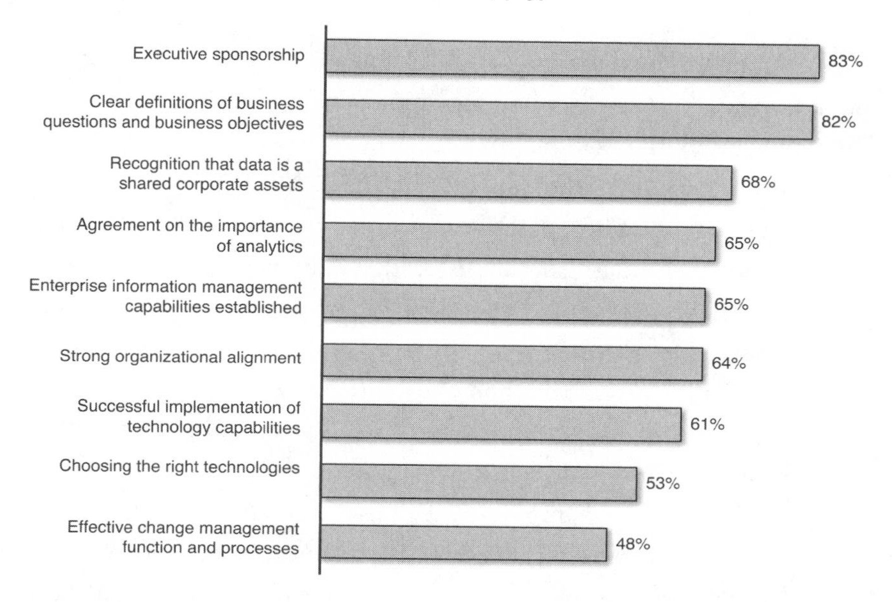

Figure 10.4 Organizational Change Issues in Big Data Projects
Source: NewVantage Partners Big Data Executive Survey 2013

helps companies to ensure separation between personal and office data, and gives them the ability to remotely track and even purge data residing on mobile phones remotely. It is an inevitable result of the move toward mobile in the digital economy but also adds one more layer of complexity to the growing security and privacy debate.

In fact, and almost ironically, the security function itself is rapidly moving toward the cloud, as companies and individuals turn away from loading data-heavy and constantly changing security software onto laptops and mobile devices and move toward cloud-based security applications that filter data before it comes into the device itself. Many groups (for example, Vormetric, Safenet, Qualsys, Zscaler) now provide cloud-based security software, security analytics and enterprise encryption, and key management for corporations. Many of these groups belong to the Cloud Security Alliance (CSA), a not-for-profit organization made up of a variety of companies and practitioners that promotes security best practices in cloud computing.

In this quickly-evolving environment, it is not just data breaches that companies need to worry about. If the data is personally identifiable information (PII), either for employees or for customers, permissions and authorizations for access need to be worked out. That will vary not only by who can see that data, but where they reside when they see it. When data is transferred into the cloud (or when SaaS Hadoop-like platforms are used) that data may be stored all over the world, making it subject to a wide variety of (often different and sometimes contradictory) data privacy laws, including laws covering ownership, use, control, and even retrieval of that data. It is one thing to apply encryption for data at rest; it is something altogether more complex when that data is in motion. There may be insurance implications to storing important data assets in a variety of national jurisdictions at the same time. There are mutual assistance treaties between nations, but government search, seizure, and warrant laws vary enormously between nations, and it is probably only a matter of time before company data—like money and other assets—becomes subject to tariffs, quarantines, sanctions, and other restrictions. Data privacy laws are being altered day-to-day in nations all over the world, and the move is, if anything, away from standardization. (We explore the different data privacy laws of the United States, the European Union, China, Australia, and others in Chapter 11, "Living in a Big Data World.")

Who is responsible for a data breach of personally identifiable customer data if that occurs through the mobile phone of an employee using a cloud-based business application (especially if the employee was never authorized to transfer company data to that service)? Is the data running through your Hadoop cluster subject to regulation? What happens when multiple parties claim ownership or access to that data? These are not easy questions to answer, and it all means that as companies opt for Big Data initiatives, company data managers increasingly must take into account a wide variety of data ownership and use laws that they may know little about and that they certainly have never encountered in the past. We discuss some of these laws in the next chapter, but suffice to say, these are the types of issues that will present a serious challenge for any company attempting a Big Data project today.

11

Living in a Big Data World

Key Chapter Points

- Civil liberties advocates suggest that a new legal framework is needed to protect personal privacy in the digital economy.
- Personal data has been made increasingly vulnerable through hacking, fraud, and company negligence.
- The nature of the Internet means that once published, personal data is irretrievable.
- The Snowden revelations on NSA monitoring activities alarmed privacy advocates and undermined trust in US businesses.
- Conflicting data privacy laws are creating friction between the United States and other nations and undermining US company competitiveness.
- If not resolved, these Big Data issues could lead to the "Balkanization" of the Internet.

Until this point, we have looked at Big Data through the eyes of the businesses and technologists actively involved in making it happen, but everyone—luddites or technologists, old and young, rich and poor, like it or not—is affected personally by the tectonic changes occurring in the digital economy.

As we've seen, Big Data can be a tremendous power for good, bringing efficiencies and insight to a variety of data-intensive areas such as medicine, research, and economics. The same is true of the supply chain-related efficiencies that come from smart parts and the business performance-related analytics that can help identify component faults or process bottlenecks. On the consumer side, there is the Faustian bargain—the fact that most people are happy to trade some loss of privacy for convenience, savings, or even novelty. This trade-off is integral to Google search and Gmail, to Facebook and other social media, and to Twitter and messaging. It is also a bargain agreed to by people who allow their car to be monitored in exchange for lower insurance premiums, or to a lesser degree when we use E-ZPass, which records traveling habits in exchange for a convenient way of paying tolls electronically. This bargain, though, means that for the first time in history, and on an ever-increasing basis, personal data has become a currency for barter. And the bargain has been entered into without much in the way of complaint. For many years now, surveys consistently show that, when asked if they would prefer to pay for content or receive the service for free (along with targeted advertising and the loss of personal data), around 90% of people opted for the latter.[1] Most of us, at least until recently, have simply not perceived the threat to personal privacy to be enough to entice us to give up the panoply of free services offered over the Web.

But how far is the consumer willing to extend that bargain? With a rapidly exploding Big Data market, the cloud, and the confluence of both the Consumer and Industrial Internets into the Internet of Things, individuals are suddenly facing very different levels of data monitoring and exposure in the coming years. Even in these relatively early days, almost anyone can find out almost anything about another individual that they want to know—where they live, where they work, how much their house costs, their personal history, their foibles and crimes, their accomplishments, and who their friends are. And, as discussed earlier, data collection groups of various stripes are happy to sell much more intimate information than that—information that was for all of human history either nonexistent or protected by the private nature of a paper folder in a locked file cabinet.

We've also seen that many of the groups on the other side of the Faustian bargain—including the Internet tech conglomerates and the massive credit bureaus—actually have much more personal data on us than they openly admit. To all that can now be added data from the electronic "signatures" of the toaster, the washer, or the hair dryer, leaving clues of how the users spend their time at home.

Add to this the combination of mobile phones and improved RFID chips, closed-circuit cameras, and facial-recognition software, and citizens now find themselves monitored physically: tracked when they leave the house, wherever they walk, bicycle, or drive. We are on the verge of a wearables revolution that will extend that monitoring to users' bodies, capturing health statistics—blood pressure, pulse, temperature. Location technologies can alert the staff when a smartphone user approaches a store or restaurant, providing them with personal data and prior purchases—even collating what the user looks at while he or she browses there with what interested them the day before in an online search. Google, Facebook, and Amazon are investing heavily in drone technology, capable of providing independent communications and (conceivably) spying on people or places from thousands of feet in the sky. Most major Internet conglomerates—Google, Facebook, Yahoo!, AOL—provide a filtered news feed for their readers with news and entertainment items selected, at least in part, to elicit a response from the reader (a like or a dislike, a comment or forwarding the item to a friend). The response itself provides the group with even more personal data. As we saw with Facebook's now-notorious behavioral experiment (see the "Power of Persuasion" sidebar), if news feeds and friend comments can influence our attitude and responses, then we are vulnerable to manipulation. The fact that these Internet companies can filter news and, increasingly, make their own content, gives them a lot of potential persuasive power.

George Orwell, in his dystopian novel *1984*, could never have dreamt of this level of intrusion, surveillance, and influence. But in this case, Big Brother isn't just big government; it's also big business. And it is invited in by us, rather than being imposed.

Not everyone is happy with the way things are moving. Some civil liberties advocates suggest that we need to have a stringent new legal framework to protect our privacy and civil liberties in a time of unfettered digital exposure. Others say that we're past the point of no return and that we've essentially already seen the "end of privacy" as it was traditionally understood.

Recently, though, a greater number of people are beginning to reflect on these personal privacy concerns and the possibility that this level of personal data collection is getting out of hand. A Pew Research poll taken in September 2013 showed how a majority of Americans (possibly influenced by the highly publicized Big Data monitoring efforts by the US government and the NSA) now are concerned about their privacy. In fact, 86% said they actively take steps to "remove or mask" their online digital footprints.[2] An astute quotation is floating around, attributed to Andrew Lewis of the MetaFilter community, warning that "If you're not paying for it, you're not the customer. You're the product being sold."

Some cite the doctrine of *caveat emptor*, explaining that users willingly sign up for the Faustian bargain, and they get what they (don't) pay for, or at least, what they deserve. Others lament that nothing much in the way of an uprising is likely to occur from the majority of users who can't even be bothered to empty their browsers once a day, or install basic data security and protection tools on their tablets.

One thing is for certain: Society can't simply put its head in the sand and pretend that nothing has changed, or that those with the capacity to collect and sell personal data will all voluntarily restrict themselves for the common good in the coming years. So what, as citizens (not just as businesspeople), should we do to ensure that these new technologies improve, rather than erode, the quality of life in the future?

To put this in perspective, let's begin by reviewing some of the more egregious incidents involving the collection and exposure of our personal data that have occurred in the past couple of years.

Data Theft and Fraud: Data Raiding and Hacktivism

In 2013, Experian, the credit bureau, admitted that it had been hacked into 86 times via the systems of unsecured partners such as banks and automobile dealers, and along with Equifax and Trans-Union (two other large credit agencies) admitted a data breach that exposed information on personal accounts, which included Michelle Obama and Joe Biden.[3] The year before, the state of South Carolina lost 14 years of electronic tax data—including the taxpayers' Social Security numbers—to unknown hackers.[4]

Sony admitted losing 77 million user records in April 2013 (12 million of those accounts had unencrypted credit card numbers).[5] TJX Co., the parent company of T. J. Maxx and other retailers, had more than 45 million credit and debit card numbers stolen from its IT systems, and these data were then used to steal nearly $8 million from Walmart stores (the TJX customer data was used to create dummy credit cards for purchasing Walmart and Sam's Club gift cards).[6] Through a laptop theft, NASA compromised the names, birth dates, Social Security numbers, and background check details of 10,000 employees.[7] Target, Michaels, Niemen Marcus, Adobe, Microsoft—all have suffered recent security breaches. In fact, here are just a few of the well-known companies that have reported data losses to hackers:

Automatic Data Processing Inc. (ADP)	BP	Baker Hughes Inc.	Bank of Swiss
Billabong	Booz Allen Hamilton	CIA	Citibank
Citigroup Bank	Commerce Bank	ConocoPhillips	Domino's Pizza
Exxon	Google	HBGary	Lockheed Martin
Marathon Oil Corp.	Mitsubishi Heavy Industries	Mobil Corp.	Oak Ridge National Laboratories
Public Broadcasting Service (PBS)	RSA	Royal Dutch Shell	Sony
Sovereign Bank	The International Monetary Fund	The United States Senate	Twitter
US Bank	Visa and MasterCard	The World Health Organization (WHO)	Yahoo!

Source: NuWave Backup[8]

These are only a few among the ones we know about. A British survey in 2014 found that 43% of large (more than 250 employees) UK companies suffered a theft or unauthorized disclosure of confidential information in the past 12 months (but that only 30% of those breaches were publicly acknowledged).[9] These companies have well-funded IT programs with executives that are highly aware of the data security threats that they face. And yet they continue to lose sensitive customer data to fraudsters.

Crimes and Misdemeanors

Equally troubling is the fact that, given a poorly-defined legal framework and an all-encompassing Terms of Agreement, many companies are selling their customer data to all comers as a means of earning a second income stream. As we've already seen, that includes the credit bureaus, the Internet technology conglomerates, and a vast array of retailers and unnoticed online trackers. Groups like the online data service OKCupid, for example, sell anonymized information on gender, age, ZIP codes, sexual orientation, and even admitted drug use from their dating applications.[10] A GPS travel service in Holland provides a "quick routing" service to drivers, at the same time selling the data of its users back to the police so that they can be caught for speeding.[11] The Big Data aggregators, including Experian, Acxiom, and Equifax, admitted to a Senate Commerce Committee panel in 2013, that they passed on (unspecified) personal details on the "X-tra needy" categories of people (also sold under their headings of "Financially Challenged" and "Struggling Societies"), including highly sensitive information not only on income and credit denials but even lists of those who had been victims of rape and other crimes. The callous honesty of the category names (which include "Relying On Aid: Retired Singles" and "Tough Start: Young Single Parents") underlines the concerns that these details can be used by fraudsters or those who prey on the most vulnerable (payday loans, risky credit-clearance schemes, and so on) to target and take advantage of unsuspecting individuals through telemarketing calls and other means.[12]

There has been a spate of recent prosecutions for illegal selling of digitized personal data. CVS, for example, was found guilty in 2011 by a state court in Pennsylvania of selling the details of its customers—name, date of birth, and medications—to large pharmaceutical companies.[13] Google has found itself in court a number of times: over its monitoring of Gmail (and non-Gmail users) and for vacuuming up personal information, including e-mails and passwords, from unsuspecting residents during its Street View (dubbed by the press as the "Wi-Spy" program) while cameras were taking photos of houses around the world. They were fined $22.5 million in 2012 by the Federal Trade Commission (FTC) for bypassing Apple Safari's security settings and antitracking features, allowing Google to track the personal information of millions of the browser's users without their knowing it[14] (Apple's Safari browser only allows first-party cookies—from sites the user has visited—and by default blocks third-party tracking cookies).[15] That same year, Google agreed to pay $500 million to the federal government as part of a settlement for knowingly (and illegally) allowing unlicensed pharmacies to advertise fake prescription medicines and illegal drugs on Google's site, based on user data provided by Google.[16]

Data aggregators, data brokers, application developers, and employment sites manage to keep the FTC busy with prosecutions. HireRight, the employment background screening company, was fined $2.6 million in August 2012 for, among other violations, failing to follow-up when those being investigated disputed their findings. Two months earlier, Spokeo paid $800,000 in civil penalties after the FTC accused it of selling personal profiles to third parties in violation of the Fair Credit Reporting Act (FCRA). A year later Certegy, the check authorization company, was fined $3.5 million for FCRA noncompliance. And in May 2013, the Commission settled with Filiquarian, the mobile app developer, after accusing the company of violating the FCRA in compiling and selling criminal background reports on consumers.[17] In 2014, Snapchat admitted to the FTC that its disappearing instant messages were not as ephemeral as they had suggested to users, and that in fact, messages and photos were stored on the smartphone of those receiving the message, and could be later reproduced by connecting to a PC. They also admitted to downloading users' address books and contacts, and monitoring user location—all in violation of their own privacy policy. They too were hacked, and the usernames and phone numbers of 4.6m Snapchat users were posted online.[18]

LexisNexis settled a class action suit brought by more than 30,000 consumers for $13.5 million after selling its Accurint reports (defined by the FCRA as "consumer reports") to debt collectors.[19] In an absolute howler, the FTC settled with InfoTrack Information Services for $1 million (reduced to $60,000 for inability to pay), over accusations that the employment background investigation company sold information on potential hires that inaccurately suggested that they might be sex offenders (InfoTrack matched up only the first and last names of prospective employees against the National Sex Offender Registry without cross-referencing those names with other validating data like date of birth, address, and so on).[20] The *New York Times* reported the plight of an Illinois man who recently received a marketing offer from OfficeMax that inadvertently included the words "Daughter Killed in Car Crash" (which was true) between his name and his address.[21]

The Senate Commerce Committee, in its recent investigation, noted that some data brokers were collecting and selling consumer data, including personally sensitive data covering rape victims or those with genetic diseases, for 7.9 cents per name. In its December 2013 report, it found that these data brokers:

- Collect a huge volume of detailed information on hundreds of millions of consumers.
- Sell products that identify financially vulnerable consumers.
- Provide information about consumer offline behavior to tailor online outreach by marketers.
- Operate behind a veil of secrecy.[22]

The Re-Anonymizing Debate

Part of the problem from a consumer point of view is that it is difficult to know just how anonymous the data being collected and sold by groups like Google, Facebook, Experian, or the myriad of other data collectors and brokers actually are. The online ad industry defines anonymous as meaning that a computer-generated code is used to replace a consumer's actual name when selling the consumer's data, thereby eliminating any link to personally-identifiable information (PII). But Hadoop-type technologies are capable of crunching through many millions of data points to find correlations, which means that a data broker (or anyone else with access to these technologies) can input various pieces of information (an e-mail, a phone number, a ZIP code, or even less obviously identifiable information such as personal interests, employment history, or relationships) and potentially uncover the real identity of those names sold to them under an anonymized code. That means that, despite assurances that much of this personal data is "anonymized," and being sold without any real names or e-mail identifiers, in reality, de-anonymizing it (sometimes known as *re-identification*) is not that difficult.

The data breach that AOL suffered as far back as 2006 provides a good example. Cooperating with research concerning online information retrieval, AOL released data on 20 million search queries collected during a three-month period, anonymizing the data by replacing the user identifiers with randomly generated numbers. Using just the Web (that is, not in-house Hadoop-type technologies), reporters from the *New York Times* were able to uncover the identities of several of the anonymous users, simply by cross-matching various data points that appeared during the search history of those users (for example, local retailers, medical complaints, and so on).[23] Today this is often referred to as the *mosaic effect*—that when various apparently unrelated data points are combined, they reveal a surprisingly clear picture of the user—and a good deal of information (including, often, their identity).

In fact, most companies probably don't want to know a user's actual identity—or at least not their actual names. It doesn't really matter to their software or marketers if the identifier says Bob Smith or 98X649MT6. For advertising purposes, they really only want an identifier that provides them consistent and accurate data on that individual's interests and purchases, and a reliable way of contacting (that is, advertising to) that person through the IP or MAC address of an identifiable computer, tablet, or smartphone. But others, from debt collectors to employment screening agencies—and even assorted evildoers—may want to associate all that information with an actual name.

We see this much more frequently now that the analytical power of Hadoop-type technologies is becoming more widely available. Universities, employers, loan, and house or apartment rental screening companies, all today routinely search the Internet and mine social media sites for information on a candidate—not just to verify past employment history or addresses, but to check for revealing Tweets, pictures, or postings. Universities look for indicators of bad (or good) behavior for applicants, and assess their previous postings and the types of friends they have. Data brokers routinely provide information on race and ethnicity (derived from friends, social media comments, photos, or the restaurants frequented).[24] Lending groups like LendUp scan Facebook and other social media sites to see whether a potential borrower has posted something revealing about previous defaults or job losses. They look for family problems and the number of young children at home. They even take into account the number of "friends" the candidate has online. And it works the other way around, as well: Lenddo, a loan company, posts a delinquent borrower's repayment notices to his or her friends on social media networks.[25]

Not only do these groups routinely mine the Internet and social media for these types of personal details, but they are also increasingly turning to predictive analytics: Big Data tools that estimate the likelihood that a candidate will succeed in college, be good at a particular job, or default on a loan. These systems can surmise from online data what church or political parties you belong to, and how likely you are to be unhealthy in the future (by looking at food purchasing, smoking, or obesity indicators). Target even has a pregnancy prediction score, triggered by the purchase of about 25 products, and boast that it can derive the baby's delivery date from those purchases so that it can provide the mother-to-be with coupons and other incentives to buy things at appropriate points throughout her pregnancy.[26] That program went famously wrong in 2012 when Target mailed promotional products to the outraged father of a high school-aged daughter, alerting him to her pregnancy. It seems that Target knew of his daughter's pregnancy before he did.[27]

More to the point, the combination of online personal data and Big Data tools that can predict behavior (accurately or otherwise) moves society into a completely new post-Orwellian realm—with the idea that what can be predicted can also be controlled. A lottery company recently admitted that it timed its advertisements to coincide with the payment dates of government benefits (to be able to coax welfare recipients, who have a much higher level of lottery play, into buying tickets). This level of predictability (and influence) was underlined with Facebook's experiment in 2014 that subjected a test group of users to only good, or only bad, news feeds to gauge their reactions (see "The Power of Persuasion" sidebar). Facebook's conclusion was, not so surprisingly, that depressing news makes people depressed. But more important was the fact that Facebook felt that it could conduct behavioral experiments with users without their knowledge or consent. The results also underscore the potential power that those who control the Internet (as for those who control the news or other media, which, increasingly, may be the same groups) could have over our thoughts, opinions, and emotions. That type of control becomes more worrying if put in the context of political elections or when a nation is deliberating whether or not to go to war.

The Power of Persuasion

In the spring of 2014, Facebook announced that it had done a week-long experiment with 690,000 users that entailed feeding them filtered positive or negative news feeds, likes, and dislikes, in order to see whether good news or bad news, skepticism or optimism, affected their users' attitudes and behaviors—in Facebook's words, would it create "emotional contagion." This was not the first time that Facebook engaged in this type of behavioral testing on its users; in 2010, a Facebook research team did an experiment to see how "political mobilization messages" sent to 61 million Facebook users—having friends and other Facebook users endorse a "get out the vote" campaign—would affect their voting patterns.

Other groups have done similar experiments with their users. OKCupid announced around the same period that it had run behavioral experiments—removing photos, extracting text from profiles, and telling applicants that they were well matched even when they weren't—all to gauge how well its system really worked.

In their defense, both organizations pointed out that these types of experiments were a necessary part of product testing, and like any other media company, Internet tech companies are always presenting to users only a filtered version of the totality of information at their disposal. Both companies also pointed out that they openly reserve the right to use user data in "research" in their Terms of Use Agreement. (Critics pointed out that research based on user data collected in a normal way is different from actively providing users misinformation—or filtered information—to alter behavior.)

Curiously, a recent study found that more than 60% of Facebook users didn't realize that their news feeds were individually generated for them using an algorithm, in part, based on their preferences and what Facebook believes they will like (and therefore will draw them back to read more).

Whether this type of behavioral manipulation is legitimate, or even unusual, at a time when news, political opinion, and brand placement can often co-mingle, the results of the Facebook experiment (that is, that it does have the ability to manipulate behavior) will not go unnoticed by advertisers, politicians, or civil libertarians.[28]

Spies Like Us

Which, of course, brings us to the NSA and the intelligence services.

Maybe no event has led to greater appreciation of the power and potential problems of Big Data than the revelations by Edward Snowden about the digital data monitoring activities of America's National Security Agency (NSA). It has all the good and bad aspects of the broader Big Data debate: the collection of huge amounts of widely varying digital data; distributed computing using Hadoop technologies over the cloud; powerful new data mining and analytics technologies; a collect-everything, everywhere, all-the-time strategy; the storage of years' worth of data in massive data warehouses; and a single company view (SCV) framework that means that a data breach by one person—Edward Snowden (or Bradley Manning before him)—provides access to millions of classified documents from hundreds of different departments. In fact, part of the reason that Snowden's revelations so resonated with the public was that the NSA's monitoring was similar to, and in fact integrally involved with, the Internet tech giants and data aggregators that also monitor us—Google, Facebook, Microsoft, Experian, and so on. (A less than compelling argument, made both by Google with its Wi-spy Street View program and by the NSA, was that it was okay to collect private data on everyone because they didn't actually read it anyway.) And although over the past year both the US and the UK governments were largely successful at deflecting the media discussion toward the issue of telephone metadata, in fact, Snowden's leaks reveal a situation where the private online data of many millions of individuals is being captured and analyzed by both commercial companies and government security agencies, often using the same technology or even shared platforms. For some this means that, in terms of real as opposed to potential harm, the case against the private sector spying is at least on par with that of government surveillance.

It could be argued that at least there is some measure of accountability and transparency with government. Oracle's Larry Ellison was provoked to suggest that we should worry first about what banks and companies are up to with our data and put the NSA at number two on the list.[29] The problem is that, given the propensity of the corporate data collectors to sell personal data, the NSA (or any other intelligence service) can and does simply add to its growing number of profiles by augmenting its files with consumer data purchased from these private companies. And because of the average citizen's willingness over the past two decades to share personal data, much of that information is available in the public domain anyway. After all, as private companies know, a lot of personal information can be gleaned from scanning Tweets, following blog posts, or monitoring how a customer reviews a book on Barnes & Noble or Amazon.

It is also important to remember how closely linked Silicon Valley and the Internet are, and always have been, to the Department of Defense. After all, defense-inspired technological innovation and the Military Industrial Complex have been at the center of US economic growth since the 1950s. From silicon chips for the guidance systems of ICBMs (Intercontinental Ballistic Missiles) to the Internet itself, much of the postwar technological boom is attributable to government research funding, and more specifically, grants from the Defense Advanced Research Projects Agency (DARPA). Even Siri, the voice of the Apple iPhone, was a result of DARPA funding.[30] In 2012, the US Defense Department invested $2.3 billion in electrical engineering or computer science research, and the National Science Foundation invested $900 million more.[31]

When in 2013, leaks from the Snowden files revealed the extent to which the NSA was leveraging private groups such as Google, Yahoo!, Facebook, and other IT and telecommunications leaders (even going so far as creating "back doors" to tap into their data cables, rigging encryption algorithms and standards, and building monitoring technologies directly into commercial hardware), Mark Zuckerberg and others protested against what they claimed was a pernicious level of interference by the government. Their contention was that they had not been fully informed about PRISM, the NSA's system authorized by the Foreign Intelligence Surveillance Act in 2008, which has (allegedly) been monitoring the private communications of users directly from the servers of nine of the largest Internet services groups, including Google, Yahoo!, Microsoft, and Facebook.[32] And this wasn't only the NSA. According to the Snowden documents released by *The Guardian* newspaper in the United Kingdom, by tapping the undersea cables leading into these Internet giants, Britain's GCHQ (the rough equivalent of America's NSA) was able to monitor up to 600 million communications every day.[33]

How much each of these Internet companies knew about NSA monitoring is still not clear in part because, even with a compromise reached between the big five companies and the US government in January 2014, the Internet groups are still restricted in what they can reveal to the public about their communications and transactions with the NSA. But from what we do know, it is apparent that there are many examples of cooperation between the intelligence community and private firms, which blur the distinction between public and private, and civil liberties versus national security interests.

The ultimate Big Data aspirant (since Admiral John Poindexter, himself the director of the DARPA Information Awareness Office, proposed the ominous-sounding Total Information Awareness program in 2002), have been the US intelligence services. For many years, they have sought, as much as possible, to create a system that collects everything on everyone and with a single click shares that data among various security and law enforcement agencies, including Homeland Security, the Drug Enforcement Agency, the CIA, and the FBI. This drive for data integration and sharing, even seeking to break down the long-standing barriers between foreign counterterrorism and domestic criminal investigations, has serious implications for jurisprudence, especially because many of these have been enshrined in post-9/11 terrorism-related laws made by Congress. The

Communications Assistance for Law Enforcement Act (CALEA), for example, requires Internet providers and phone companies to maintain data for government wiretaps. The Cyber Intelligence Sharing and Protection Act (CISPA) provides for (voluntary) information sharing between the government and private companies in the event of a cyber attack.

There are many more examples of this government accommodated, commercial-security service collaboration. Beginning in 2007, for example, the NSA funded and helped design the Accumulo open-source database released by Apache (and reverse-engineered from Google's BigTable database) to store and analyze the huge amounts of data for its PRISM program. The system can capture, analyze, and store data from a wide variety of formats, and currently operates the storage and retrieval system on thousands of distributed computer nodes in NSA data centers.[34] In 2012, Ely Khan, former White House cyber security strategy director, joined with ex-NSA employees to create Sqrrl, an analytics tool that is a commercial version of Apache Accumulo. By October 2013, they had raised more than $5 million in venture capital.[35] The Transportation Safety Administration (TSA) has sought tenders from private companies to support it in providing the risk analysis when administering its "trusted traveler program." Booz Allan Hamilton, the company that employed Edward Snowden, is majority owned by the Carlyle Group and employs 24,500 people, providing consulting services to defense contractors, government, and the intelligence agencies—much of that involving digital data collection. It had a net profit of $219 million on $5.8 billion revenue in 2012–2013.[36] The consultancy has close ties to the intelligence services: Its vice chairman, Mike McConnell, was the director of national intelligence (DNI) in the George W. Bush administration. James Woolsey, the former CIA director, was a Booz Allen Hamilton vice president. Even James Clapper, the current director of national intelligence, is a former company executive.[37]

As far back as 1999, the Central Intelligence Agency formed In-Q-Tel, its own nonprofit company, to support commercial sector research that it believed would also be helpful in capturing and analyzing intelligence-related data. According to In-Q-Tel's first director of business operations, the company today helps fund 59 IT companies, many in Silicon Valley. One of those CIA-funded companies is Visible Technologies, which reportedly reviews more than 500,000 web sites, blogs, and forums every day, including Twitter, Amazon, and YouTube, and various newspapers, TV programs, video, and radio reports.[38] The In-Q-Tel-sponsored Big Data groups also include Palantir, which was talking about a possible valuation in late 2013 of up to $8 billion (and whose advisors include former CIA director George Tenet and Condoleezza Rice, former national security advisor to President George W. Bush), and Cloudera, which will be integrating with the NSA's Apache Accumulo database.[39]

Possibly the most revealing example of this growing private/public Big Data cooperation is the CIA's open announcement in November 2013 that Amazon's (Hadoop-MapReduce-based) cloud services were selected over IBM for the $600 million bid to provide the intelligence agency with data analytics and massive data storage.[40] That's on top of more than 600 agencies (including the Air Force and the Navy) already now signed up to Amazon's cloud services.[41]

It is too early to tell what blowback effect the Snowden revelations will have on gathering and storing of personal data by the intelligence community, but the revelations have certainly undermined the reputation of the US government (particularly with allies such as Germany). It is likely (reflecting the law of unintended consequences) that the fallout from the NSA's wide-ranging data monitoring policies will also have an effect on American IT and Internet companies both at home and abroad. US companies from Google to Apple to Cisco have already found themselves facing charges by foreign governments (and in particular China) that they are a security risk because they have either willingly or unwillingly become pawns of the US security services. Cisco's CEO, John Chambers, complained directly to President Obama in May 2014, saying that new standards of conduct were needed after an internal NSA report released by Edward Snowden contained photographs showing NSA employees intercepting Cisco servers, routers, and other network gear in order to implant monitoring firmware before delivery.[42] Even the European Parliament has called for a reassessment of a long-standing data transfer agreement with the United States known as the Safe Harbor provisions (see the section "International Relations" later in the chapter) to be withdrawn, and apart from implementing more stringent data privacy requirements, have even pushed for all digital data of EU citizens to be contained within European borders. There is an ongoing investigation of Microsoft regarding its use of Hotmail to collect private personal data, and Google, specifically, is the subject of the stringent ruling on "right to be forgotten" policies (see sidebar). The European Court of Justice even recently ruled that laws by member nations that require telecommunications companies to store customer data for two years (in case these data were needed by the intelligence services) were illegal under warrantless search laws.[43]

Long the leaders in IT innovation, American companies may find that the NSA's uncompromising determination to use Big Data in its most expansive form could result not only in the "Balkanization" of the Internet (where each nation or region maintains a separate, secure Internet) but could ultimately undermine American companies eager to expand against growing competition overseas. It is not just other national governments that have become suspicious; a survey by the Truste company in September 2013 found that a third of American Internet users now say they have stopped using a company's web site (or have stopped doing business with a company) because of concerns about privacy.[44] All this means that American companies are suddenly in an unenviable position of having to prove that their products and approach don't compromise another nation's security or a user's privacy, and to demonstrate that the headlong rush for collecting personal data that has become so much a part of US business these days is compatible with both security and personal privacy legislation in other countries. This is something that should concern American citizens, politicians, intelligence agencies, and businesses alike.

This level of intelligence gathering, increasingly, is trickling down to the local level. Police all around America today use automatic license plate scanners to routinely photograph (and thereby track) cars and trucks, and that photo data is often stored in a database that can also be accessed by other authorities, including Homeland Security and the FBI, as part of 71 intelligence fusion organizations set up by the federal government after 9/11. Those photos are often analyzed with the same Palantir software that is used extensively by the NSA (and is partly funded by In-Q-Tel) and that can (according to Palantir) search the 500 million license plate photos kept by the New York Police Department in less than five seconds.[45]

For many, this confluence of government, business, and Big Data calls for a number of changes to our antiquated, pre-Big Data privacy legislation. Unfortunately, those changes are not going to come quickly or easily.

Not So Straightforward

Developing a modern data privacy framework in a Big Data economy requires us to confront some difficult issues. For example, is it a crime to publish accurate but personally sensitive data if that publication harms someone (for example, revenge porn versus investigative journalism)? Do photos belong to anyone who is in a picture (with full property and use rights), or to everyone who is in the picture (giving any one person a right of veto for its use)? Can that ownership be transferred through a user agreement even if others in the photo don't consent? What exactly constitutes the public domain when almost any piece of digital data can be published on the Internet (that is, is it suddenly public domain simply because it is published)? Can data be used for purposes entirely different from its original intent (as can be the case with data purchased from a credit bureau that is then used by a debt collector)?

The US Supreme Court said (in *United States vs. Jones*) that using a tracking device on a vehicle by the police (without a court order) constitutes an illegal search under the Fourth Amendment. If an individual tracks another person's movements and activities, she can be prosecuted for stalking. So why can companies monitor our private e-mails, online search activity, television programs, and location (through GPS and mobile telephone tracking technologies)? What about in-store tracking? Are there any limits to the rights that can be "signed away" through a user agreement? Can you sign away ownership of your house and children if you press "Agree" to an unread 37-page Terms of Use agreement? Revealing someone's confidential medical history is a crime under Health Insurance Portability and Accountability Act (HIPAA) regulations. If a person's medical history can be inferred from his Facebook or blog postings or online search history is that a violation of HIPAA? Does the NSA's policy of collecting metadata constitute warrantless search? How long can a company keep your personal data? What if you want it back? What if it is inaccurate and you want to correct it or eliminate it from the Web altogether? Can malicious or libelous Tweeting be prosecuted?

These are the types of fundamental questions being asked around the world as more and more personal data are being produced and collected, and companies and courts begin to wrestle with privacy issues never before contemplated. The answers to these questions tend to vary widely between jurisdictions and cultures.

Broadly, digital data policy issues fall into several areas. One of the most fundamental and vexing issues is that of *ownership*. Does digital data belong to the person who created it, to the group who controls it, or to the person or group that it concerns most? For example, if someone asks whether we have a right of control over our own photo, most of us would intuitively say that we do. But what if we didn't take the photo? What if there are others in the photo? What happens if it is posted online? What if it was done without our consent? What if we first agree to post it but then change our minds?

In an era when personal e-mails, photos, and even our belt size can be quickly distributed anonymously around the Internet, there is no more perplexing problem than establishing ownership and responsibility for the use or reuse of digital data. Are these data our property with all the rights attached to that concept legally? It is not straightforward, because ownership usually implies some element of control, use, and disposition. But practically speaking, individuals have almost no control over use, reuse, or disposal of their data once it is loose on the Internet, if only because locating it and controlling it (both physically and logically) is all but impossible.

So what can you do if an online report wrongly indicates that you were declared bankrupt? Or what if it accurately shows you as a teenager smoking marijuana? And what if you suspect that these data were responsible for a job rejection or a higher premium (or denial) of health insurance? What rights do you now have to gain access to, to alter, or to delete these data?

Right now, the answer is very few rights. Because the average user has so little real control over personal data once it is online, authorities have instinctively turned to those who do. That's the direction that the EU moved in May 2014. Under its Right to Be Forgotten ruling, the European Court of Justice held that EU citizens have the right to require Google (specifically) to remove or block online publication of information that is "irrelevant, inaccurate, or outdated." Of course, Google itself doesn't maintain or store that data; its search engine simply crawls the Web looking for key words. But it illustrates a growing concern with a fundamental flaw in the nature of the Internet: It never forgets.

The ruling also highlights a growing worldwide concern about the loss of personal privacy that is, after all, at the heart of a Big Data economy. Internet and Big Data purists argue that freely accessible data is at the heart of the Internet. That contrasts sharply with a growing opposition that feels that personal data is personal property and that individuals should be able to exercise control over what information about them appears in public. Finding the balance between the individual's right to privacy and the public's right to know requires a debate that is long overdue.

For all its import, though, the EU court ruling isn't very practical in terms of providing a system for legitimately deciding what personal data should or should not be left online. First, it requires that Google employees decide whether the user's request to remove the data is valid. But Google-appointed adjudicators have no special knowledge as to whether the information in question—anything from a badly conceived blog posting to a decade-old bankruptcy notice—is legitimate. Given the billions of data sets that now reside on the Internet, the burden for Google to block any data for which it receives a complaint will be enormous. To make those changes, Google also needs to verify the identity of the requester and make certain that the requester has legitimate claim on the data. What's more, the incentives are misguided. Google doesn't care whether the information presented through its search engine is true or not. Why would it want to get bogged down in protracted arguments with users? In practical terms, the ruling simply means that Google will be forced to filter through its search engine very personal data about themselves that its millions of users object to, as people across Europe decide to do a bit of housecleaning on their online image.

Critics point out that not only does this undermine the transparency and neutrality of the Web, but that important, revealing information (criminal records, former political pronouncements, and so on) could be airbrushed out of online history. Even more important in practical terms is that Google doesn't have access to the data itself; the company can block it from appearing on Google searches, but it will still exist on the Internet and can still be accessed through another, non-Google search engine. One of the most frightening characteristics of the Internet is that tracking everywhere that data has been on the Web is simply impossible. And in the unlikely event that Google refuses to remove information, the user can refer the request to assessment bodies set up by national governments to adjudicate on data removal, a situation that moves the process of personal data removal from the Internet very near to due process, with evidence, judges, and appeals. It is a first foray by the modern world's judiciary into shifting the balance of power back toward the consumer, but critics and supporters alike appreciate that the ruling potentially creates a practical and bureaucratic nightmare.

Part of the problem is that the case was brought specifically against Google under the mistaken impression that the search engine has any real control over the personal data it finds when crawling the Internet. More logically, and no doubt the next step in the evolution of Right to Be Forgotten, will be for the courts to focus on those groups who collect and publish (or at least sell or distribute) personal data. But again, simply identifying the origins of bad data doesn't mean you can erase it from all the other places where it is found on the Internet. And web site publishers have protected rights of free speech, too—if the data they publish is true, the original owner may have no legal right to have it expunged (any more than those being reported in the offline media have the right to demand that information about them be removed without a court order).

But how is a user to know what personal data a group—say one of the credit bureaus—has been collecting about him? After all, a data broker has no real incentive to be certain that the data it has collected on any individual is accurate. Do individuals have the right to see that data, or to change it if it is wrong?

A corollary of the Right to Be Forgotten is the Right to Know, a movement gaining momentum worldwide. Right to Know laws require that companies of all types—Internet search engines, online tracker companies, or offline credit bureaus—allow individuals to see exactly what data a company has stored on them and to know how (and with whom) that data is being shared. This level of transparency is commonplace in European law but still fairly rare in the United States (although California is moving quickly in that direction). More commonly, US laws require companies to allow individuals to see their data and make corrections, but that usually comes only after a complex process of identification, which often provides the company with even more personal data (now personally verified by the users themselves).

But what if a user consents (as part of the Faustian bargain) to transfer the use of his or her personal data to Facebook, Amazon, or any of the millions of other online web sites on the Internet through a Terms of Use contract? They may be long and filled with legalese, but courts have consistently held that these online contracts are binding, and in those agreements companies often explain that a user has a choice to restrict how personal data is used and shared (although many sites reserve the right to change those privacy policies without notice at any time). A 2012 survey by Siegel+Gale asked Facebook and Google users to review and rate their understanding of the companies' privacy policies on a scale of 100: The results were 36 for Google's agreement and only a slightly better 39 for Facebook.[46] In fact, apropos to the idea of a Faustian bargain, an online company in the United Kingdom recently added a clause to its Terms of Agreement that said that by accepting, users were giving permission for the site to "claim, now and for evermore, your immortal soul," a successful legal maneuver that the *Spectator* points out harvested some 7,000 souls in one day.[47]

Another question central to the Big Data privacy debate is whether that data can be integrated across a company's various offerings or reused for purposes different from those that the user originally intended. For example, can a social media site like Facebook sell a user's data to a debt collection agency? In some contracts, that right to transfer or integrate personal data is assumed unless the user explicitly checks a box and opts out, or in some other way actively intervenes to change the site's default privacy settings. This is also true for Do Not Track settings, which have become a key area of concern for privacy advocates. This is because for many years, major Internet companies and advertising industry groups did all they could to make that opting out of the tracking process confusing, technically difficult, or time-consuming (often in the past, despite the straightforward wording, selecting the Do Not Track configuration simply meant that a user no longer received targeted ads, even though the site would continue to follow the user's online activity). Google, Facebook, Yahoo!, and AOL have all said that they will no longer comply with Do Not Track signals sent by web browsers even when users indicate specifically that they don't want to receive digital ads.[48] That's why regulation of default privacy settings is so hotly contested in the United States between the privacy advocates, who want to limit data collection and want the process simple and transparent, and several powerful companies and industry groups that want to protect the right of web sites and trackers to collect data for what they call "operational" reasons (scanning for malware or misuse, for example), even if that is against the wishes of the user.[49]

Whether because of the heightened attention to personal data privacy highlighted by the Snowden leaks, or simply because of the obvious parallels being drawn between the tracking policies of commercial firms and the intelligence agencies, Americans are beginning to worry. In an August 2013 poll, Revolution Analytics found that 80% of respondents said that they would like to see an ethical framework for collecting and using data.[50] And the natural place to turn for that type of framework is the federal government.

US Law and Big Data

There is no overarching "omnibus" data privacy legislation that attempts to regulate how companies use personal data in America. At the federal level, there is a patchwork of Congressional laws and regulations dealing with the protection of personal health care or credit data, or data concerning children, housing, or employment (the Fair Credit Reporting Act [FCRA], the Patriot Act, the Children's Online Privacy Protection Act [COPPA], the Health Insurance Portability & Accountability Act [HIPPA], the Health Information Technology for Economic & Clinical Health Act [HITECH], and so on), but these tend to be limited and industry-specific, with no coordinated approach to the issues now being raised with the onset of Big Data and the digital economy.

For the most part, the FTC carries the regulatory burden for protecting the rights of consumers online, and, as we saw earlier, it has been fairly active in prosecuting companies that violate existing data privacy laws under the Fair Credit Reporting Act. The FTC tends to be more reactive (responding to consumer complaints) than proactive at providing guidance or making rules and has collaborated with the US Senate Commerce Committee recently on some important investigations into the activities of Big Data brokers. But many of the issues in question are related more to technology and privacy laws than to trade, and require complex, innovative solutions. Even the Commission's chairman has described the FTC's rule-making approach as "complex, cumbersome and time-consuming."[51] With a Big Data Big Bang occurring all around us, it is likely that the FTC will remain more a rule enforcer than a solution provider.

As an indicator of how important issues of data privacy have become, even the White House is involved, with the Obama Administration as far back as 2010 sponsoring the President's Privacy Blueprint and the Consumer Privacy Bill of Rights. These are part of a broader initiative that includes an Internet Policy Task Force driven by the US Commerce Department, which has been tasked with coordinating various governmental bodies in a comprehensive review of what it describes as the "nexus between privacy policy, copyright, global free flow of information, cyber security, and innovation in the Internet economy." This Internet Policy Task Force, active since 2012, includes representatives from the National Telecommunications and Information Administration (NTIA), the Patent and Trademark Office (PTO), the National Institute of Standards and Technology (NIST), and the International Trade Administration (ITA), pulled together with the view to identifying "leading public policy and operational challenges in the Internet environment."[52]

Skeptics may cringe at the thought of another government Internet policy task force, but the focus of the Consumer Privacy Bill of Rights is completely appropriate—in its words, guiding "efforts to give users more control over how their personal information is used on the Internet and to help businesses maintain consumer trust and grow in the rapidly changing digital environment."[53] It sets out basic principles on key issues, which include the following:

- **Individual control:** Consumers have a right to exercise control over what personal data organizations collect from them and how they use it.
- **Transparency:** Consumers have a right to easily understandable information about privacy and security practices.
- **Respect for context:** Consumers have a right to expect that organizations will collect, use, and disclose personal data in ways consistent with the context in which consumers provide the data.
- **Security:** Consumers have a right to secure and responsible handling of personal data.
- **Access and accuracy:** Consumers have a right to access and correct personal data in usable formats, in a manner appropriate to the sensitivity of the data and the risk of adverse consequences to consumers if the data are inaccurate.

- **Focused collection:** Consumers have a right to reasonable limits on the personal data that companies collect and retain.
- **Accountability:** Consumers have a right to have personal data handled by companies with appropriate measures in place to ensure they adhere to the Consumer Privacy Bill of Rights.[54]

As laudable as these principles are, making certain that they are applied throughout the economy is a daunting task and will primarily depend on the support of businesses. There has been some progress. Encouragingly, as part of the White House's initiative, The Digital Advertising Alliance, a working group that includes the National Advertising Initiative (NAI), the FTC, the Internet Advertising Bureau, and various advisors, agreed to a clear and simple method for users to opt out of being tracked through a Do Not Track policy that has now also been accepted by Microsoft, AOL, Yahoo!, and Google, as well as by other companies which represent some 90% of online advertising.[55] Equally important, the advertising industry (but *only* the advertising industry) has committed to no longer selling a user's browsing data to companies to use for reasons other than advertising (for example, employee screening, debt collection, insurance companies, and so on).[56] These are small steps forward, but important ones.

State governments, too, have plunged into the consumer data privacy debate, with Colorado, Delaware, Connecticut, and California all adopting consumer online privacy laws. Responding to the sophistry by Internet companies regarding the Do Not Track mechanism, California's bill AB 370, which went into effect in January 2014, requires companies to disclose clearly what a user's options are if he or she wants to opt out of tracking, and to reveal to consumers when they intend to share their personally identifiable information (PII) with third parties. California now even requires that online companies provide an erase button, so that teenagers can delete misguided postings.[57]

And, of course, an increasing number of court cases are being filed against companies based on just these types of issues. In addition to the cases cited before, in the spring of 2014, Google faced a lawsuit in California launched by nine plaintiffs who assert that Google's scanning of student e-mails through Gmail accounts violated wiretap laws. Once again, the issue revolves around the "operational" features of Gmail—spell check, malware, spam, and virus protection—which provide an opportunity (or an excuse, depending on your point of view) to also scan e-mails for data that can be used for its targeted advertising.[58]

Still, neither the Internet companies nor the credit bureaus in particular are going to cede their rights to collect data and track online activity without a fight. After all, data collection, digital data sales, and online advertising is their *raison d'être*. And their influence in Washington is significant. When the Sunlight Foundation and the Center for Responsive Politics collected figures for credit bureau lobbying and political contributions during the 2007–2010 period, they revealed that Experian spent $3.35 million in lobbying expenditures during that period and an additional $520 million in campaign contributions. During that time, they received more than $10 million in federal contracts. Equifax spent $1.75 million on lobbying and was awarded nearly $56 million in federal contracts.[59] And, in a reflection of the confidence and power of their position, data brokers Acxiom, Experian, and Epsilon rebuffed requests by Senators Rockefeller and Markey of the Senate's Commerce Committee to reveal their specific data sources, or in Experian's case, even to name the companies to which they sold their data.[60] According to the Center for Media Justice, between 2008 and 2013, Walmart spent almost $34 million lobbying the federal government on issues concerned with data protection, privacy, and online advertising.[61] Google spent $8.85 million lobbying Washington in just the first two quarters of 2014 alone.[62]

International Relations

In today's digital economy, users can access accounts, trade e-mails or photos with contacts abroad, or buy goods internationally through the Internet—regardless of national boundaries or time zones. Companies in one nation can transact business—ordering products, exchanging contracts, paying bills—with other companies, small and large, throughout the world, and the records of those transactions may be captured and stored on server networks that extend around the globe. Amazon's cloud service platform, for example, boasts servers in the US, Japan, Brazil, Ireland, and Singapore.[63] Huge amounts of data exist—"unowned"—in the global cloud. These types of cross-border online data flows are crucial to the Internet economy and an integral aspect of international trade. And yet this cross-jurisdictional, global infrastructure is fraught with issues concerning cyber security, fraud, data ownership, and use. If Big Data and the digital economy are to flourish, governments need to agree on ways to ensure that these trans-national exchanges are protected from those who would block, copy, reveal, or repurpose that data, contrary to the wishes of their citizens.

The natural tendency is for countries to treat cyberspace much the way they do their natural borders, particularly because as both the incubator for innovation and the infrastructure for communication and commerce, in many ways the Internet has become one of the most important elements in geo-political positioning for the modern nation. The obvious problem is that different countries have different perceptions of the role of government, espionage, and terrorism, and, most particularly, on data ownership and privacy issues. Americans, generally profess to be fairly relaxed about the idea of companies (or the NSA) capturing their online activities or collecting huge amounts of personal data, and prefer to encourage self-regulation (on the part of both consumers and businesses) in the name of entrepreneurialism. The Europeans tend to have a much more restrictive view of what personal data businesses or the state can collect on an individual citizen. Nations like Turkey and China, and to an even greater extent Russia and Iran, see the Internet as both a tool of government power and a dangerous platform for free expression that may threaten national security—something to be monitored and manipulated.

All of this means that one man's open Internet is another man's potential threat to personal liberty or political stability. It hasn't helped that both Western and Chinese spy agencies have further tainted the "free and open Internet" by making it a primary tool for political and industrial espionage.

Most EU national laws are based on the EU Data Protection Directive, which is even now being updated by a set of regulations (the General Data Protection Regulation or GDPR), which will provide a consistent set of strict data privacy standards and protections across all EU member nations, enforced with significant fines (which can reach as high as 2% of a multinational's worldwide turnover for negligent security breaches).[64] The EU has a much more explicit Do Not Track directive and requires explicit consent before cookies can be dropped on a user's computer.[65] And the GDPR framework defines personal data broadly as "any information relating to an individual, whether it relates to his or her private, professional, or public life. It can be anything from a name, a photo, an email address, bank details, posts on social networking web sites, medical information, or a computer's IP address."[66]

The UK government has an Information Commissioner's Office, an independent authority set up in 2010 that has the power to investigate breaches of both its Data Protection Act and its Privacy and Electronic Regulations (PECR), and to assess fines of up to £500,000 (roughly $850,000).[67] And it is not just EU member states that have moved toward more comprehensive data protection laws. Similar directives have appeared in more than 100 countries, including New Zealand, Canada, Singapore, Australia, and Mexico.[68]

Over the years, before the Big Data Big Bang, the United States, Europe, and the Asia-Pacific nations worked together to devise various practices and rules that would allow the exchange of data internationally, including the FTC's Fair Information Practice Principles (FIPPs) (voluntary guidelines governing data exchange between companies) and the Cross Border Privacy Rules (CBPR) system (the United States has been a member since 2011), which now includes 21 members of the Asian and Pacific Economic Cooperation framework and deals with, among other things, information exchange between nations with different privacy regimes. Most important of all, the US Department of Commerce in 2000 first developed a framework known as Safe Harbor for ensuring that UK and EU data (there is also a US-Swiss version) stored in the United States (by a myriad of multinational companies) complies with generally more stringent EU rules concerning data privacy collection and storage. The Safe Harbor provisions require yearly certification by companies that agree to comply with seven principles:

- **Notice:** Individuals must be informed that their data is being collected and about how it will be used.
- **Choice:** Individuals must have the option to opt out of the collection and forward transfer of the data to third parties.
- **Onward transfer:** Transfers of data to third parties may only occur to other organizations that follow adequate data protection principles.
- **Security:** Reasonable efforts must be made to prevent loss of collected information.
- **Data integrity:** Data must be relevant and reliable for the purpose it was collected for.
- **Access:** Individuals must be able to access information held about them and correct or delete it if it is inaccurate.
- **Enforcement:** There must be effective means of enforcing these rules.[69]

The Safe Harbor provisions were meant to provide a way for American companies, without having to change US law, to continue to move data between their US headquarters and their European offices or subsidiaries, as long as they agreed to ensure adequate protection for personal data and generally adhered to the stricter personal data privacy provisions of the EU's Data Protection Act. By early 2014, more than 3,000 US companies had signed up to the provisions.[70]

But much has changed since the Safe Harbor provisions were created in 2000, including the development of cloud computing, and, more controversially, the US Patriot Act, which allows the US government access to foreign data stored in US servers and even data held in the EU by US-based companies. And, according to the Patriot Act, all that data, including the personal data of European citizens, can be accessed by the US government at any time without the knowledge or consent of European authorities or the citizens themselves. The Patriot Act also mandates that any EU data that is collected or stored by a non-US company in the United States, or even by a subsidiary of the Internet giants—Google, Amazon, Salesforce, Microsoft, Facebook—is subject to inspection by the US intelligence services without the knowledge or permission of the foreign company or subsidiary. That means, for example, that personal data of EU citizens held by Google UK or Google Germany could be accessed and read at any time by US authorities (and those companies and their EU citizen-employees don't even need to be told).[71]

Needless to say, the all-encompassing nature of the Patriot Act puts it in direct conflict with new EU data protection regulations and raises a lot of hackles in Europe. It also means that the long-standing Safe Harbor provisions have come under fire, particularly from the EU Parliament, which in November 2013 (and, again, in part as a reaction to the Snowden revelations about the NSA's ubiquitous data collection policies) called for suspension of the agreement after the EU Home Affairs Commissioner said that the NSA had "grown into an uncontrollable monster." In the end, the Commission agreed to look at the possibilities of a compromise solution by the summer of 2014, but negotiations since that time have, if anything, highlighted the growing differences between how EU and US authorities view personal data privacy in light of national security.

Interestingly, the Right to Be Forgotten ruling by the EU court in May 2014 is loosely parallel in its implications to the Patriot Act, because it means that the national subsidiaries of US firms (for example, Google Spain) are subject to EU laws, even if their customer data is stored and analyzed by servers in the United States. It is the first skirmish in what promises to be a significant ideological and legal war over data privacy in an international setting.

This international data privacy divide is not lost on the Internet tech companies, which see conflicting national rules as a threat to the open nature of the Internet and particularly a restriction on their ability to do what they want with the data they want to collect. That has even led critics—including Mathias Döpfner, the CEO of Germany's digital publishing house, Axel Springer—to charge that groups as powerful as Google may attempt to avoid the clutches of regulators and privacy laws by creating off-shore, digital superstates[72] (possibly not so far-fetched, considering Google has constructed two massive, mystery floating barges—one in San Francisco Bay, the other in the harbor at Portland, Maine).

All this leaves us with more questions than answers. Can there be continued innovation with acceptable levels of privacy protection or will restrictions on data collection and use undermine innovation? Can all the important players in a global digital economy ever come to agreement, even in principle, on the major issues surrounding Big Data privacy and use? Do we trust companies (and governments) to regulate themselves through internal codes of conduct, or do we need formal mandated policies enforced through audits and court-imposed penalties?

These questions need to be resolved, and quickly, to tame the Wild West of unfettered digitization that has been going on for the last decade but now threatens to undermine data security, privacy, civil liberties—and possibly the success of the Big Data phenomenon itself.

Bibliography

Adams, Guy, "Is Your TV Spying On You?," *Daily Mail,* November 25, 2013, http://www.dailymail.co.uk/sciencetech/article-2513592/Is-TV-spying-YOU.html.

Ahmed, Murad, "Google adopts 'soft power' Europe lobbying," *Financial Times*, September 18, 2014, p. 20.

Albergotti, Reed, "Facebook App Knows What You're Hearing, Watching," *WSJ.D,* May 21, 2014, http://blogs.wsj.com/digits/2014/05/21/facebook-app-knows-what-youre-hearing-and-watching/.

Alden, William, "Start-Up Data Storage Firm Actifio Hits $1 Billion Mark," *New York Times*, March 23, 2014, http://dealbook. nytimes.com/2014/03/23/start-up-data-storage-firm-actifio-hits-1-billion-mark/?src=recg.

Anderson, Ian, "Signal - Big Brother Software for Recruiters Is Coming," ArcticStartUp, December 18, 2013, http://arcticstartup.com/2013/12/18/signal-big-brother-software-for-recruiters-is-coming.

Angwin, Julia, "The Web's New Gold Mine: Your Secrets," *Wall Street Journal*, July 30, 2010, http://online.wsj.com/news/articles/SB10001424052748703940904575395073512989404.

Anthony, Sebastian, "Google Admits It Wants to Put Ads on 'Fridges, Car Dashboards, Thermostats, Glasses, and Watches,'" ExtremeTech, May 21, 2014, http://www.extremetech.com/extreme/182849-google-admits-it-wants-to-put-ads-on-fridges-car-dashboards-thermostats-glasses-and-watches.

Apache Spark web site, last accessed July 15, 2014, http://spark.apache.org/.

Armerding, Taylor, "The 15 Worst Data Security Breaches of the 21st Century," CSO, February 15, 2012, http://www.csoonline.com/article/2130877/data-protection/the-15-worst-data-security-breaches-of-the-21st-century.html.

Armitage, Hugh, "Xbox One to Monitor TV Viewing, Content Matched, Numbers of Viewers," DigitalSpy, May 24, 2013, http://www.digitalspy.com/gaming/news/a484593/xbox-one-to-monitor-tv-viewing-content-watched-number-of-viewers.html.

Aslett, Matt, "Big Data Reconsidered: It's the Economics, Stupid," 451Research, December 2, 2013, https://451research.com/report-short?entityId=79479&referrer=marketing.

"The Australian Public Service Big Data Strategy," Australian Department of Finance and Deregulation, August 2013, http://www.finance.gov.au//sites/default/files/Big%20Data%20Strategy.pdf.

"Global Survey: The Business Impact of Big Data," Avanade, November 2010, http://www.avanade.com/Documents/Research%20and%20Insights/Big%20Data%20Executive%20Summary%20FINAL%20SEOv.pdf.

Babcock, Charles, "Amazon Again Beats IBM for CIA Cloud Contract," *InformationWeek*, November 8, 2013, http://www.informationweek.com/cloud/infrastructure-as-a-service/amazon-again-beats-ibm-for-cia-cloud-contract/d/d-id/1112211.

Bachman, Katy, "Senate Commerce Report Says Data Brokers 'Operate Behind a Veil of Secrecy,'" *Adweek*, December 18, 2013, http://www.adweek.com/news/technology/senate-commerce-report-says-data-brokers-operate-behind-veil-secrecy-154579.

Bacon, Jonathan, "Mobile Microtargeting," *MarketingWeek*, December 12, 2013, http://www.marketingweek.co.uk/analysis/essential-reads/mobile-microtargeting/4008800.article.

Baker, Jennifer, "EU Will Not Suspend Safe Harbor Data Privacy Agreement with the US," *PCWorld*, November 27, 2013, http://www.pcworld.com/article/2067480/eu-will-not-suspend-safe-harbor-data-privacy-agreement-with-the-us.html.

Barr, Alistair, "Amazon, with Focus on Digital Services, Is Thinking Outside the Box to Grow (Literally)," *Reuters*, April 26, 2013, http://www.huffingtonpost.com/2013/04/26/amazon-digital-services_n_3160456.html.

Barr, Alistair, "Analysis: Sleeping Ad Giant Amazon Finally Stirs," *Reuters*, April 24, 2013, http://www.reuters.com/article/2013/04/24/us-amazon-advertising-idUSBRE93N06E20130424.

Barth, Paul, "Get the Maximum Value Out of Your Big Data Initiative," HBR Blog Network and NewVantage Partners, February 1, 2013, http://newvantage.com/wp-content/uploads/2013/03/HBR-Blog-Network-020113.pdf.

Bartlett, Jamie, "iSPY: How the Internet Buys and Sells Your Secrets," *The Spectator*, December 7, 2013, http://www.spectator.co.uk/features/9093961/little-brothers-are-watching-you/.

Basulto, Dominic, "Why You Should Care About the Mobile Web's Advertising Problem," *Washington Post*, April 29, http://www.washingtonpost.com/blogs/innovations/wp/2014/04/29/why-you-should-care-about-the-mobile-webs-advertising-problem/.

Baynes, Terry, "Walgreen Accused of Selling Patient Data," *Reuters*, March 11, 2011, http://www.reuters.com/article/2011/03/11/us-walgreen-prescriptions-idUSTRE72A83I20110311.

Beckett, Lois, "Everything We Know About What Data Brokers Know About You," June 13, 2014, https://www.propublica.org/article/everything-we-know-about-what-data-brokers-know-about-you.

Bednarz, Ann, "Big Data Skills Pay Top Dollar," CIO, February 7, 2014, http://www.cio.com/article/747927/Big_Data_Skills_Pay_Top_Dollar?taxonomyId=600010.

Biegelsen, Amy, "Unregulated FICO Has Key Role in Each American's Access to Credit," May 17, 2011, http://www.publicintegrity.org/2011/05/17/4628/unregulated-fico-has-key-role-each-americans-access-credit.

"How Amazon Is Leveraging Big Data," *BigData-Startups*, last accessed July 15, 2014, http://www.bigdata-startups.com/BigData-startup/amazon-leveraging-big-data/.

Bilton, Nick, "Google S.E.C. Filing Says It Wants Ads in Your Thermostat and Car," *New York Times*, May 25, 2014, http://bits.blogs.nytimes.com/2014/05/21/google-plans-to-deliver-ads-through-your-thermostat-and-car/?action=click&module=Search®ion=searchResults&mabReward=relbias%3Ar&url=http%3A%2F%2Fquery.nytimes.com%2Fsearch%2Fsitesearch%2F%3Faction%3Dclick%26contentCollection%3Dundefined%26region%3DTopBar%26module%3DSearchSubmit%26pgtype%3DTopic%23%2Fgoogle%2Bsec%2F.

Bilton, Nick, "Intruders for the Plugged-In Home, Coming in Through the Internet," *New York Times*, June 1, 2014, http://bits.blogs.nytimes.com/2014/06/01/dark-side-to-internet-of-things-hacked-homes-and-invasive-ads/?_php=true&_type=blogs&hpw&rref=business&_r=0.

Bird, Jane, "Business Warms to Wearable Computers But Fresh Ideas Are Needed," *Financial Times*, February 23, 2014, http://www.ft.com/intl/cms/s/0/3aa877b0-94b2-11e3-9146-00144feab7de.html#axzz38t3F7ETO.

Bolle, Justin, "Mapping, and Sharing, the Consumer Genome," *New York Times*, June 17, 2012, http://www.nytimes.com/2012/06/17/technology/acxiom-the-quiet-giant-of-consumer-database-marketing.html?pagewanted=3&_r=0.

Borger, Julian, "Booz Allen Hamilton: Edward Snowden's US Contracting Firm," *The Guardian*, June 9, 2013, http://www.theguardian.com/world/2013/jun/09/booz-allen-hamilton-edward-snowden.

Bradshaw, Tim, "CES 2014: Wearables Emerge as Top Trend," *Financial Times*, January 6, 2014, http://www.ft.com/intl/cms/s/0/50264574-7485-11e3-9125-00144feabdc0.html#axzz38t3F7ETO.

Bradshaw, Tim, "Snapchat settles privacy complaint," *Financial Times*, May 8, 2014, http://www.ft.com/intl/cms/s/0/a831c9a6-d6d6-11e3-b95e-00144feabdc0.html?siteedition=uk#axzz3E9wqxy6T

Bradshaw, Tim, "Technology: All Eyes on the Future," *Financial Times*, March 28, 2014, http://www.ft.com/intl/cms/s/0/67f4904e-b665-11e3-905b-00144feabdc0.html#axzz2yxuWKjtX.

Bray, Hiawatha, "Would You Let Your TV Watch You?," *The Boston Globe*, June 14, 2013, http://www.bostonglobe.com/business/2013/06/13/capuano-seeks-curbs-spying/w5R6IL1tbQ4EzrypMH5aYJ/story.html.

Brinker, Scott, "81% of Big Firms Now Have a Chief Marketing Technologist," ChiefDigitalOfficer, January 31, 2014, http://chiefdigitalofficer.net/81-of-big-firms-now-have-a-chief-marketing-technologist/.

Brodkin, Jon, "Yahoo Is the Latest Company Ignoring Web Users' Requirements for Privacy," ARS Technica, May 1, 2014, http://arstechnica.com/information-technology/2014/05/yahoo-is-the-latest-company-ignoring-web-users-requests-for-privacy/.

Brust, Andrew, "MapReduce and MPP: Two Sides of the Big Data Coin?," ZDNet, March 2, 2012, http://www.zdnet.com/blog/big-data/mapreduce-and-mpp-two-sides-of-the-big-data-coin/121.

Bryant, Chris, "VW Chief Urges Carmakers to Fight the Rise of the 'Data Monster,'" *Financial Times*, March 10, 2014, http://www.ft.com/intl/cms/s/0/581aa95a-a81f-11e3-8ce1-00144feab7de.html#axzz2xGUZ9o4B.

Bump, Philip, "Larry Ellison, NSA Database Supplier, Approves of NSA Surveillance," *The Wire*, August 13, 2013, http://www.thewire.com/business/2013/08/guy-who-provides-nsa-databases-loves-nsa-surveillance/68280/.

"Clutch Partners with RetailNext to Take Consumer Loyalty and Engagement to Next Level," *BusinessWire*, January 13, 2014, http://www.businesswire.com/news/home/20140113006134/en/Clutch-Partners-RetailNext-Consumer-Loyalty-Engagement-Level#.U1A4Z6NOXGg.

Burns, Ed, "Hadoop Still Too Slow for Real-time Analysis Applications?," TechTarget, last accessed July 15, 2014, http://searchbusinessanalytics.techtarget.com/feature/Hadoop-still-too-slow-for-real-time-analysis-applications.

Butler, Brandon, "Nine Hadoop Companies You Should Know," *Networkworld*, March 18, 2014, http://www.networkworld.com/article/2175299/cloud-computing/nine-hadoop-companies-you-should-know.html.

"Senate Bill No. 568, Chapter 336," California Legislative Information web site, last accessed July 15, 2014, http://leginfo.legislature.ca.gov/faces/billNavClient.xhtml?bill_id=201320140SB568.

Campos, Adrian, "Why Intel Is Investing in Cloudera," The Motley Fool, March 31, 2014, http://www.fool.com/investing/general/2014/03/31/why-intel-is-investing-in-cloudera.aspx.

Carlson, Nicholas, "Facebook Is Buying Huge Messaging App WhatsApp for $19 Billion!," *Business Insider*, February 19, 2014, http://www.businessinsider.com/facebook-is-buying-whatsapp-2014-2#ixzz39pOBH4Q6.

Carpentier, Megan, "What Your Search History Says About You (And How to Shut It Up)," *The Huffington Post*, October 31, 2013, http://www.huffingtonpost.com/megan-carpentier/what-your-search-history-_b_4179728.html and https://info.yahoo.com/legal/us/yahoo/utos/terms/.

Carr, Paul, "AOL Sites Will Now Track You, Whether You Like It or Not," PandoDaily, August 18, 2014, http://pando.com/2014/08/18/aol-sites-will-now-track-you-whether-you-like-it-or-not/.

Cheng, Roger, "Walmart Exec: Mobile Can Revive Personal Touch for Shoppers," CNET, May 22, 2013, http://reviews.cnet.com/8301-12261_7-57585710-10356022/walmart-exec-mobile-can-revive-personal-touch-for-shoppers/.

"Consumers, Big Data, and Online Tracking in the Retail Industry: A Case Study of Walmart," The Center for Media Justice, November 2013, http://centerformediajustice.org/wp-content/files/WALMART_PRIVACY_.pdf.

"Kakao Talk Daily Traffic Hits 3 Billion," The Chosun Ilbo, July 27, 2012, http://english.chosun.com/site/data/html_dir/2012/07/27/2012072701392.html.

"Strategic Cloud Computing Demands Cooperation," CIO, October 28, 2013, http://zerodistance.cio.com/2013/10/vcloud/#sthash.x5ijM4Ib.dpuf.

"Cisco Visual Networking Index: Global Mobile Data Traffic Forecast Update, 2013–2018," Cisco, February 5, 2014, http://www.cisco.com/c/en/us/solutions/collateral/service-provider/visual-networking-index-vni/white_paper_c11-520862.html.

Clark, Evan, "Walmart Sets Aggressive Digital Plan," *Women's Wear Daily*," May 2, 2013, at http://www.wwd.com/retail-news/mass-off-price/wal-marts-plans-for-digital-domination-6916532?navSection=issues, as referenced in "Consumers, Big Data, and Online Tracking in the Retail Industry: A Case Study of Walmart," The Center for Media Justice, November 2013, http://centerformediajustice.org/wp-content/files/WALMART_PRIVACY_.pdf.

Clifford, Stephanie, "Attention, Shoppers: Store Is Tracking Your Cell," *New York Times*, July 15, 2013, http://www.nytimes.com/2013/07/15/business/attention-shopper-stores-are-tracking-your-cell.html.

Clover, Charles, "Chinese Internet: Mobile Wars," *Financial Times*, March 19, 2014, http://www.ft.com/intl/cms/s/2/56a160aa-a86f-11e3-a946-00144feab7de.html#axzz2xAvlKJlp.

Cohen, Heidi, "67 Mobile Facts to Develop Your 2014 Budget," Mobile, October 21, 2013, http://heidicohen.com/67-mobile-facts-from-2013-research-charts/.

Constine, Josh, "Facebook's Mobile Ad Network Is Called 'Facebook Audience Network' and Here's How It Works," TechCrunch, April 25, 2014, http://techcrunch.com/2014/04/25/facebook-audience-network/.

"Global Active/Passive RFID Market to Exceed $23 Billion in 2020," *Converting Quarterly*, October 22, 2013, http://www.convertingquarterly.com/industry-news/articles/id/6077/global-activepassive-rfid-market-to-exceed-23-billion-in-2020.aspx).

Cookson, Robert, "Google and Facebook Add Creative Verve to Their Mix," *Financial Times*, April 10, 2014, http://www.ft.com/intl/cms/s/0/440c1f46-bfdc-11e3-9513-00144feabdc0.html#axzz2yaArjflI.

Cookson, Robert, "Mercedes Online Ads Viewed More by Fraudster Robots Than Humans," *Financial Times*, May 26, 2014, http://www.ft.com/intl/cms/s/0/788d6d42-da6c-11e3-8273-00144feabdc0.html#axzz32v1myO1x.

Cookson, Robert, "Moneysupermarket to Sell Data on Customers," *Financial Times*, March 4, 2014, http://www.ft.com/intl/cms/s/0/dc169c48-a381-11e3-88b0-00144feab7de.html?siteedition=intl#axzz2xGUZ9o4B.

Cookson, Robert, "UK Mobile Ad Spend Forecast to Overtake Newspaper Expenditure," *Financial Times*, March 9, 2014, http://www.ft.com/intl/cms/s/0/120c4644-a77f-11e3-9c7d-00144feab7de.html#axzz2xIS8DERs.

Cox, Ryan, "Storage Is the Link Between Collecting, Analyzing + Acting On Big Data," SiliconAngle, June 3, 2013, http://siliconangle.com/blog/2013/06/03/storage-is-the-link-between-collecting-and-analyzing-acting-on-big-data/.

Darrow, Barb, "Acxiom Snaps Up LiveRamp and Its Data Onboarding Smarts for $310M," GIGAOM, May 14, 2014, http://gigaom.com/2014/05/14/acxiom-snaps-up-liveramp-for-its-data-collection-smarts-for-31om/.

"High Profile Data Breach Hits Experian, Equifax & Trans Union," Data Breach Watch, March 13, 2013, http://www.databreachwatch.org/high-profile-data-breach-hits-experian-equifax-trans-union/.

Datoo, Siraj, "How Tracking Customers In-Store Will Soon Be the Norm," *The Guardian*, January 10, 2014, http://www.theguardian.com/technology/datablog/2014/jan/10/how-tracking-customers-in-store-will-soon-be-the-norm.

Datoo, Siraj, "What Information Can Retailers See When They Track Customer Movements?," *The Guardian*, October 11, 2013, http://www.theguardian.com/news/datablog/2013/oct/11/information-retailers-track-customer-movements.

Davenport, Thomas, and Kim, Jinho, *Keeping Up With the Quants*, Harvard Business Review Press, Boston, 2013.

Davies, Sally, "Who Will Be the Google of the Internet of Things?," *Financial Times*, May1, 2014, http://blogs.ft.com/tech-blog/2014/05/who-will-be-the-google-of-the-internet-of-things/.

Davies, Sally, "Facebook Targets Financial Services," *Financial Times*, April 13, 2014, http://www.ft.com/intl/cms/s/0/0e0ef050-c16a-11e3-97b2-00144feabdc0.html#axzz2yxuWKjtX.

Dembosky, April, "Silicon Valley Rooted in Backing from US Military," *Financial Times*, June 9, 2013, http://www.ft.com/intl/cms/s/0/8c0152d2-d0f2-11e2-be7b-00144feab7de.html#axzz2xAvlKJlp.

Dempsey, Michael, "CIOs Must Face Up to 'Off-Radar' Spending on Online Services," *Financial Times*, January 28, 2014, http://www.ft.com/intl/cms/s/0/dd064c6c-81c5-11e3-87d5-00144feab7de.html#axzz39B66hbCN.

Dilanian, Ken, "The NSA Is Watching. So Are Google and Facebook," *LA Times*, June 30, 2013, http://articles.latimes.com/2013/jun/30/nation/la-na-consumer-tracking-20130701.

Donohue, Steve, "Verizon: Intel OnCue Acquisition Will Power New OTT Video Service, Next-Gen FiOS TV Product," FierceCable, January 21, 2014, http://www.fiercecable.com/story/verizon-intel-oncue-acquisition-will-power-new-ott-video-service-next-gen-f/2014-01-21.

Doyle, Eric, "ICO to Investigate UK Effects of Sony Data Breach," TechWeek Europe, April 28, 2011, http://www.techweekeurope.co.uk/news/ico-to-investigate-uk-effects-of-sony-data-breach-27748.

Dredge, Stuart, "Mobile Apps Revenues Tipped to Reach $26bn in 2013," *The Guardian*, September 19, 2013, http://www.theguardian.com/technology/appsblog/2013/sep/19/gartner-mobile-apps-revenues-report.

Duck, Barbara, "United Health Care to Use Data Mining Algorithms on Claim Data to Look for Those at 'Risk' of Developing Diabetes – Walgreens and the YMCA Benefit with Pay for Performance Dollars to Promote and Supply the

Tools," The Medical Quack, last accessed July 30, 2014, http://ducknetweb.blogspot.com/2010/04/unitedhealthcare-to-use-data-mining.html.

Duhigg, Charles, "How Companies Learn Your Secrets," *New York Times*, February 16, 2012, http://www.nytimes.com/2012/02/19/magazine/shopping-habits.html?pagewanted=all&_r=1&.

"Conservatives of Every Hue," *The Economist*, April 5, 2014, p. 27.

"Migrating Finches," *The Economist*, March 22, 2014, p. 66.

"Now or Naver," *The Economist*, March 1, 14, p. 68.

"Surfing a Digital Wave, or Drowning?," *The Economist*, December 7, 2014, http://www.economist.com/news/business/21591201-information-technology-everywhere-companies-it-departments-mixed.

Elgan, Mike, "Google, Facebook Go Beyond Social, Beyond Identity," *Computerworld*, August 9, 2014, http://www.computerworld.com/s/article/9250256/Google_Facebook_go_beyond_social_beyond_identity.

Elgan, Mike, "Why You Shouldn't Buy the Amazon Fire Phone," *Computerworld*, June 21, 2014, http://www.computerworld.com/s/article/9249269/Why_you_shouldn_t_buy_the_Amazon_Fire_phone?pageNumber=2.

Epstein, Robert, "Google's Gotcha," *US News and World Report*, May 10, 2013, http://www.usnews.com/opinion/articles/2013/05/10/15-ways-google-monitors-you.

Epstein, Zach, "400,000 American Homes Have Dumped Pay-TV So Far This Year," BGR, August 2, 2012, http://bgr.com/2012/08/02/cable-tv-subscriber-stats-q2-2012-satellite/.

"Most Digital Ad Growth Now Goes to Mobile as Desktop Growth Falters," eMarketer, December 16, 2013, http://www.emarketer.com/Article/Most-Digital-Ad-Growth-Now-Goes-Mobile-Desktop-Growth-Falters/1010458.

Computers-in-Use Forecast by Country, eTForecasts, last accessed July 15, 2014, http://www.etforecasts.com/products/ES_cinusev2.htm.

"Commission Proposes a Comprehensive Reform of Data Protection Rules to Increase Users' Control of Their Data and to Cut Costs for Businesses," Press Release from the European Commission, Europa Press Releases Database, January 25, 2012, http://europa.eu/rapid/press-release_IP-12-46_en.htm?locale=en.

Everson, Eric, "Big Data, Big Privacy Concerns, and Big Settlements," Lexology, April 10, 2013, http://www.lexology.com/library/detail.aspx?g=16e512fa-666f-4242-9e9d-7b93dc27204e.

"Welcome to the U.S.-EU & U.S.-Swiss Safe Harbor Frameworks," Export.gov, last accessed July 15, 2014, http://www.export.gov/safeharbor/.

"The World's Top 10 Most Innovative Companies in Big Data," Fast Company, February 10, 2014, http://www.fastcompany.com/most-innovative-companies/2014/industry/big-data.

Fearnow, Benjamin, "They Can Hear You Now: Verizon Patent Could Listen In on Customers," CBS DC, December 4, 2012, http://washington.cbslocal.com/2012/12/04/they-can-hear-you-now-verizon-patent-listens-in-on-customers/.

Fitchard, Kevin, "How You and I Could Become Bodes in the Internet of Things," GIGAOM, June 3, 2013, http://gigaom.com/2013/06/03/how-you-and-i-could-become-nodes-in-the-internet-of-things/.

Flinders, Karl, "Gartner Outsourcing Summit 2013: How Digitisation Is Shaking Up IT Outsourcing," ComputerWeekly.com, September 10, 2013, http://www.computerweekly.com/news/2240205134/Gartner-Outsourcing-Summit-2013-How-digitisation-is-shaking-up-IT-outsourcing.

Fontanella-Khan, James, "Microsoft Cloud System Wins EU Privacy Regulators' Approval," *Financial Times*, April 10, 2014, http://www.ft.com/intl/cms/s/0/aeeb7350-c0a1-11e3-a74d-00144feabdc0.html#axzz2yaArjflI.

"$16.1 Billion Big Data Market: 2014 Predictions From IDC and IIA," *Forbes*, December 12, 2013, http://www.forbes.com/sites/gilpress/2013/12/12/16-1-billion-big-data-market-2014-predictions-from-idc-and-iia/.

Foy, Henry, "Smart Technology Takes a Back Seat at Detroit Motor Show," *Financial Times*, January 15, 2014, http://www.ft.com/intl/cms/s/0/de423e9e-7dcc-11e3-95dd-00144feabdc0.html#axzz38t3F7ETO.

Gatdula, Armand, "Fleet Tracking Devices will be Installed in 22,000 UPS Trucks to Cut Costs and Improve Driver Efficiency in 2010," FieldLogix, July 20, 2010, http://www.fieldtechnologies.com/gps-tracking-systems-installed-in-ups-trucks-driver-efficiency/.

"Follow the Ones and Zeros: How the Most Critical and Complex Big Data Around Brings Productivity and Profits," GE Reports, May 20, 2014, http://www.gereports.com/post/86322233075/follow-the-ones-and-zeros-how-the-most-critical-and.

Fung, Brian, "OkCupid reveals it's been lying to some of its users. Just to see what'll happen," *Washington Post*, July 28, 2014, http://www.washingtonpost.com/blogs/the-switch/wp/2014/07/28/okcupid-reveals-its-been-lying-to-some-of-its-users-just-to-see-whatll-happen/).

Geary, Joanna, "Adnxs (AppNexus): What Is It and What Does It Do?," *The Guardian*, April 23, 2012, http://www.theguardian.com/technology/2012/apr/23/adnxs-tracking-trackers-cookies-web-monitoring.

Geary, Joanna, "Facebook: What Is It and What Does It Do?," *The Guardian*, April 23, 2012, http://www.theguardian.com/technology/2012/apr/23/facebook-tracking-trackers-cookies-web-monitoring.

Gittleson, Kim, "How Big Data Is Changing the Cost of Insurance," BBC News, November 14, 2013, http://www.bbc.co.uk/news/business-24941415 and http://www.progressive.com/auto/snapshot/.

Greenberg, Andy, "How a 'Deviant' Philosopher Built Palantir, A CIA-Funded Data-Mining Juggernaut," *Forbes*, August 14, 2013, http://www.forbes.com/sites/andygreenberg/2013/08/14/agent-of-intelligence-how-a-deviant-philosopher-built-palantir-a-cia-funded-data-mining-juggernaut/3/.

Greenleaf, Graham, "Global Data Privacy Laws 2013: 99 Countries and Counting," *Privacy Laws & Business International Report*, Issue 123, UNSW Law Research Paper No. 2013-58, June 2013, http://ssrn.com/abstract=2305882).

Griswold, Alison, "Big Data Can Help Marketers Unlock Up To $200 Billion," *Business Insider*, November 22, 2013, http://www.businessinsider.com/big-data-can-boost-marketing-roi-2013-11.

Hadoop web site, http://hadoop.apache.org/docs/r1.2.1/mapred_tutorial.html.

Hamblen, Matt, "App Economy Expected to Double by 2017 to $151," *Computerworld*, July 15, 2013, http://www.computerworld.com/s/article/9240794/App_economy_expected_to_double_by_2017_to_151B.

Hamby, Steve, "3 Factors Contributing to Lack of Data Efficacy," *The Huffington Post*, April 19, 2013, http://www.huffingtonpost.com/steve-hamby/3-factors-contributing-to_b_3109600.html.

Hammond, Ed, "TMT's Add Verve to Global Deal Activity, *Financial Times*, March 30, 2014, http://www.ft.com/intl/cms/s/0/ebee9b42-b52a-11e3-a746-00144feabdc0.html#axzz2xeJV5gtd.

Hardy, Quentin, "Cisco Bets a Billion on the Cloud," *New York Times*, March 24, 2014, http://bits.blogs.nytimes.com/2014/03/24/cisco-bets-a-billion-on-the-cloud/?src=recg.

Hardy, Quentin, "IBM to Announce More Powerful Watson Via the Internet," *New York Times*, November 14, 2014, http://www.nytimes.com/2013/11/14/technology/ibm-to-announce-more-powerful-watson-via-the-internet.html.

Harris, Derrick, "MapR Raises $110M to Fuel Its Enterprise Hadoop Push," GIGAOM,June30,2014,http://gigaom.com/2014/06/30/mapr-raises-110m-to-fuel-its-enterprise-hadoop-push/.

Harris, Derrick, "Under the Covers of the NSA's Big Data Effort," GIGAOM, June 7, 2013, http://gigaom.com/2013/06/07/under-the-covers-of-the-nsas-big-data-effort/.

Hassman, John, "Lofty Expectations for Big Data," USSCO Speaks, February 26, 2013, http://usscospeaks.com/lofty-expectations-for-big-data/.

Heath, Thomas, "NSA Revelations Put Booz Allen Hamilton, Carlyle Group in Uncomfortable Limelight," *Washington Post*, June 11, 2013, http://www.washingtonpost.com/business/economy/nsa-revelations-put-booz-allen-hamilton-carlyle-group-in-uncomfortable-limelight/2013/06/11/8f4d9138-d2ca-11e2-a73e-826d299ff459_story.html.

Heggestuen, John, "One in Every 5 People in the World Own a Smartphone, One in Every 17 Own a Tablet," *Business Insider*, December 15, 2013, http://www.businessinsider.com/smartphone-and-tablet-penetration-2013-10.

Hern, Alex, "Google Faces Lawsuit over Email Scanning and Student Data," *The Guardian*, March 19, 2014, http://www.theguardian.com/technology/2014/mar/19/google-lawsuit-email-scanning-student-data-apps-education.

Hof, Robert, "Marketers' Customer Data Web Widens with Acxiom's $310 Million Purchase of LiveRamp," *Forbes*, May 14, 2014, http://www.forbes.com/sites/roberthof/2014/05/14/marketers-customer-data-web-widens-with-acxioms-310-million-purchase-of-liveramp/.

Hsu, Tiffany, "Target CEO Resigns as Fallout from Data Breach Continues," *LA Times*, May 5, 2014, http://www.latimes.com/business/la-fi-target-ceo-20140506-story.html.

"Cookies on Mobile 101," iab, November 2013, http://www.iab.net/media/file/CookiesOnMobile101Final.pdf.

"The Digital Universe of Opportunities," IDC and EMC Digital Universe, April 2014, http://www.emc.com/collateral/analyst-reports/idc-digital-universe-2014.pdf.

"Android and iOS Combine for 91.1% of the Worldwide Smartphone OS Market in 4Q12 and 87.6% for the Year," IDC Press Release, February 14, 2013, http://www.businesswire.com/news/home/20130214005415/en/Android-iOS-Combine-91.1-Worldwide-Smartphone-OS#.VCLcEst0w_w.

"Worldwide Smartphone Shipments Top One Billion Units for the First Time," IDC Press Release, January 27, 2014, http://www.idc.com/getdoc.jsp?containerId=prUS24645514.

Indvik, Lauren, "Forrester: Mobile Commerce to Quadruple to $31 Billion in Next 5 Years," Mashable, January 16, 2013, http://mashable.com/2013/01/16/mcommerce-31-billion-2017-forrester/.

Informatica web site, http://www.informatica.com/us/#fbid=p5mYlM884hF.

"T. J. Maxx Parent Company Data Theft Is the Worst Ever," *Informationweek*, March 29, 2007, http://www.informationweek.com/tj-maxx-parent-company-data-theft-is-the-worst-ever/d/d-id/1053522?.

Jeffries, Adrianne, "FICO May Start Including Your Facebook Presence in Your Credit Score," The Verge, January 9, 2014, http://www.theverge.com/2014/1/9/5292568/fico-may-start-including-your-facebook-presence-in-your-credit-score.

Johnsen, Michael, "Nielsen Finds Loyalty Programs Resonate with Shoppers," *Retailing Today*, November 13, 2013, http://www.retailingtoday.com/article/nielsen-finds-loyalty-programs-resonate-shoppers.

Johnston, Leslie, "How Many Libraries of Congress Does It Take?," Library of Congress, March 23, 2012, http://blogs.loc.gov/digitalpreservation/2012/03/how-many-libraries-of-congress-does-it-take/.

Jones Harbour, Pamela, "Careful! Your Company May Be a Defacto Data Broker: Are Privacy Regulators Going for Broke(rs) as Part of the 2014 Legislative and Privacy Enforcement Agenda?," *Data Privacy Monitor*, January 10, 2014, http://www.dataprivacymonitor.com/enforcement/careful-your-company-may-be-a-defacto-data-broker-are-privacy-regulators-going-for-brokers-as-part-of-the-2014-legislative-and-privacy-enforcement-agenda/.

Jones Harbour, and Steel, Emily, "Senators Seek New Rules for Data Brokers," *Financial Times*, February 23, 2014, http://www.ft.com/intl/cms/s/0/06a78f5e-94b3-11e3-9146-00144feab7de.html#axzz39B66hbCN.

Jopson, Barney, "Amazon Cloud Seeks to Revamp Corporate IT," *Financial Times*, September 25, 2012, http://www.ft.com/intl/cms/s/0/d822679c-0694-11e2-abdb-00144feabdc0.html#axzz2xAvlKJlp.

Jopson, Barney, "Amazon Gets Clearance to Provide More Cloud Services to Pentagon," *Financial Times*, March 26, 2014, http://www.ft.com/cms/s/0/22a91a08-b504-11e3-9166-00144feabdc0.html#ixzz2xAwV5Cqs.

Kaplan, James, "Protecting Information in the Cloud," McKinsey&Company, January 2013, http://www.mckinsey.com/insights/business_technology/protecting_information_in_the_cloud.

Kelly, Jeff, "Big Data Market Size and Vendor Revenues," Wikibon, January 3, 2014, http://wikibon.org/wiki/v/Big_Data_Market_Size_and_Vendor_Revenues.

Kenney, Martin, "Silicon Valley's Spy Problem," Project Syndicate, print, July 2, 2014, http://www.project-syndicate.org/commentary/martin-kenney-warns-that-the-nsa-s-actions-are-undermining-the-american-it-sector-s-global-dominance#pg3dSfs7aHpy5JFP.99.

Kirk, Jeremy, "Yahoo to Scrub Personal Data After Three Months," *PCWorld*, December 17, 2008, http://www.pcworld.com/article/155610/yahoo_privacy_support.html.

Kleinman, Alexis, "Americans Will Spend More Time on Digital Devices Than Watching TV This Year: Research," *Huffington Post*, August 1, 2013, http://www.huffingtonpost.com/2013/08/01/tv-digital-devices_n_3691196.html.

Klosowski, Thorin, "How Facebook Uses Your Data to Target Ads, Even Offline," Lifehacker, April 11, 2013, http://lifehacker.com/5994380/how-facebook-uses-your-data-to-target-ads-even-offline.

Knapp, Alex, "Forecasting the Weather with Big Data and the Fourth Dimension," *Forbes*, June 13, 2013, http://www.forbes.com/sites/alexknapp/2013/06/13/forecasting-the-weather-with-big-data-and-the-fourth-dimension/.

Krehel, Ondrej, "10 Worst Government Data Breaches," MSN Money, December 10, 2012, http://money.msn.com/identity-theft/10-worst-government-data-breaches.

Kolakowski, Nick, "Zuckerberg Wants Facebook to 'Glue' Internet of Things Together," Dice, January 29, 2014, http://news.dice.com/2014/01/29/zuckerberg-wants-facebook-to-glue-internet-of-things-together/.

Kosinski, Michal, and Stillwell, David, "Private Traits and Attributes Are Predictable from Digital Records of Human Behavior," *Proceedings of the National Academy of Sciences of the United States of America*, vol. 110, no. 15, April 9, 2013, http://www.pnas.org/content/110/15/5802.full.

Kuchler, Hannah, "Adobe Says 38m Customers Hit by Cyber Security Breach," *Financial Times*, October 30, 2013, http://www.ft.com/intl/cms/s/0/83e0aa90-417b-11e3-9073-00144feabdc0.html#axzz2xAvlKJlp.

Kuchler, Hannah, "CES 2014: Yahoo Unveils New Ad Platforms," *Financial Times*, January 8, 2014, http://www.ft.com/intl/cms/s/0/3fc7ecd0-77f7-11e3-afc5-00144feabdc0.html#axzz2xGUZ9o4B.

Kuchler, Hannah, "Cyber Criminals Target Smaller Companies," *Financial Times*, February 10, 2014, http://www.ft.com/intl/cms/s/0/3bb5e5b2-901a-11e3-aee9-00144feab7de.html#axzz39B66hbCN.

Kuchler, Hannah, "Facebook Reels in Advertising Cash," *Financial Times*, January 30, 2014, http://www.ft.com/intl/cms/s/2/d54cea88-8951-11e3-bb5f-00144feab7de.html#axzz2zWpfUGkS.

Kuchler, Hannah, "Investors Flock to Cyber Security Start-ups," *Financial Times*, March 12, 2014, http://www.ft.com/intl/cms/s/0/f5c87808-a883-11e3-b50f-00144feab7de.html#axzz2xAvlKJlp.

Kuchler, Hannah, "Twitter Beats Facebook to Mobile Advertising Launch," *Financial Times*, April 17, 2014, http://www.ft.com/intl/cms/s/0/0d278c9c-c633-11e3-9839-00144feabdc0.html#axzz2zWpfUGkS.

Kuchler, Hannah, "Twitter Eyes Rapid Asia Growth Despite China Ban," *Financial Times*, May 27, 2014, http://www.ft.com/intl/cms/s/0/f32c0d9a-e2c5-11e3-a829-00144feabdc0.html#axzz32v1myO1x.

Kuchler, Hannah, "WhatsApp 'Sticker Shock' Purchase Offers Facebook Mobile Leverage," *Financial Times*, February 20, 2014, http://www.ft.com/intl/cms/s/0/abd4a734-99d9-11e3-b3a2-00144feab7de.html?siteedition=intl#axzz38sCjnZss.

Kuchler, Hannah, "Yahoo to Axe Google and Facebook Sign-ins in Data Collection Drive," *Financial Times*, March 5, 2014, http://www.ft.com/intl/cms/s/0/41455370-a418-11e3-aa85-00144feab7de.html#axzz2xGUZ9o4B.

Lardinois, Frederic, "Google Launches BigQuery Streaming for Real-Time, Big-Data Analytics," TechCrunch, March 25, 2014, http://techcrunch.com/2014/03/25/google-launches-bigquery-streaming-for-real-time-big-data-analytics/.

"Why You Need to Care About This 'Internet of Things' Thing," Laserfiche, July 29, 2013, http://simplicity.laserfiche.com/content/why-you-need-care-about-internet-things-thing.

Leber, Jessica, "Amazon Woos Advertisers with What It Knows About Consumers," *MIT Technology Review*, January 21, 2013, http://www.technologyreview.com/news/509471/amazon-woos-advertisers-with-what-it-knows-about-consumers/.

Lee, Timothy B., "Here's Everything We Know about PRISM to Date," *Washington Post*, June 12, 2013, http://www.washingtonpost.com/blogs/wonkblog/wp/2013/06/12/heres-everything-we-know-about-prism-to-date/.

"ERP System" graphic on LKD Technologies web site, http://www.lkdtech.com/ServiceDetail.aspx?id=8.

Lohr, Steve, "The Origins of 'Big Data': An Etymological Detective Story," *New York Times*, February 1, 2013, http://bits.blogs.nytimes.com/2013/02/01/the-origins-of-big-data-an-etymological-detective-story/?action=click&module=Search®ion=searchResults%231&version=&url=http%3A%2F%2Fquery.nytimes.com%2Fsearch%2Fsitesearch%2F%3Faction%3Dclick%26region%3DMasthead%26pgtype%3DHomepage%26module%

3DSearchSubmit%26contentCollection%3DHomepage%26t%3Dqry633%23%2Fbig%2Bdata%2Fsince1851%2Fallresults%2F2%2F.

Lopez, Isaac, "Report: Big Data Will Represent Billions in Automotive," datanami, November 21, 2013, http://www.datanami.com/2013/11/21/report_big_data_will_represent_billions_in_automotive/.

Mac, Ryan, "CIA-Funded Data-Miner Palantir Not Yet Profitable But Looking for $8 Billion Valuation," *Forbes*, August 16, 2013, http://www.forbes.com/sites/ryanmac/2013/08/16/cia-funded-data-miner-palantir-not-yet-profitable-but-looking-for-8-billion-valuation/.

Machanavajjhala, Ashwin, "Big Privacy: Protecting Confidentiality in Big Data," Duke University, last accessed July 15, 2014, http://www.cs.duke.edu/~ashwin/pubs/BigPrivacyACMXRDS_final.pdf.

Mackintosh, James, "Investment: A Better Bubble," *Financial Times*, March 5, 2014, http://www.ft.com/intl/cms/s/3/31223cc2-a438-11e3-b915-00144feab7de.html#slide0.

"Facebook Scoops Up Remnant of Microsoft's Ill-Fated aQuantive," *Maclean's*, February 28, 2013, http://www.macleans.ca/news/facebook-scoops-up-remnant-of-microsofts-ill-fated-aquantive/.

Madrigal, Alexis C., "I'm Being Followed: How Google—and 104 Other Companies—Are Tracking Me on the Web," *The Atlantic*, February 29, 2012, http://www.theatlantic.com/technology/archive/2012/02/im-being-followed-how-google-151-and-104-other-companies-151-are-tracking-me-on-the-web/253758/.

Mandel, Michael, "The Data Economy Is Much, Much Bigger Than You (and the Government) Think," *The Atlantic*, July 25, 2013, http://www.theatlantic.com/business/archive/2013/07/the-data-economy-is-much-much-bigger-than-you-and-the-government-think/278113/.

Manyika, James, "Big Data: The Next Frontier for Innovation, Competition, and Productivity," McKinsey Global Institute, May, 2011, http://www.mckinsey.com/insights/business_technology/big_data_the_next_frontier_for_innovation.

Marr, Bernard, "Why the 'Big Data' Hype Is NOT About Big or Data!," LinkedIn, September 11, 2013, http://www.linkedin.com/today/post/article/20130911045931-64875646-why-the-big-data-hype-is-not-about-big-or-data.

Maruma, Misha, "Five Important Ecommerce Trends in China During 2014," Econsultsancy, June 9, 2014, https://econsultancy.com/blog/64958-five-important-ecommerce-trends-in-china-during-2014#i.1mus9f6crudavy.

Mayer-Schonberger, Victor, and Cukier, Kenneth, *Big Data: A Revolution That Will Transform How We Live, Work, and Think*, Eamon Dolan/Houghton Mifflin Harcourt; London, 2013.

McDuling, John, "Proof That 'Big Data' Is One of the Most Overused Corporate Buzzwords of 2013," Quartz, November 27, 2013, http://qz.com/151109/proof-that-big-data-is-one-of-the-most-overused-corporate-buzzwords-of-2013/.

McFarland, Michael, "Ethical Implications of Data Aggregation," Santa Clara University, June 2012, http://www.scu.edu/ethics/practicing/focusareas/technology/internet/privacy/data-aggregation.html.

Meyer, David, "'Facebook for Things' Company Evrythng Teams Up with ARM on Internet of Things," GIGAOM, February 22, 2013, https://gigaom.com/2013/02/22/facebook-for-things-company-evrything-teams-up-with-arm-on-internet-of-things/.

"Millennial Media Signs Definitive Agreement to Acquire Jumptap," Millennial Media Press Release, August 13, 2013, http://www.millennialmedia.com/pressroom/press-releases/millennial-media-signs-definitive-agreement-to-acquire-jumptap/.

Millward, Steven, "Now China's WeChat App Is Censoring Its Users Globally," TECHINASIA, January 10, 2013, http://www.techinasia.com/china-wechat-censoring-users-globally/ and https://en.wikipedia.org/wiki/WeChat.

Mishkin, Sarah, "China's YouTube Taps Surge in Online Viewership," *Financial Times*, March 9, 2014, http://www.ft.com/intl/cms/s/0/ff7a3e00-a3b9-11e3-88b0-00144feab7de.html#axzz2xIS8DERs.

Mizroch, Amir, "UK Firms Increasingly Hit by Data Theft, But Aren't Reporting It," *Wall Street Journal Digits*, April 29, 2014, http://blogs.wsj.com/digits/2014/04/29/uk-firms-increasingly-hit-by-data-theft-but-arent-reporting-it/.

"Global Mobile Statistics 2014," MobiThinking, May 2014, http://mobithinking.com/mobile-marketing-tools/latest-mobile-stats/a.

Montón, Màrius, "The Internet of Things is Knocking on Your Door," *CMSWire*, January 29, 2014, http://www.cmswire.com/cms/internet-of-things/the-internet-of-things-is-knocking-on-your-door-023959.php.

Moyse, Ian, "Cloudy Data Sovereignty in Europe (part two)," Cloudtech, September 28, 2012, http://www.cloudcomputing-news.net/news/2012/sep/28/cloudy-data-sovereignty-europe-part-two/.

Mundy, Simon, "Investors Take $275bn Bite Out of Big Tech Groups," *Financial Times*, April 8, 2014, http://www.ft.com/intl/cms/s/0/00596a2e-bedd-11e3-a4af-00144feabdc0.html#axzz2yaArjflI.

Munshi, Neil, "Farming Advances with Appliance of Science to Tractor Technology," *Financial Times*, October 25, 2013, http://www.ft.com/intl/cms/s/0/a48ad98c-36c7-11e3-aaf1-00144feab7de.html?siteedition=intl#axzz38t3F7ETO.

Internet Policy Task Force web page, National Telecommunications and Information Administration, last accessed on July 15, 2014, http://www.ntia.doc.gov/category/internet-policy-task-force.

Needham, Jeffrey, *Disruptive Possibilities: How Big Data Changes Everything*, O'Reilly, 2013, http://chimera.labs.oreilly.com/books/1234000000914/ch04.html#_the_actual_internet.

Newman, Nathan, "Why Google's Spying on User Data Is Worse than the NSA's," *Huffington Post*, July 1, 2013, http://www.huffingtonpost.com/nathan-newman/why-googles-spying-on-use_b_3530296.html.

"Big Data Executive Survey: Themes & Trends," NewVantage Partners, 2012, http://newvantage.com/wp-content/uploads/2012/12/NVP-Big-Data-Survey-Themes-Trends.pdf.

"A Second Front in the Privacy Wars," *New York Times*, February 2, 2014, http://www.nytimes.com/2014/02/24/opinion/a-second-front-in-the-privacy-wars.html.

"More Mobile Phones in NZ Than People: Study," *New Zealand Herald*, April 24, 2012, http://www.nzherald.co.nz/nz/news/article.cfm?c_id=1&objectid=10801183.

Noble, Josh, "Weibo Jeading for IPO with $7bn-$8bn Valuation Target," *Financial Times*, February 25, 2014, http://www.ft.com/intl/cms/s/0/d596fe74-9d02-11e3-b535-00144feab7de.html?siteedition=intl#axzz38mnfQXBE.

NuWave Backup web site, last accessed July 15, 2014, http://nwbackup.net/wordpress/computer-security/.

Ogg, Jon, "Why Apple Should Just Buy Netflix," *24/7 Wall St.*, March 24, 2014, http://247wallst.com/media/2014/03/24/why-apple-should-just-buy-netflix/#ixzz30at3qZ00.

Olavsrud, Thor, "Red Hat and Hortonworks Expand Strategic Big Data Alliance," CIO, February 10, 2014, http://www.cio.com/article/748045/Red_Hat_and_Hortonworks_Expand_Strategic_Big_Data_Alliance?page=2&taxonomyId=600010.

Ong, Josh, "Report: Twitter's Most Active Country Is China," TNW Blog, September26,2012,http://thenextweb.com/asia/2012/09/26/surprise-twitters-active-country-china-where-blocked/.

Packer, George, "Cheap Words: Amazon Is Good for Customers. But Is It Good for Books?," *The New Yorker*, February 17, 2014, http://www.newyorker.com/reporting/2014/02/17/140217fa_fact_packer?currentPage=all.

Palmer, Maija, "How to Get Ahead in Social Media Advertising," *Financial Times*, May 27, 2014, http://www.ft.com/intl/cms/s/0/0be25712-df61-11e3-86a4-00144feabdc0.html?siteedition=intl#axzz32v1myO1x.

Patel, Zarna, "Survey: Majority of Employees Ready to Break BYOD Policies," Bank Systems and Technology, October 24, 2013, http://www.banktech.com/survey-majority-of-employees-ready-to-break-byod-policies/d/d-id/1296657.

Pearson, Sophia, "CVS Accused in Suit of Selling Customer Data to Drugmakers," Bloomberg, March 9, 2011, http://www.bloomberg.com/news/2011-03-09/cvs-accused-in-suit-of-using-customers-pharmacy-data-for-drug-companies.html.

Perez, Sarah, "Sqrrl Raises $5.2M to Provide Deeper Granularity for NSA-Born Database Technology," Techcrunch, October 21, 2013, http://techcrunch.com/2013/10/21/sqrrl-raises-2-5m-to-provide-deeper-granularity-for-nsa-born-database-technology/.

Peterson, Tim, "Did Apple's 'Spotlight' Update Just Sideline Google Search Ads?," AdAge, June 2, 2014, http://adage.com/article/digital/apple-s-spotlight-update-sideline-google-s-ads/293497/.

Picardo, Elvis, "Apple? Google? Tesla? Which Will Be the First to Reach $1 Trillion Market Cap?," Investopedia, http://www.investopedia.com/articles/investing/070714/apple-google-tesla-which-will-be-first-reach-1-trillion-market-cap.asp.

Pitcher, Pat, "Staggering Tech in an F1 Car Produces 3tb of Data per Second," *The Queensland Times*, March 24, 2014, http://www.qt.com.au/news/Staggering-technology-in-F1-produces-3tb-of-data-p/2207027/.

Popelka, Larry, "What We Learned from Twitter's IPO: The Value of Innovation Is at an All-Time High," *Businessweek*, November 18, 2013, http://www.businessweek.com/articles/2013-11-18/what-we-learned-from-twitter-s-ipo-the-value-of-innovation-is-at-an-all-time-high.

Popken, Ben, "FTC Fines Data Broker for Suggesting Potential Hires Were Sex Offenders," NBC News, April 10, 2014, http://www.nbcnews.com/business/consumer/ftc-fines-data-broker-suggesting-potential-hires-were-sex-offenders-n77071.

Mobile Messaging Futures 2012-2016, PortioResearch, http://www.portioresearch.com/en/market-briefings/budget-reports/mobile-messaging-futures-2012-2016.aspx.

Prasath, Arun, "The @WalmartLabs Social Media Analytics project," @Walmartlabs, January 11, 2013, http://walmartlabs.blogspot.com/2013/01/the-walmartlabs-social-media-analytics.html.

Press, Gil, "$16.1 Billion Big Data Market: 2014 Predictions from IDC and IIA," *Forbes*, December 12, 2013, http://www.forbes.com/sites/gilpress/2013/12/12/16-1-billion-big-data-market-2014-predictions-from-idc-and-iia/.

Pritchard, Stephen, "Data Privacy: US Revelations Put Heat on Business," *Financial Times*, February 23, 2014, http://www.ft.com/intl/cms/s/0/8ef6af94-94b2-11e3-9146-00144feab7de.html#axzz39FQ2PJDb.

Pritchard, Stephen, "Moral and Legal Points Weigh on Information Use," *Financial Times*, March 25, 2014, http://www.ft.com/intl/cms/s/0/2507750c-adb5-11e3-9ddc-00144feab7de.html?siteedition=intl#axzz2xAvlKJlp.

"Fact Sheet 18: Online Privacy: Using the Internet Safely," Privacy Rights Clearinghouse, July 2014, https://www.privacyrights.org/online-privacy-using-internet-safely.

Proffitt, Brian, "Hadoop Could Save You Money over a Traditional RDBMS," *ComputerworldUK*, January 10, 2012, http://www.computerworlduk.com/in-depth/applications/3329092/hadoop-could-save-you-money-over-a-traditional-rdbms/.

"Capitalizing on the Promise of Big Data," PWC, January, 2013, p. 2, http://www.pwc.com/us/en/increasing-it-effectiveness/assets/capitalizing-on-the-promise-of-big-data.pdf.

Quinn, Evan, "Getting Real About Big Data: Build Versus Buy," Enterprise Strategy Group, February 2013, https://www.yumpu.com/en/document/view/10987281/esg-big-data-wp-1914112/9.

Rainie, Lee, "Anonymity, Privacy, and Security Online," Pew Research, September 5, 2013, http://www.pewinternet.org/2013/09/05/anonymity-privacy-and-security-online/.

Raval, Anjli, "Amazon Joins Screen Battle with Fire TV Video Streaming Device," *Financial Times*, April 2, 2014, http://uk.news.voxquo.com/noticia-detalhe-media.asp?id=70218&t=Amazon-joins-screen-battle-with-Fire-TV.

Reifel, Joe, "Telematics: The Game Changer—Reinventing Auto Insurance," AT Kearney, 2010, http://www.atkearney.co.uk/documents/10192/19079b53-8042-43ea-b870-ef42b1f033a6.

Reno, Jim, "Big Data, Little Privacy," CA Technologies, 2012, http://www.ca.com/us/~/media/files/articles/ca-technology-exchange/big-data-little-privacy-reno.aspx.

"A New Solution for Mobile Engagement," *RetailingToday*, February 18, 2014, http://www.retailingtoday.com/article/new-solution-mobile-engagement.

"Global Tech Startup Personalizes Shopping Experience," *RetailingToday*, January 14, 2013,
http://www.retailingtoday.com/article/global-tech-startup-personalizes-shopping-experience.

"Glaxo Links with Top Labs on 'Big Data' Drug Project, *Reuters*, March 28, 2014 http://www.reuters.com/article/2014/03/27/pharmaceuticals-data-idUSL5N0MN3AI20140327.

"Hortonworks Raises $100 Million in Funding, Eyes M&A," *Reuters,* March 25, 2014, http://www.reuters.com/article/2014/03/25/hortonworks-funding-idUSL1N0ML1KP20140325.

Riley, James, "Cut Big Data Down to Size," ComputerWeekly.com, July 2013, http://www.computerweekly.com/feature/Cut-big-data-down-to-size.

Robinson, Duncan, "Mobile Commerce: Stores Caught by Surprise as Shoppers Take Their Tablets," *Financial Times*, February 23, 2014, http://www.ft.com/intl/cms/s/0/e6fde794-94b1-11e3-9146-00144feab7de.html#axzz38t3F7ETO.

Rosenbush, Steve, "Kleiner's Ted Schlein on Cyber Risk: 'It Only Gets Worse," *WallStreetJournal*,February4,2014,http://blogs.wsj.com/cio/2014/02/04/kleiners-ted-schlein-on-cyber-risk-it-only-gets-worse/.

Rosenbush, Steve, "The Morning Download: More Companies, Drowning in Data, Are Turning to Hadoop," *Wall Street Journal*, April 14, 2014, http://blogs.wsj.com/cio/2014/04/14/the-morning-download-more-companies-drowning-in-data-are-turning-to-hadoop/.

Rosenfeld, Steven, "4 Ways Google Is Destroying Privacy and Collecting Your Data," *Salon*, February 5, 2014, http://www.salon.com/2014/02/05/4_ways_google_is_destroying_privacy_and_collecting_your_data_partner/.

Rudarakanchana, Nat, "Big Data: Cat-And-Mouse Escalates on Privacy Concerns, As NRF Retail Conference Looms," *International Business Times*, January 9, 2014,http://www.ibtimes.com/big-data-cat-mouse-escalates-privacy-concerns-nrf-retail-conference-looms-1533616.

Rudarakanchana, Nat, "Big Data: Retailers, Supermarkets, Medical Markets All Dive in to Extract Information from and about Consumers," *International Business Times*, December 20, 2013, http://www.ibtimes.com/big-data-retailers-supermarkets-medical-markets-all-dive-extract-information-about-consumers-1517510.

Sabat, Sunil, "Real Time Big Data Options," Big Data Know How, February 28, 2014, http://bigdataknowhow.weebly.com/blog/category/nosql.

Sartain, J. D., "What the Internet of Things Will Mean for CIOs," CIO, February 3, 2014, http://www.cio.com/article/747634/What_the_Internet_of_Things_Will_Mean_for_CIOs?page=2&taxonomyId=600010.

Savitz, Eric, "Big Data: Big Hype?, *Forbes*, February 4, 2013, http://www.forbes.com/sites/ciocentral/2013/02/04/big-data-big-hype/

Sermeño, Rodrigo, "Data Brokers Gathering Dossiers on Millions of Americans by Income, Disease, and More," PJMedia, December 26, 2013, http://pjmedia.com/blog/data-brokers-gathering-dossiers-on-millions-of-americans-by-income-disease-and-more/.

Shachtman, Noah, "Exclusive: U.S. Spies Buy Stake in Firm That Monitors Blogs, Tweets," *Wired,* October 19, 2009, http://www.wired.com/dangerroom/2009/10/exclusive-us-spies-buy-stake-in-twitter-blog-monitoring-firm/

Singer, Natasha, "You for Sale: Mapping, and Sharing, the Consumer Genome," *New York Times*, June 16, 2012, http://www.nytimes.com/2012/06/17/technology/acxiom-the-quiet-giant-of-consumer-database-marketing.html?_r=0.

Stambor, Zak, "Wal-Mart Factors Popularity into Site Search Results," internetRetailer,August30,2012,http://www.internetretailer.com/2012/08/30/wal-mart-factors-popularity-site-search-results.

Steel, Emily, "Data Brokers Change Labels Describing Poor," *Financial Times*, March 28, 2014, http://www.ft.com/intl/cms/s/0/a6a0783e-b107-11e3-bbd4-00144feab7de.html#axzz2xGUZ9o4B.

Steel, Emily, "US Internet Ad Spending Surpasses Broadcast TV," *Financial Times*, April 10, 2014, http://www.ft.com/intl/cms/s/0/594a1856-c0ca-11e3-bd6b-00144feabdc0.html#axzz2yaArjflI.

Stone, Brad, "Can Marissa Mayer Save Yahoo?," *Bloomberg Businessweek*, August 1, 2013, http://www.businessweek.com/articles/2013-08-01/can-marissa-mayer-save-yahoo#p4.

"Big Data and the CMO: What's Changing for Marketing Leadership?," CMO Summit Survey Results, Research and Insight, SpencerStuart, April, 2013, https://www.spencerstuart.com/research-and-insight/big-data-and-the-cmo-whats-changing-for-marketing-leadership-cmo-summit-survey-results.

Swidey, Neil, "Cambridge's Bluefin Labs Decodes Social Media Chatter," *The Boston Globe*, November 25, 2012, http://www.bostonglobe.com/2012/11/25/cambridge-bluefin-labs-decodes-social-media-chatter/SLDp9nflJK0tFQKBPuVZhP/story.html.

Taylor, Paul, "Corporate 'Digital IQ' Linked to Performance," *Financial Times*, March 26, 2014, http://www.ft.com/intl/cms/s/0/8ad17f4c-b52e-11e3-af92-00144feabdc0.html?siteedition=intl#axzz2xAvlKJlp.

Temple, James, "Stale Cookies: How Companies Are Tracking You Online Today," *SFGate*, October 2, 2013, http://blog.sfgate.com/techchron/2013/10/02/stale-cookies-how-companies-are-tracking-you-online-today/.

Teradata Aster Database, Teradata, last accessed July 15, 2014, http://assets.teradata.com/resourceCenter/downloads/Brochures/Teradata_Aster_Database_EB6950.pdf?processed=1.

Thielman, Sam, "Comcast to Tap Set-Top Data for Advanced Advertising Service NBCU+ Powered by Comcast 'open for business,'" *Adweek*, January 30, 2014, http://www.adweek.com/news/television/comcast-tap-set-top-data-advanced-advertising-service-155335.

Thomas, Daniel, "China's Mobile Sector Grows Up Superfast," *Financial Times*, March 2, 2014, http://www.ft.com/intl/cms/s/0/2ee4891c-9b21-11e3-b0d0-00144feab7de.html#axzz38t3F7ETO.

Thomas, Daniel, "Cisco boss calls on Obama to rein in surveillance," *Financial Times*, May 18, 2014, http://www.ft.com/intl/cms/s/0/a697c292-de80-11e3-9640-00144feabdc0.html#axzz3E9wqxy6T

Thomas, Daniel, "WhatsApp in Voice Threat to Telecoms Sector," *Financial Times*, February 24, 2014, http://www.ft.com/intl/cms/s/0/0cc98b28-9d76-11e3-a599-00144feab7de.html#axzz38sCjnZss.

"Surge in Mobile Malware Affects 11.6 Million Devices," Tripwire, January 29, 2014, http://www.tripwire.com/state-of-security/top-security-stories/surge-mobile-malware-affects-11-6-million-devices/.

Troy, Mike, "Digital Future Director Predicts Facebook Decline," *Retailing Today*, February 3, 2014, http://www.retailingtoday.com/article/digital-future-director-predicts-facebook-decline.

Troy, Mike, "Kroger Initiative Digitizes Stores," *RetailingToday*, April 2, 2014, http://www.retailingtoday.com/article/kroger-initiative-digitizes-stores.

Twentyman, Jessica, "Data Can Be Source of Power," *Financial Times*, January 28, 2014, http://www.ft.com/intl/cms/s/0/89bad71c-81c5-11e3-87d5-00144feab7de.html#axzz38mfCvuyf.

"About Twitter," Twitter.com, last accessed July 15, 2014, https://about.twitter.com/company.

"Review of the Impact of the ICO's Civil Monetary Penalties," UK Information Commissioner's Office, last accessed July 15, 2014, http://ico.org.uk/about_us/research/data_protection.

Valentino-DeVries, Jennifer, "They Know What You're Shopping For," *Wall Street Journal*, December 7, 2012, http://online.wsj.com/news/articles/SB10001424127887324784404578143144132736214?mod=WSJ_WhatTheyKnowPrivacy_LeftTopNews&mg=reno64-wsj&url=http%3A%2F%2Fonline.wsj.com%2Farticle%2FSB10001424127887324784404578143144132736214.html%3Fmod%3DWSJ_WhatTheyKnowPrivacy_LeftTopNews.

Van Rijmenam, Mark, "A Self-Driving Car Will Create 1 Gigabyte of Data Per Second: New Big Data Opportunity?," SmartData Collective, July 22, 2013, http://smartdatacollective.com/bigdatastartups/135291/self-driving-cars-will-create-2-petabytes-data-what-are-big-data-opportunitie.

Vasagar, Jeevan, "Axel Springer Accuses Google of Seeking Digital 'Superstate,'" *Financial Times*, April 16, 2014, http://www.ft.com/intl/cms/s/0/41507d26-c575-11e3-89a9-00144feabdc0.html#axzz2zWpfUGkS.

Ward, Andrew, "Technology Companies Eye Health Market," *Financial Times*, March 6, 2014, http://www.ft.com/intl/cms/s/0/604c9308-9fb0-11e3-b6c7-00144feab7de.html#axzz2xGUZ9o4B.

Waters, Richard, "Apple Seeks to Work Jobs Magic on the Internet of Things," *Financial Times,* May 30, 2014, http://www.ft.com/intl/cms/s/0/3c6e330a-e74b-11e3-8b4e-00144feabdc0.html#axzz38rcNAqLk.

Waters, Richards, "IBM Must Keep Head Above the Clouds to Claim Glory," *Financial Times*, January 22, 2014, http://www.ft.com/intl/cms/s/0/7f45ff04-82f7-11e3-8119-00144feab7de.html#axzz399g8L7ZT.

Waxer, Cindy, "Big Data Blues: The Dangers of Data Mining," *Computerworld*, November 4, 2013, http://www.computerworld.com/s/article/9243719/Big_data_blues_The_dangers_of_data_mining?taxonomyId=18&pageNumber=3.

Weil, Ari, "I'm Not a Hollywood Actor Because I Haven't Been Discovered Yet," Akiban, March 7, 2013, http://blog.akiban.com/im-not-a-hollywood-actor-because-i-havent-been-discovered-yet/.

Wheatley, Mike, "Acxiom Gets into Big Data 'Onboarding' = Cue More Targeted Ads," SiliconAngle, May 15, 2014, http://siliconangle.com/blog/2014/05/15/acxiom-gets-into-big-data-onboarding-cue-more-targeted-ads/.

"We Can't Wait: Obama Administration Unveils Blueprint for a 'Privacy Bill of Rights' to Protect Consumers Online," White House Press Release, The White House web site, February 23, 2012, http://www.whitehouse.gov/the-press-office/2012/02/23/we-can-t-wait-obama-administration-unveils-blueprint-privacy-bill-rights.

"A Comprehensive List of Big Data Statistics," Wikibon, August 1, 2012, http://wikibon.org/blog/big-data-statistics.

"International Safe Harbor Privacy Principles," Wikipedia, last accessed July 15, 2014, https://en.wikipedia.org/wiki/International_Safe_Harbor_Privacy_" Principles.

"The Internet of Things," Wind River, 2013, http://www.windriver.com/iot/ZDNet/Wind-River-IoT-infographic.pdf.

Womack, Brian, "Facebook Market Value Tops $100 Billion Amid Mobile Push," Bloomberg.com, August 26, 2013, http://www.bloomberg.com/news/2013-08-26/facebook-market-value-tops-100-billion-amid-mobile-ad-push.html.

Woodward, Curt, "Twitter Shows Off Bluefin Labs Buy with New TV Ad Targeting," FG Press, May 23, 2013, http://www.xconomy.com/boston/2013/05/23/twitter-shows-off-bluefin-labs-buy-with-new-tv-ad-targeting/.

Yang, Nu, "Digital Marketplace: How Publishers Can Use Data to Sell Ads," Editor & Publisher, October 17, 2013, http://www.editorandpublisher.com/Features/Article/Digital-Marketplace--How-Publishers-Can-Use-Data-to-Sell-Ads#sthash.iTHjXXv4.izz0A9Rb.dpuf.

Zaino, Jennifer, "HealthCare.Gov: Progress Made But BackEnd Struggles Continue," Semanticweb.com, December 2, 2013, http://semanticweb.com/healthcare-gov-progress-made-backend-struggles-continue_b40816.

Endnotes

Chapter 1

1. Johnston, Leslie, "How Many Libraries of Congress Does It Take?," Library of Congress, March 23, 2012, http://blogs.loc.gov/digitalpreservation/2012/03/how-many-libraries-of-congress-does-it-take/.

2. "The Digital Universe of Opportunities," IDC and EMC Digital Universe, April 2014, http://www.emc.com/collateral/analyst-reports/idc-digital-universe-2014.pdf.

3. "A Comprehensive List of Big Data Statistics," Wikibon, August 1, 2012, http://wikibon.org/blog/big-data-statistics.

4. Lohr, Steve, "The Origins of 'Big Data': An Etymological Detective Story," *New York Times*, February 1, 2013, http://bits.blogs.nytimes.com/2013/02/01/the-origins-of-big-data-an-etymological-detective-story/?action=click&module=Search®ion=searchResults%231&version=&url=http%3A%2F%2Fquery.nytimes.com%2Fsearch%2Fsitesearch%2F%3Faction%3Dclick%26region%3DMasthead%26pgtype%3DHomepage%26module%3DSearchSubmit%26contentCollection%3DHomepage%26t%3Dqry633%23%2Fbig%2Bdata%2Fsince1851%2Fallresults%2F2%2F.

5. Singer, Natasha, "You for Sale: Mapping, and Sharing, the Consumer Genome," *New York Times*, June 16, 2012, http://www.nytimes.com/2012/06/17/technology/acxiom-the-quiet-giant-of-consumer-database-marketing.html?_r=0.

6. "The Internet of Things," Wind River, 2013, http://www.windriver.com/iot/ZDNet/Wind-River-IoT-infographic.pdf.

7. "Cisco Visual Networking Index: Global Mobile Data Traffic Forecast Update, 2013–2018," Cisco, February 5, 2014, http://www.cisco.com/c/en/us/solutions/collateral/service-provider/visual-networking-index-vni/white_paper_c11-520862.html.

8. Gartner, "The Importance of 'Big Data': A Definition," http://www.gartner.com/id=2057415.

9. "Capitalizing on the promise of Big Data," PWC, January, 2013, p. 2, http://www.pwc.com/us/en/increasing-it-effectiveness/assets/capitalizing-on-the-promise-of-big-data.pdf.

10. "Follow the Ones and Zeros: How the Most Critical and Complex Big Data Around Brings Productivity and Profits," GE Reports, May 20, 2014, http://www.gereports.com/post/86322233075/follow-the-ones-and-zeros-how-the-most-critical-and.

11. Manyika, James, et al.,"Big Data: The Next Frontier for Innovation, Competition, and Productivity," McKinsey Global Institute, May 2011, http://www.mckinsey.com/insights/business_technology/big_data_the_next_frontier_for_innovation.

12. Marr, Bernard, "Why the 'Big Data' Hype Is NOT About Big or Data!," LinkedIn, September 11, 2013, http://www.linkedin.com/today/post/article/20130911045931-64875646-why-the-big-data-hype-is-not-about-big-or-data.

13. "Glaxo Links with Top Labs on 'Big Data' Drug Project, *Reuters*, March 28, 2014, http://www.medscape.com/viewarticle/822736.

14. Knapp, Alex, "Forecasting the Weather with Big Data and the Fourth Dimension," *Forbes*, June 13, 2013, http://www.forbes.com/sites/alexknapp/2013/06/13/forecasting-the-weather-with-big-data-and-the-fourth-dimension/.

15. Twentyman, Jessica, "Data Can Be Source of Power," *Financial Times*, January 28, 2014, http://www.ft.com/intl/cms/s/0/89bad71c-81c5-11e3-87d5-00144feab7de.html#axzz38mfCvuyf.

16. Packer, George, "Cheap Words: Amazon Is Good for Customers. But Is It Good for Books?," *The New Yorker*, February 17, 2014, http://www.newyorker.com/reporting/2014/02/17/140217fa_fact_packer?currentPage=all.

17. Baynes, Terry, "Walgreen Accused of Selling Patient Data," *Reuters*, March 11, 2011, http://www.reuters.com/article/2011/03/11/us-walgreen-prescriptions-idUSTRE72A83I20110311.

18. "Big Data and the CMO: What's Changing for Marketing Leadership?," CMO Summit Survey Results, *Research and Insight*, SpencerStuart, April 2013, https://www.spencerstuart.com/research-and-insight/big-data-and-the-cmo-whats-changing-for-marketing-leadership-cmo-summit-survey-results.

19. Hsu, Tiffany, "Target CEO Resigns as Fallout from Data Breach Continues," *LA Times*, May 5, 2014, http://www.latimes.com/business/la-fi-target-ceo-20140506-story.html.

20. Twentyman, Jessica, "Data Can Be Source of Power," *Financial Times*, January 28, 2014, http://www.ft.com/intl/cms/s/0/89bad71c-81c5-11e3-87d5-00144feab7de.html#axzz38mfCvuyf.

21. Kelly, Jeff, "Big Data Market Size and Vendor Revenues," Wikibon, January 3, 2014, http://wikibon.org/wiki/v/Big_Data_Market_Size_and_Vendor_Revenues.

Chapter 2

1. FutureTimeline.Net at http://www.futuretimeline.net/subject/computers-internet.htm.

2. MacKintosh, James, "Investment: A Better Bubble," *Financial Times*, March 5, 2014, http://www.ft.com/intl/cms/s/3/31223cc2-a438-11e3-b915-00144feab7de.html#slide0.

3. Hardy, Quentin, "IBM to Announce More Powerful Watson Via the Internet," *New York Times*, November 13, 2013, http://www.nytimes.com/2013/11/14/technology/ibm-to-announce-more-powerful-watson-via-the-internet.html, and Barr, Alistair, "Amazon, with Focus on Digital Services, Is Thinking Outside the Box to Grow (Literally)," *Reuters*, April 26, 2013, http://www.huffingtonpost.com/2013/04/26/amazon-digital-services_n_3160456.html.

4. Womack, Brian, "Facebook Market Value Tops $100 Billion Amid Mobile Push," Bloomberg.com, August 26, 2013, http://www.bloomberg.com/news/2013-08-26/facebook-market-value-tops-100-billion-amid-mobile-ad-push.html.

5. Womack, Brian, "Facebook Market Value Tops $100 Billion Amid Mobile Push," Bloomberg.com, August 26, 2013, http://www.bloomberg.com/news/2013-08-26/facebook-market-value-tops-100-billion-amid-mobile-ad-push.html.

6. Popelka, Larry, "What We Learned from Twitter's IPO: The Value of Innovation Is at an All-Time High," *Bloomberg Businessweek*, November 18, 2013, http://www.businessweek.com/articles/2013-11-18/what-we-learned-from-twitter-s-ipo-the-value-of-innovation-is-at-an-all-time-high.

7. Clover, Charles, "Chinese internet: Mobile wars," *Financial Times*, March 19, 2014, http://www.ft.com/intl/cms/s/2/56a160aa-a86f-11e3-a946-00144feab7de.html#axzz2xAvlKJlp.

8. Picardo, Elvis, "Apple? Google? Tesla? Which Will Be the First to Reach a $1 Trillion Market Cap?," Investopedia, http://www.investopedia.com/articles/investing/070714/apple-google-tesla-which-will-be-first-reach-1-trillion-market-cap.asp.

9. Stone, Brad, "Can Marissa Mayer Save Yahoo?," *Bloomberg Businessweek*, August 1, 2013, http://www.businessweek.com/articles/2013-08-01/can-marissa-mayer-save-yahoo#p4.

10. Noble, Josh, "Weibo Heading for IPO with $7bn-$8bn Valuation Target," *Financial Times*, February 25, 2014, http://www.ft.com/intl/cms/s/0/d596fe74-9d02-11e3-b535-00144feab7de.html?siteedition=intl#axzz38mnfQXBE.

11. Angwin, Julia, "The Web's New Gold Mine: Your Secrets," *Wall Street Journal*, July 30, 2010, http://online.wsj.com/news/articles/SB10001424052748703940904575395073512989404.

12. Hammond, Ed, "TMT's Add Verve to Global Deal Activity, *Financial Times*, March 30, 2014, http://www.ft.com/intl/cms/s/0/ebee9b42-b52a-11e3-a746-00144feabdc0.html#axzz2xeJV5gtd.

Chapter 3

1. Kleinman, Alexis, "Americans Will Spend More Time on Digital Devices Than Watching TV This Year: Research," *Huffington Post*, August 1, 2013, http://www.huffingtonpost.com/2013/08/01/tv-digital-devices_n_3691196.html.

2. Epstein, Zach, "400,000 American Homes Have Dumped Pay-TV So Far This Year," BGR, August 2, 2012, http://bgr.com/2012/08/02/cable-tv-subscriber-stats-q2-2012-satellite/.

3. Raval, Anjli, "Amazon Joins Screen Battle with Fire TV Video Streaming Device," *Financial Times*, April 2, 2014, http://uk.news.voxquo.com/noticia-detalhe-media.asp?id=70218&t=Amazon-joins-screen-battle-with-Fire-TV.

4. Thielman, Sam, "Comcast to Tap Set-Top Data for Advanced Advertising Service NBCU+ Powered by Comcast 'open for business,'" Adweek, January 30, 2014, http://www.adweek.com/news/television/comcast-tap-set-top-data-advanced-advertising-service-155335.

5. Dilanian, Ken, "The NSA Is Watching. So Are Google and Facebook," *LA Times*, June 30, 2013, http://articles.latimes.com/2013/jun/30/nation/la-na-consumer-tracking-20130701.

6. It is a curious anomaly that in most European and Asian countries, the cables that carry the Internet into houses and offices—the pipes of the Internet—have long been open to competition; as many as seven broadband providers are available in London, for example. By contrast, in the United States, in 2002 the Federal Communications Commission made the decision that only one provider could "own" and maintain the cable running into American homes and businesses, so that regional monopolies exist and the average American has only one or possibly two Internet carrier options. This had two major effects. First, it created a lack of competition and poorer service levels for telephone and broadband (compared with other nations). Although cable Internet is now available to users in about 90% of the United States, fiber-optic cable (Fiber-to-the-Premises or FTTP) is available in less than 25% of the country. Comcast, America's largest cable

Internet provider, for example, still uses the older copper cable (or telephone) lines, which always limit the faster speeds being attained by fiber-optic lines. This leaves average Internet speed in the United States a fraction of that in Europe and Asia (about a tenth of the average speed they get in Tokyo). This arrangement also prevented existing and would-be content providers like Amazon or Netflix from moving into the infrastructure business themselves—forcing these innovators to "do deals" with the existing cable providers—whereby they pay higher fees for "caching boxes," servers that provide higher bandwidth for select customers. The caching servers don't really solve the fundamental infrastructure constraints, and, at least in the view of the FCC, these types of pay-for-better-service deals threaten Net Neutrality. Internet service providers are now even threatening usage caps on high-data users. Google has taken the bit in its teeth, of course, and is establishing Google Fiber—laying fiber-optic cable to select cities around the country (Comcast is in negotiations with 34 cities in nine metro areas) that it claims will provide Internet speeds up to 100 times faster than basic broadband over copper wire.

7. Ogg, Jon, "Why Apple Should Just Buy Netflix," 24/7 Wall St., March 24, 2014, http://247wallst.com/media/2014/03/24/why-apple-should-just-buy-netflix/#ixzz30at3qZ00.

8. Kuchler, Hannah, "CES 2014: Yahoo Unveils New Ad Platforms," *Financial Times*, January 8, 2014, http://www.ft.com/intl/cms/s/0/3fc7ecd0-77f7-11e3-afc5-00144feabdc0.html#axzz2xGUZ9o4B.

9. Fearnow, Benjamin, "They Can Hear You Now: Verizon Patent Could Listen In on Customers," CBS DC, December 4, 2012, http://washington.cbslocal.com/2012/12/04/they-can-hear-you-now-verizon-patent-listens-in-on-customers/.

10. Donohue, Steve, "Verizon: Intel OnCue Acquisition Will Power New OTT Video Service, Next-Gen FiOS TV Product," FierceCable, January 21, 2014, http://www.fiercecable.com/story/verizon-intel-oncue-acquisition-will-power-new-ott-video-service-next-gen-f/2014-01-21.

11. Bray, Hiawatha, "Would You Let Your TV Watch You?," *The Boston Globe*, June 14, 2013, http://www.bostonglobe.com/business/2013/06/13/capuano-seeks-curbs-spying/w5R6IL1tbQ4EzrypMH5aYJ/story.html, and Armitage, Hugh, "Xbox One to Monitor TV Viewing, Content Watched, Numbers of Viewers," DigitalSpy, May 24, 2013, http://www.digitalspy.com/gaming/news/a484593/xbox-one-to-monitor-tv-viewing-content-watched-number-of-viewers.html.

12. Fearnow, Benjamin, "They Can Hear You Now: Verizon Patent Could Listen In on Customers," CBS DC, December 4, 2012, http://washington.cbslocal.com/2012/12/04/they-can-hear-you-now-verizon-patent-listens-in-on-customers/.

13. Adams, Guy, "Is Your TV Spying On You?" *The Daily Mail,* November 25, 2013, http://www.dailymail.co.uk/sciencetech/article-2513592/Is-TV-spying-YOU.html.

14. Albergotti, Reed, "Facebook App Knows What You're Hearing, Watching," *WSJ.D*, May 21, 2014, http://blogs.wsj.com/digits/2014/05/21/facebook-app-knows-what-youre-hearing-and-watching/.

15. Woodward, Curt, "Twitter Shows Off Bluefin Labs Buy with New TV Ad Targeting," FG Press, May 23, 2013, http://www.xconomy.com/boston/2013/05/23/twitter-shows-off-bluefin-labs-buy-with-new-tv-ad-targeting/.

Chapter 4

1. "Worldwide Smartphone Shipments Top One Billion Units for the First Time," IDC Press Release, January 27, 2014, http://www.idc.com/getdoc.jsp?containerId=prUS24645514.

2. "More Mobile Phones in NZ Than People: Study," *New Zealand Herald*, April 24, 2012, http://www.nzherald.co.nz/nz/news/article.cfm?c_id=1&objectid=10801183.

3. "Global Mobile Statistics 2014," MobiThinking, May 2014, http://mobithinking.com/mobile-marketing-tools/latest-mobile-stats/a.

4. Heggestuen, John, "One in Every 5 People in the World Own a Smartphone, One In Every 17 Own a Tablet," *Business Insider*, December 15, 2013, http://www.businessinsider.com/smartphone-and-tablet-penetration-2013-10.

5. Robinson, Duncan, "Mobile Commerce: Stores Caught by Surprise as Shoppers Take Their Tablets," *Financial Times*, February 23, 2014, http://www.ft.com/intl/cms/s/0/e6fde794-94b1-11e3-9146-00144feab7de.html#axzz38t3F7ETO.

6. "Android and iOS Combine for 91.1% of the Worldwide Smartphone OS Market in 4Q12 and 87.6% for the Year," IDC Press Release, February 14, 2013, http://www.businesswire.com/news/home/20130214005415/en/Android-iOS-Combine-91.1-Worldwide-Smartphone-OS#.VCLcEst0w_w.

7. Indvik, Lauren, "Forrester: Mobile Commerce to Quadruple to $31 Billion in Next 5 Years," Mashable, January 16, 2013, http://mashable.com/2013/01/16/mcommerce-31-billion-2017-forrester/.

8. Davies, Sally, "Facebook Targets Financial Services," *Financial Times*, April 13, 2014, http://www.ft.com/intl/cms/s/0/0e0ef050-c16a-11e3-97b2-00144feabdc0.html#axzz2yxuWKjtX.

9. Richard Waters, "Apple Seeks to Work Jobs Magic on the Internet of Things," *Financial Times*, May 30, 2014, http://www.ft.com/intl/cms/s/0/3c6e330a-e74b-11e3-8b4e-00144feabdc0.html#axzz38rcNAqLk.

10. Dredge, Stuart, "Mobile Apps Revenues Tipped to Reach $26bn in 2013," *The Guardian*, September 19, 2013, http://www.theguardian.com/technology/appsblog/2013/sep/19/gartner-mobile-apps-revenues-report.

11. Mandel, Michael, "The Data Economy Is Much, Much Bigger Than You (and the Government) Think," *The Atlantic*, July 25, 2013, http://www.theatlantic.com/business/archive/2013/07/the-data-economy-is-much-much-bigger-than-you-and-the-government-think/278113/.

12. Hamblen, Matt, "App Economy Expected to Double by 2017 to $151," *Computerworld*, July 15, 2013, http://www.computerworld.com/s/article/9240794/App_economy_expected_to_double_by_2017_to_151B.

13. Cohen, Heidi, "67 Mobile Facts to Develop Your 2014 Budget," Mobile, October 21, 2013, http://heidicohen.com/67-mobile-facts-from-2013-research-charts/.

14. Bradshaw, Tim, "Technology: All Eyes on the Future," *Financial Times*, March 28, 2014, http://www.ft.com/intl/cms/s/0/67f4904e-b665-11e3-905b-00144feabdc0.html#axzz2yxuWKjtX.

15. Peterson, Tim, "Did Apple's 'Spotlight' Update Just Sideline Google Search Ads?," AdAge, June 2, 2014, http://adage.com/article/digital/apple-s-spotlight-update-sideline-google-s-ads/293497/.

16. Steel, Emily, "US Internet Ad Spending Surpasses Broadcast TV," *Financial Times*, April 10, 2014, http://www.ft.com/intl/cms/s/0/594a1856-c0ca-11e3-bd6b-00144feabdc0.html#axzz2yaArjflI, and "Most Digital Ad Growth Now Goes to Mobile as Desktop Growth Falters," *eMarketer*, December 16, 2013, http://www.emarketer.com/Article/Most-Digital-Ad-Growth-Now-Goes-Mobile-Desktop-Growth-Falters/1010458.

17. Cookson, Robert, "UK Mobile Ad Spend Forecast to Overtake Newspaper Expenditure," *Financial Times*, March 9, 2014, http://www.ft.com/intl/cms/s/0/120c4644-a77f-11e3-9c7d-00144feab7de.html#axzz2xIS8DERs.

Chapter 5

1. Cookson, Robert, "Google and Facebook Add Creative Verve to Their Mix," *Financial Times,* April 10, 2014, http://www.ft.com/intl/cms/s/0/440c1f46-bfdc-11e3-9513-00144feabdc0.html#axzz2yaArjflI, and Basulto, Dominic, "Why You Should Care about the Mobile Web's Advertising Problem," *Washington Post*, April 29, http://www.washingtonpost.com/blogs/innovations/wp/2014/04/29/why-you-should-care-about-the-mobile-webs-advertising-problem/.

2. Palmer, Maija, "How to Get Ahead in Social Media Advertising," *Financial Times,* May 27, 2014, http://www.ft.com/intl/cms/s/0/0be25712-df61-11e3-86a4-00144feabdc0.html?siteedition=intl#axzz32v1myO1x.

3. MacKintosh, James, "Investment: a Better Bubble," *Financial Times*, March 5, 2014, http://www.ft.com/intl/cms/s/3/31223cc2-a438-11e3-b915-00144feab7de.html#slide0.

4. Kuchler, Hannah, "Yahoo to Axe Google and Facebook Sign-ins in Data Collection Drive," *Financial Times*, March 5, 2014, http://www.ft.com/intl/cms/s/0/41455370-a418-11e3-aa85-00144feab7de.html#axzz2xGUZ9o4B.

5. Palmer, Maija, "How to Get Ahead in Social Media Advertising," *Financial Times*, May 27, 2014, http://www.ft.com/intl/cms/s/0/0be25712-df61-11e3-86a4-00144feabdc0.html?siteedition=intl#axzz32v1myO1x.

6. Troy, Mike, "Digital Future Director Predicts Facebook Decline," *Retailing Today*, February 3, 2014, http://www.retailingtoday.com/article/digital-future-director-predicts-facebook-decline.

7. Mobile Messaging Futures 2012-2016, PortioResearch, http://www.portioresearch.com/en/market-briefings/budget-reports/mobile-messaging-futures-2012-2016.aspx.

8. Kuchler, Hannah, "WhatsApp 'Sticker Shock' Purchase Offers Facebook Mobile Leverage," *Financial Times*, February 20, 2014, http://www.ft.com/intl/cms/s/0/abd4a734-99d9-11e3-b3a2-00144feab7de.html?siteedition=intl#axzz38sCjnZss.

9. Carlson, Nicholas, "Facebook Is Buying Huge Messaging App WhatsApp For $19 Billion!," *Business Insider*, February 19, 2014, http://www.businessinsider.com/facebook-is-buying-whatsapp-2014-2#ixzz39pOBH4Q6.

10. Thomas, Daniel, "WhatsApp in Voice Threat to Telecoms Sector," *Financial Times*, February 24, 2014, http://www.ft.com/intl/cms/s/0/0cc98b28-9d76-11e3-a599-00144feab7de.html#axzz38sCjnZss.

11. Kuchler, Hannah, "Facebook Reels in Advertising Cash," *Financial Times*, January 30, 2014, http://www.ft.com/intl/cms/s/2/d54cea88-8951-11e3-bb5f-00144feab7de.html#axzz2zWpfUGkS.

12. Constine, Josh, "Facebook's Mobile Ad Network Is Called 'Facebook Audience Network' and Here's How It Works," TechCrunch, April 25, 2014, http://techcrunch.com/2014/04/25/facebook-audience-network/.

13. "Millennial Media Signs Definitive Agreement to Acquire Jumptap," Millennial Media Press Release, August 13, 2013, http://www.millennialmedia.com/pressroom/press-releases/millennial-media-signs-definitive-agreement-to-acquire-jumptap/.

14. Popelka, Larry, "What We Learned from Twitter's IPO: The Value of Innovation Is at an All-Time High," *Businessweek*, November 18, 2013, http://www.businessweek.com/articles/2013-11-18/what-we-learned-from-twitter-s-ipo-the-value-of-innovation-is-at-an-all-time-high.

15. Kuchler, Hannah, "Twitter Beats Facebook to Mobile Advertising Launch," *Financial Times*, April 17, 2014, http://www.ft.com/intl/cms/s/0/0d278c9c-c633-11e3-9839-00144feabdc0.html#axzz2zWpfUGkS.

16. Ha, Anthony, "Twitter Confirms Acquisition of Mobile Ad Retargeting Startup TapCommerce," *TechCrunch*, June 30, 2014, http://techcrunch.com/2014/06/30/twitter-acquires-tapcommerce/.

17. "About Twitter," *Twitter.com*, last accessed July 15, 2014, https://about.twitter.com/company.

18. "Facebook Scoops Up Remnant of Microsoft's Ill-Fated aQuantive," Maclean's, February 28, 2013, http://www.macleans.ca/news/facebook-scoops-up-remnant-of-microsofts-ill-fated-aquantive/.

Chapter 6

1. Computers-in-Use Forecast by Country, eTForecasts, last accessed July 15, 2014, http://www.etforecasts.com/products/ES_cinusev2.htm.

2. Bradshaw, Tim, "Technology: All Eyes on the Future," *Financial Times*, March 28, 2014, http://www.ft.com/intl/cms/s/0/67f4904e-b665-11e3-905b-00144feabdc0.html#axzz2yxuWKjtX.

3. Thomas, Daniel, "China's Mobile Sector Grows Up Superfast," *Financial Times*, March 2, 2014, http://www.ft.com/intl/cms/s/0/2ee4891c-9b21-11e3-b0d0-00144feab7de.html#axzz38t3F7ETO.

4. "Kakao Talk Daily Traffic Hits 3 Billion," The Chosun Ilbo, July 27, 2012, http://english.chosun.com/site/data/html_dir/2012/07/27/2012072701392.html.

5. "Now or Naver," *The Economist*, March 1, 14, p. 68.

6. Maruma, Misha, "Five Important Ecommerce Trends in China During 2014," Econsultsancy, June 9, 2014, https://econsultancy.com/blog/64958-five-important-ecommerce-trends-in-china-during-2014#i.1mus9f6crudavy.

7. Mishkin, Sarah, "China's YouTube Taps Surge in Online Viewership," *Financial Times*, March 9, 2014, http://www.ft.com/intl/cms/s/0/ff7a3e00-a3b9-11e3-88b0-00144feab7de.html#axzz2xIS8DERs.

8. Millward, Steven, "Now China's WeChat App Is Censoring Its Users Globally," TECHINASIA, January 10, 2013, https://en.wikipedia.org/wiki/WeChat.

9. Mundy, Simon, "Investors Take $275bn Bite Out of Big Tech Groups," *Financial Times*, April 8, 2014, http://www.ft.com/intl/cms/s/0/00596a2e-bedd-11e3-a4af-00144feabdc0.html#axzz2yaArjflI.

10. Kuchler, Hannah, "Twitter Eyes Rapid Asia Growth Despite China Ban," *Financial Times*, May 27, 2014, http://www.ft.com/intl/cms/s/0/f32c0d9a-e2c5-11e3-a829-00144feabdc0.html#axzz32v1myO1x.

11. Ong, Josh, "Report: Twitter's Most Active Country Is China," TNW Blog, September 26, 2012, http://thenextweb.com/asia/2012/09/26/surprise-twitters-active-country-china-where-blocked/.

12. Ong, Josh, "Report: Twitter's Most Active Country Is China," TNW Blog, September 26, 2012, http://thenextweb.com/asia/2012/09/26/surprise-twitters-active-country-china-where-blocked/.

13. "Migrating Finches," *The Economist*, March 22, 2014, p. 66.

Chapter 7

1. Montón, Màrius, "The Internet of Things Is Knocking on Your Door," CMSWire, January 29, 2014, http://www.cmswire.com/cms/internet-of-things/the-internet-of-things-is-knocking-on-your-door-023959.php.

2. "Global Active/Passive RFID Market to Exceed $23 Billion in 2020," *Converting Quarterly*, October 22, 2013, http://www.convertingquarterly.com/industry-news/articles/id/6077/global-activepassive-rfid-market-to-exceed-23-billion-in-2020.aspx).

3. "The Internet of Things," Wind River, 2013, http://www.windriver.com/iot/ZDNet/Wind-River-IoT-infographic.pdf.

4. Gatdula, Armand, "Fleet Tracking Devices Will Be Installed in 22,000 UPS Trucks to Cut Costs and Improve Driver Efficiency in 2010," FieldLogix, July 20th, 2010, http://www.fieldtechnologies.com/gps-tracking-systems-installed-in-ups-trucks-driver-efficiency/.

5. "The Internet of Things," Wind River, 2013, http://www.windriver.com/iot/ZDNet/Wind-River-IoT-infographic.pdf.

6. Pitcher, Pat, "Staggering Tech in an F1 Car Produces 3tb of Data per Second," *The Queensland Times*, March 24, 2014, http://www.qt.com.au/news/Staggering-technology-in-F1-produces-3tb-of-data-p/2207027/.

7. Munshi, Neil, "Farming Advances with Appliance of Science to Tractor Technology," *Financial Times*, October 25, 2013, http://www.ft.com/intl/cms/s/0/a48ad98c-36c7-11e3-aaf1-00144feab7de.html?siteedition=intl#axzz38t3F7ETO.

8. Bird, Jane, "Business Warms to Wearable Computers but Fresh Ideas Are Needed," *Financial Times*, February 23, 2014, http://www.ft.com/intl/cms/s/0/3aa877b0-94b2-11e3-9146-00144feab7de.html#axzz38t3F7ETO, and Sartain, J. D., "What the Internet of Things Will Mean for CIOs," CIO, February 3, 2014, http://www.cio.com/article/747634/What_the_Internet_of_Things_Will_Mean_for_CIOs?page=2&taxonomyId=600010.

9. Kolakowski, Nick, "Zuckerberg Wants Facebook to 'Glue' Internet of Things Together," Dice, January 29, 2014, http://news.dice.com/2014/01/29/zuckerberg-wants-facebook-to-glue-internet-of-things-together/.

10. "Why You Need to Care About This 'Internet of Things' Thing," Laserfiche, July 29, 2013, http://simplicity.laserfiche.com/content/why-you-need-care-about-internet-things-thing.

11. Davies, Sally, "Who Will Be the Google of the Internet of Things?," *Financial Times*, May 1, 2014, http://blogs.ft.com/tech-blog/2014/05/who-will-be-the-google-of-the-internet-of-things/.

12. Bryant, Chris, "VW Chief Urges Carmakers to Fight the Rise of the 'Data Monster,'" *Financial Times*, March 10, 2014, http://www.ft.com/intl/cms/s/0/581aa95a-a81f-11e3-8ce1-00144feab7de.html#axzz2xGUZ9o4B.

13. Lopez, Isaac, "Report: Big Data Will Represent Billions in Automotive," datanami, November 21, 2013, http://www.datanami.com/2013/11/21/report_big_data_will_represent_billions_in_automotive/.

14. Gittleson, Kim, "How Big Data Is Changing the Cost of Insurance," BBC News, November 14, 2013, http://www.bbc.co.uk/news/business-24941415 and http://www.progressive.com/auto/snapshot/.

15. Reifel, Joe, "Telematics: the Game Changer—Reinventing Auto Insurance," AT Kearney, 2010, http://www.atkearney.co.uk/documents/10192/19079b53-8042-43ea-b870-ef42b1f033a6.

16. Foy, Henry, "Smart Technology Takes a Back Seat for Carmakers," *Financial Times*, January 15, 2014, http://www.ft.com/intl/cms/s/0/de423e9e-7dcc-11e3-95dd-00144feabdc0.html#axzz38t3F7ETO.

17. Van Rijmenam, Mark, "A Self-Driving Car Will Create 1 Gigabyte of Data Per Second: New Big Data Opportunity?," SmartData Collective, July 22, 2013, http://smartdatacollective.com/bigdatastartups/135291/self-driving-cars-will-create-2-petabytes-data-what-are-big-data-opportunitie.

18. Bilton, Nick, "Intruders for the Plugged-In Home, Coming in Through the Internet," *New York Times*, June 1, 2014, http://bits.blogs.nytimes.com/2014/06/01/dark-side-to-internet-of-things-hacked-homes-and-invasive-ads/?_php=true&_type=blogs&hpw&rref=business&_r=0.

19. Fitchard, Kevin, "How You and I Could Become Nodes in the Internet of Things," GIGAOM, June 3, 2013, http://gigaom.com/2013/06/03/how-you-and-i-could-become-nodes-in-the-internet-of-things/.

20. Marr, Bernard, "Why the 'Big Data' Hype Is NOT About Big or Data!," LinkedIn, September 11, 2013, http://www.linkedin.com/today/post/article/20130911045931-64875646-why-the-big-data-hype-is-not-about-big-or-data.

21. Ward, Andrew, "Technology Companies Eye Health Market," *Financial Times*, March 6, 2014, http://www.ft.com/intl/cms/s/0/604c9308-9fb0-11e3-b6c7-00144feab7de.html#axzz2xGUZ9o4B.

22. Bradshaw, Tim, "CES 2014: Wearables Emerge as Top Trend," *Financial Times*, January 6, 2014, http://www.ft.com/intl/cms/s/0/50264574-7485-11e3-9125-00144feabdc0.html#axzz38t3F7ETO.

23. Bradshaw, Tim, "Technology: All Eyes on the Future," *Financial Times*, March 28, 2014, http://www.ft.com/intl/cms/s/0/67f4904e-b665-11e3-905b-00144feabdc0.html#axzz2yxuWKjtX

24. Meyer, David, "'Facebook for Things' Company Evrythng Teams Up with ARM on Internet of Things," GIGAOM, February 22, 2013, https://gigaom.com/2013/02/22/facebook-for-things-company-evrything-teams-up-with-arm-on-internet-of-things/.

25. Montón, Màrius, "The Internet of Things Is Knocking on Your Door," CMSWire, January 29, 2014, http://www.cmswire.com/cms/internet-of-things/the-internet-of-things-is-knocking-on-your-door-023959.php.

26. Hardy, Quentin, "Consortium Wants Standards for 'Internet of Things,'" *The New York Times,* March 27, 2014, http://bits.blogs.nytimes.com/2014/03/27/consortium-wants-standards-for-internet-of-things/?_php=true&_type=blogs&_r=0.

27. "Why You Need to Care About This 'Internet of Things' Thing," Laserfiche, July 29, 2013, http://simplicity.laserfiche.com/content/why-you-need-care-about-internet-things-thing.

28. Anthony, Sebastian, "Google Admits It Wants to Put Ads on 'fridges, car dashboards, thermostats, glasses, and watches,'" *ExtremeTech*, May 21, 2014, http://www.extremetech.com/extreme/182849-google-admits-it-wants-to-put-ads-on-fridges-car-dashboards-thermostats-glasses-and-watches.

29. Bilton, Nick, "Google S.E.C. Filing Says It Wants Ads in Your Thermostat and Car," *New York Times*, May 25, 2014, http://bits.blogs.nytimes.com/2014/05/21/google-plans-to-deliver-ads-through-your-thermostat-and-car/?action=click&module=Search®ion=searchResults&mabReward=relbias%3Ar&url=http%3A%2F%2Fquery.nytimes.com%2Fsearch%2Fsitesearch%2F%3Faction%3Dclick%26contentCollection%3Dundefined%26region%3DTopBar%26module%3DSearchSubmit%26pgtype%3DTopic%23%2Fgoogle%2Bsec%2F.

Chapter 8

1. Sermeño, Rodrigo, "Data Brokers Gathering Dossiers on Millions of Americans by Income, Disease, and More," PJMedia, December 26, 2013, http://pjmedia.com/blog/data-brokers-gathering-dossiers-on-millions-of-americans-by-income-disease-and-more/.

2. Singer, Natasha, "You for Sale: Mapping, and Sharing, the Consumer Genome," *New York Times*, June 16, 2012, http://www.nytimes.com/2012/06/17/technology/acxiom-the-quiet-giant-of-consumer-database-marketing.html?_r=0.

3. Ibid.

4. Biegelsen, Amy, "Unregulated FICO Has Key Role in Each American's Access to Credit," May 17, 2011, http://www.publicintegrity.org/2011/05/17/4628/unregulated-fico-has-key-role-each-americans-access-credit.

5. Beckett, Lois, "Everything We Know About What Data Brokers Know About You," June 13, 2014, https://www.propublica.org/article/everything-we-know-about-what-data-brokers-know-about-you.

6. Cookson, Robert, "Moneysupermarket to sell data on customers," *Financial Times*, March 4, 2014, http://www.ft.com/intl/cms/s/0/dc169c48-a381-11e3-88b0-00144feab7de.html?siteedition=intl#axzz2xGUZ9o4B.

7. "The World's Top 10 Most Innovative Companies in Big Data," Fast Company, February 10, 2014, http://www.fastcompany.com/most-innovative-companies/2014/industry/big-data.

8. Anderson, Ian, "Signal - Big Brother Software for Recruiters Is Coming," ArcticStartUp, December 18, 2013, http://arcticstartup.com/2013/12/18/signal-big-brother-software-for-recruiters-is-coming.

9. McFarland, Michael, "Ethical Implications of Data Aggregation," Santa Clara University, June, 2012, http://www.scu.edu/ethics/practicing/focusareas/technology/internet/privacy/data-aggregation.html.

10. Rosenfeld, Steven, "4 Ways Google Is Destroying Privacy and Collecting Your Data," *Salon*, February 5, 2014, http://www.salon.com/2014/02/05/4_ways_google_is_destroying_privacy_and_collecting_your_data_partner/.

11. Epstein, Robert, "Google's Gotcha," *US News and World Report*, May 10, 2013, http://www.usnews.com/opinion/articles/2013/05/10/15-ways-google-monitors-you.

12. Kuchler, Hannah, "Yahoo to Axe Google and Facebook Sign-ins in Data Collection Drive," *Financial Times*, March 5, 2014, http://www.ft.com/intl/cms/s/0/41455370-a418-11e3-aa85-00144feab7de.html#axzz2xGUZ9o4B.

13. Carpentier, Megan, "What Your Search History Says About You (And How to Shut It Up)," *The Huffington Post*, October 31, 2013, http://www.huffingtonpost.com/megan-carpentier/what-your-search-history-_b_4179728.html and https://info.yahoo.com/legal/us/yahoo/utos/terms/.

14. Kirk, Jeremy, "Yahoo to Scrub Personal Data After Three Months," *PCWorld*, December 17, 2008, http://www.pcworld.com/article/155610/yahoo_privacy_support.html, and "Fact Sheet 18: Online Privacy: Using the Internet Safely," *Privacy Rights Clearinghouse*, July 2014, https://www.privacyrights.org/online-privacy-using-internet-safely.

15. Elgan, Mike, "Why You Shouldn't Buy the Amazon Fire Phone," *Computerworld*, June 21, 2014, http://www.computerworld.com/s/article/9249269/Why_you_shouldn_t_buy_the_Amazon_Fire_phone?pageNumber=2.

16. Barr, Alistair, "Analysis: Sleeping Ad Giant Amazon Finally Stirs," *Reuters*, April 24, 2013, http://www.reuters.com/article/2013/04/24/us-amazon-advertising-idUSBRE93N06E20130424, and Leber, Jessica, "Amazon Woos Advertisers with What It Knows About Consumers," *MIT Technology Review*, January 21, 2013, http://www.technologyreview.com/news/509471/amazon-woos-advertisers-with-what-it-knows-about-consumers/.

17. "How Amazon Is Leveraging Big Data," *BigData-Startups*, last accessed July 15, 2014, http://www.bigdata-startups.com/BigData-startup/amazon-leveraging-big-data/.

18. Bartlett, Jamie, "iSPY: How the Internet Buys and Sells Your Secrets," *The Spectator*, December 7, 2013, http://www.spectator.co.uk/features/9093961/little-brothers-are-watching-you/.

19. Valentino-DeVries, Jennifer, "They Know What You're Shopping For," *Wall Street Journal*, December 7, 2012, http://online.wsj.com/news/articles/SB10001424127887324784404578143144132736214?mod=WSJ_WhatTheyKnowPrivacy_LeftTopNews&mg=reno64-wsj&url=http%3A%2F%2Fonline.wsj.com%2Farticle%2FSB10001424127887324784404578143144132736214.html%3Fmod%3DWSJ_WhatTheyKnowPrivacy_LeftTopNews.

20. Geary, Joanna, "Facebook: What Is It and What Does It Do?," *The Guardian*, April 23, 2012, http://www.theguardian.com/technology/2012/apr/23/facebook-tracking-trackers-cookies-web-monitoring.

21. Kosinski, Michal and Stillwell, David, "Private Traits and Attributes Are Predictable from Digital Records of Human Behavior," *Proceedings of the National Academy of Sciences of the United States of America*, vol. 110, no. 15, April 9, 2013, http://www.pnas.org/content/110/15/5802.full.

22. Swidey, Neil, "Cambridge's Bluefin Labs Decodes Social Media Chatter," *The Boston Globe*, November 25, 2012, http://www.bostonglobe.com/2012/11/25/cambridge-bluefin-labs-decodes-social-media-chatter/SLDp9nflJK0tFQKBPuVZhP/story.html.

23. Klosowski, Thorin, "How Facebook Uses Your Data to Target Ads, Even Offline," Lifehacker, April 11, 2013, http://lifehacker.com/5994380/how-facebook-uses-your-data-to-target-ads-even-offline, and Elgan, Mike, "Google, Facebook Go Beyond Social, Beyond Identity," *Computerworld*, August 9, 2014, http://www.computerworld.com/s/article/9250256/Google_Facebook_go_beyond_social_beyond_identity.

24. Ibid., Valentino-DeVries, Jennifer.

25. Johnsen, Michael, "Nielsen Finds Loyalty Programs Resonate with Shoppers," *RetailingToday*, November 13, 2013, http://www.retailingtoday.com/article/nielsen-finds-loyalty-programs-resonate-shoppers.

26. "Consumers, Big Data, and Online Tracking in the Retail Industry: A Case Study of Walmart," The Center for Media Justice, November 2013, http://centerformediajustice.org/wp-content/files/WALMART_PRIVACY_.pdf.

27. "Global Tech Startup Personalizes Shopping Experience," *RetailingToday*, January 14, 2013, http://www.retailingtoday.com/article/global-tech-startup-personalizes-shopping-experience.

28. Rudarakanchana, Nat, "Big Data: Cat-And-Mouse Escalates on Privacy Concerns, As NRF Retail Conference Looms," *International Business Times*, January 9, 2014, http://www.ibtimes.com/big-data-cat-mouse-escalates-privacy-concerns-nrf-retail-conference-looms-1533616.

29. Datoo, Siraj, "How Tracking Customers in-Store Will Soon Be the Norm," *The Guardian*, January 10, 2014, http://www.theguardian.com/technology/datablog/2014/jan/10/how-tracking-customers-in-store-will-soon-be-the-norm.

30. "A New Solution for Mobile Engagement," *RetailingToday*, February 18, 2014, http://www.retailingtoday.com/article/new-solution-mobile-engagement.

31. Rudarakanchana, Nat, "Big Data: Retailers, Supermarkets, Medical Markets All Dive in to Extract Information from and About Consumers," *International Business Times*, December 20, 2013, http://www.ibtimes.com/big-data-retailers-supermarkets-medical-markets-all-dive-extract-information-about-consumers-1517510.

32. Bacon, Jonathan, "Mobile Microtargeting," *MarketingWeek*, December 12, 2013, http://www.marketingweek.co.uk/analysis/essential-reads/mobile-micro-targeting/4008800.article.

33. Clifford, Stephanie, "Attention, Shoppers: Store Is Tracking Your Cell," *New York Times*, July 15, 2013, http://www.nytimes.com/2013/07/15/business/attention-shopper-stores-are-tracking-your-cell.html.

34. "Clutch Partners with RetailNext to Take Consumer Loyalty and Engagement to Next Level," *BusinessWire*, January 13, 2014, http://www.businesswire.com/news/home/20140113006134/en/Clutch-Partners-RetailNext-Consumer-Loyalty-Engagement-Level#.U1A4Z6NOXGg.

35. Troy, Mike, "Kroger Initiative Digitizes Stores," *RetailingToday*, April 2, 2014, http://www.retailingtoday.com/article/kroger-initiative-digitizes-stores.

36. Palmer, Maija, "How to Get Ahead in Social Media Advertising," *Financial Times*, May 27, 2014, http://www.ft.com/intl/cms/s/0/0be25712-df61-11e3-86a4-00144feabdc0.html?siteedition=intl#axzz32v1myO1x.

37. Cheng, Roger, "Walmart Exec: Mobile Can Revive Personal Touch for Shoppers," *CNET*, May 22, 2013, http://reviews.cnet.com/8301-12261_7-57585710-10356022/walmart-exec-mobile-can-revive-personal-touch-for-shoppers/.

38. Stambor, Zak, "Wal-Mart Factors Popularity into Site Search Results," internet Retailer, August 30, 2012, http://www.internetretailer.com/2012/08/30/wal-mart-factors-popularity-site-search-results.

39. Prasath, Arun, "The @WalmartLabs Social Media Analytics Project," @Walmartlabs, January 11, 2013, http://walmartlabs.blogspot.com/2013/01/the-walmart-labs-social-media-analytics.html.

40. Clark, Evan, "Walmart Sets Aggressive Digital Plan." *Women's Wear Daily*," May 2, 2013, http://centerformediajustice.org/wp-content/files/WALMART_PRIVACY_.pdf.

41. Ibid., Valentino-DeVries.

42. "Consumers, Big Data, and Online Tracking in the Retail Industry: A Case Study of Walmart," The Center for Media Justice, November 2013, http://centerformediajustice.org/wp-content/files/WALMART_PRIVACY_.pdf.

43. Ibid., Beckett, Lois.

44. Duck, Barbara, "United Health Care to Use Data Mining Algorithms on Claim Data to Look for Those at 'Risk' of Developing Diabetes—Walgreens and the YMCA Benefit with Pay for Performance Dollars to Promote and Supply the Tools," The Medical Quack, last accessed July 30, 2014, http://ducknetweb.blogspot.com/2010/04/unitedhealthcare-to-use-data-mining.html.

45. Ibid., Valentino-DeVries.

46. Madrigal, Alexis C., "I'm Being Followed: How Google—and 104 Other Companies—Are Tracking Me on the Web," *The Atlantic*, February 29, 2012, http://www.theatlantic.com/technology/archive/2012/02/im-being-followed-how-google-151-and-104-other-companies-151-are-tracking-me-on-the-web/253758/.

47. Angwin, Julia, "The Web's New Gold Mine: Your Secrets," *Wall Street Journal*, July 30, 2010, http://online.wsj.com/news/articles/SB10001424052748703940904575395073512989404.

48. Temple, James, "Stale Cookies: How Companies Are Tracking You Online Today," *SFGate*, October 2, 2013, http://blog.sfgate.com/techchron/2013/10/02/stale-cookies-how-companies-are-tracking-you-online-today/.

49. Yang, Nu, "Digital Marketplace: How Publishers Can Use Data to Sell Ads," Editor & Publisher, October 17, 2013, http://www.editorandpublisher.com/Features/Article/Digital-Marketplace--How-Publishers-Can-Use-Data-to-Sell-Ads#sthash.iTHjXXv4.izz0A9Rb.dpuf.

50. Geary, Joanna, "Adnxs (AppNexus): What Is It and What Does It Do?," *The Guardian*, April 23, 2012, http://www.theguardian.com/technology/2012/apr/23/adnxs-tracking-trackers-cookies-web-monitoring.

51. Cookson, Robert, "Mercedes Online Ads Viewed More by Fraudster Robots Than Humans," *Financial Times*, May 26, 2014, http://www.ft.com/intl/cms/s/0/788d6d42-da6c-11e3-8273-00144feabdc0.html#axzz32v1myO1x.

52. Hof, Robert, "Marketers' Customer Data Web Widens with Acxiom's $310 Million Purchase of LiveRamp," *Forbes*, May 14, 2014, http://www.forbes.com/sites/roberthof/2014/05/14/marketers-customer-data-web-widens-with-acxioms-310-million-purchase-of-liveramp/.

53. Wheatley, Mike, "Acxiom Gets into Big Data 'Onboarding' = Cue More Targeted Ads," SiliconAngle, May 15, 2014, http://siliconangle.com/blog/2014/05/15/acxiom-gets-into-big-data-onboarding-cue-more-targeted-ads/, and Ibid., Hof.

54. Darrow, Barb, "Acxiom Snaps Up LiveRamp and Its Data Onboarding Smarts for $310M," GIGAOM, May 14, 2014, http://gigaom.com/2014/05/14/acxiom-snaps-up-liveramp-for-its-data-collection-smarts-for-31om/.

55. Datoo, Siraj, "What Information Can Retailers See When They Track Customer Movements?," *The Guardian*, October 11, 2013, http://www.theguardian.com/news/datablog/2013/oct/11/information-retailers-track-customer-movements.

Chapter 9

1. Hamby, Steve, "3 Factors Contributing to Lack of Data Efficacy," *The Huffington Post*, April 19, 2013, http://www.huffingtonpost.com/steve-hamby/3-factors-contributing-to_b_3109600.html.

2. Needham, Jeffrey, *Disruptive Possibilities: How Big Data Changes Everything*, O'Reilly, 2013, http://chimera.labs.oreilly.com/books/1234000000914/ch04.html#_the_actual_internet.

3. "ERP System," LKD Technologies, http://www.lkdtech.com/ServiceDetail.aspx?id=8.

4. Hassman, John, "Lofty Expectations for Big Data," USSCO Speaks, February 26, 2013, http://usscospeaks.com/lofty-expectations-for-big-data/.

5. Griswold, Alison, "Big Data Can Help Marketers Unlock Up To $200 Billion," *Business Insider*, November 22, 2013, http://www.businessinsider.com/big-data-can-boost-marketing-roi-2013-11.

6. Rosenbush, Steve, "The Morning Download: More Companies, Drowning in Data, Are Turning to Hadoop," *Wall Street Journal*, April 14, 2014, http://blogs.wsj.com/cio/2014/04/14/the-morning-download-more-companies-drowning-in-data-are-turning-to-hadoop/.

7. http://hadoop.apache.org/docs/r1.2.1/mapred_tutorial.html.

8. Proffitt, Brian, "Hadoop Could Save You Money over a Traditional RDBMS," *ComputerworldUK*, January 10, 2012, http://www.computerworlduk.com/in-depth/applications/3329092/hadoop-could-save-you-money-over-a-traditional-rdbms/.

9. Barth, Paul, "Get the Maximum Value Out of Your Big Data Initiative," HBR Blog Network and NewVantage Partners, February 1, 2013, http://newvantage.com/wp-content/uploads/2013/03/HBR-Blog-Network-020113.pdf.

10. Butler, Brandon, "Nine Hadoop Companies You Should Know," *Networkworld*, March 18, 2014, http://www.networkworld.com/article/2175299/cloud-computing/nine-hadoop-companies-you-should-know.html.

11. Apache Spark web site, last accessed July 15, 2014, http://spark.apache.org/.

12. Brust, Andrew, "MapReduce and MPP: Two Sides of the Big Data Coin?," ZDNet, March 2, 2012, http://www.zdnet.com/blog/big-data/mapreduce-and-mpp-two-sides-of-the-big-data-coin/121.

13. Burns, Ed, "Hadoop Still Too Slow for Real-Time Analysis Applications?," TechTarget, http://searchbusinessanalytics.techtarget.com/feature/Hadoop-still-too-slow-for-real-time-analysis-applications.

14. Informatica web site at http://www.informatica.com/us/#fbid=p5mYlM884hF.

15. Teradata Aster Database, Teradata, last accessed July 15, 2014, http://assets.teradata.com/resourceCenter/downloads/Brochures/Teradata_Aster_Database_EB6950.pdf?processed=1.

16. Lardinois, Frederic, "Google Launches BigQuery Streaming for Real-Time, Big-Data Analytics," TechCrunch, March 25, 2014, http://techcrunch.com/2014/03/25/google-launches-bigquery-streaming-for-real-time-big-data-analytics/.

17. Sabat, Sunil, "Real Time Big Data Options," Big Data Know How, February 28, 2014, http://bigdataknowhow.weebly.com/blog/category/nosql.

18. Zaino, Jennifer, "HealthCare.Gov: Progress Made But BackEnd Struggles Continue," Semanticweb.com, December 2, 2013, http://semanticweb.com/healthcare-gov-progress-made-backend-struggles-continue_b40816.

19. Aslett, Matt, "Big Data Reconsidered: It's the Economics, Stupid," 451Research, December 2, 2013, https://451research.com/report-short?entityId=79479&referrer=marketing.

20. Savitz, Eric, "Big Data: Big Hype?, *Forbes*, February 4, 2013, http://www.forbes.com/sites/ciocentral/2013/02/04/big-data-big-hype/.

21. McDuling, John, "Proof That "Big Data" Is One of the Most Overused Corporate Buzzwords of 2013," Quartz, November 27, 2013, http://qz.com/151109/proof-that-big-data-is-one-of-the-most-overused-corporate-buzzwords-of-2013/.

22. Cox, Ryan, "Storage Is the Link Between Collecting, Analyzing + Acting On Big Data," SiliconAngle, June 3, 2013, http://siliconangle.com/blog/2013/06/03/storage-is-the-link-between-collecting-and-analyzing-acting-on-big-data/.

23. Press, Gil, "$16.1 Billion Big Data Market: 2014 Predictions from IDC and IIA," *Forbes*, December 12, 2013, http://www.forbes.com/sites/gilpress/2013/12/12/16-1-billion-big-data-market-2014-predictions-from-idc-and-iia/.

24. Kaplan, James, "Protecting Information in the Cloud," McKinsey&Company, January 2013, http://www.mckinsey.com/insights/business_technology/protecting_information_in_the_cloud.

25. "The Australian Public Service Big Data Strategy," Australian Department of Finance and Deregulation, August 2013, http://www.finance.gov.au//sites/default/files/Big%20Data%20Strategy.pdf.

26. Hardy, Quentin, "Cisco Bets a Billion on the Cloud," *New York Times*, March 24, 2014, http://bits.blogs.nytimes.com/2014/03/24/cisco-bets-a-billion-on-the-cloud/?src=recg.

27. Jopson, Barney, "Amazon Cloud Seeks to Revamp Corporate IT," *Financial Times*, September 25, 2012, http://www.ft.com/intl/cms/s/0/d822679c-0694-11e2-abdb-00144feabdc0.html#axzz2xAvlKJlp.

28. Lardinois, Frederic, "Google Launches BigQuery Streaming for Real-Time, Big-Data Analytics," TechCrunch, March 25, 2014, http://techcrunch.com/2014/03/25/google-launches-bigquery-streaming-for-real-time-big-data-analytics/.

29. Hardy, Quentin, "IBM to Announce More Powerful Watson Via the Internet," *New York Times*, November 14, 2014, http://www.nytimes.com/2013/11/14/technology/ibm-to-announce-more-powerful-watson-via-the-internet.html.

30. "Hortonworks Raises $100 Million in Funding, Eyes M&A," *Reuters*, March 25, 2014, http://www.reuters.com/article/2014/03/25/hortonworks-funding-idUSL1N0ML1KP20140325.

31. Campos, Adrian, "Why Intel Is Investing in Cloudera," The Motley Fool, March 31, 2014, http://www.fool.com/investing/general/2014/03/31/why-intel-is-investing-in-cloudera.aspx.

32. Harris, Derrick, "MapR Raises $110M to Fuel Its Enterprise Hadoop Push," GIGAOM, June 30, 2014, http://gigaom.com/2014/06/30/mapr-raises-110m-to-fuel-its-enterprise-hadoop-push/.

33. Alden, William, "Start-Up Data Storage Firm Actifio Hits $1 Billion Mark," *The New York Times*, March 23, 2014, http://dealbook.nytimes.com/2014/03/23/start-up-data-storage-firm-actifio-hits-1-billion-mark/?src=recg.

34. Press, Gil, "$16.1 Billion Big Data Market: 2014 Predictions From IDC and IIA," *Forbes*, December 12, 2013, http://www.forbes.com/sites/gilpress/2013/12/12/16-1-billion-big-data-market-2014-predictions-from-idc-and-iia/.

35. Waters, Richards, "IBM Must Keep Head above the Clouds to Claim Glory," *Financial Times*, January 22, 2014, http://www.ft.com/intl/cms/s/0/7f45ff04-82f7-11e3-8119-00144feab7de.html#axzz399g8L7ZT.

36. "The World's Top 10 Most Innovative Companies in Big Data," Fast Company, February 10, 2014, http://www.fastcompany.com/most-innovative-companies/2014/industry/big-data.

Chapter 10

1. "Big Data Executive Survey: Themes & Trends," NewVantage Partners, 2012, http://newvantage.com/wp-content/uploads/2012/12/NVP-Big-Data-Survey-Themes-Trends.pdf.

2. Ibid., NewVantage Partners.

3. Ibid., NewVantage Partners.

4. "Global Survey: The Business Impact of Big Data," Avanade, November 2010, http://www.avanade.com/Documents/Research%20and%20Insights/Big%20Data%20Executive%20Summary%20FINAL%20SEOv.pdf.

5. Weil, Ari, "I'm Not a Hollywood Actor Because I Haven't Been Discovered Yet," Akiban, March 7, 2013, http://blog.akiban.com/im-not-a-hollywood-actor-because-i-havent-been-discovered-yet/.

6. "Surfing a Digital Wave, or Drowning?," *The Economist*, December 7, 2014, http://www.economist.com/news/business/21591201-information-technology-everywhere-companies-it-departments-mixed.

7. Ibid., NewVantage Partners.

8. Taylor, Paul, "Corporate 'Digital IQ' Linked to Performance," *Financial Times*, March 26, 2014, http://www.ft.com/intl/cms/s/0/8ad17f4c-b52e-11e3-af92-00144feabdc0.html?siteedition=intl#axzz2xAvlKJlp.

9. Brinker, Scott, "81% of Big Firms Now Have a Chief Marketing Technologist," Chief Digital Officer, January 31, 2014, http://chiefdigitalofficer.net/81-of-big-firms-now-have-a-chief-marketing-technologist/.

10. Ibid., *The Economist*.

11. Quinn, Evan, "Getting Real About Big Data: Build Versus Buy," Enterprise Strategy Group, February 2013, https://www.yumpu.com/en/document/view/10987281/esg-big-data-wp-1914112/9.

12. Ibid., NewVantage Partners.

13. Ibid., Quinn.

14. Olavsrud, Thor, "Red Hat and Hortonworks Expand Strategic Big Data Alliance," CIO, February 10, 2014, http://www.cio.com/article/748045/Red_Hat_and_Hortonworks_Expand_Strategic_Big_Data_Alliance?page=2&taxonomyId=600010.

15. Ibid., NewVantage Partners.

16. Bednarz, Ann, "Big Data Skills Pay Top Dollar," CIO, February 7, 2014, http://www.cio.com/article/747927/Big_Data_Skills_Pay_Top_Dollar?taxonomyId=600010.

17. Riley, James, "Cut Big Data Down to Size," ComputerWeekly.com, July 2013, http://www.computerweekly.com/feature/Cut-big-data-down-to-size.

18. Ibid., NewVantage Partners.

19. "Strategic Cloud Computing Demands Cooperation," CIO, October 28, 2013, http://zerodistance.cio.com/2013/10/vcloud/#sthash.x5ijM4Ib.dpuf.

20. Flinders, Karl, "Gartner Outsourcing Summit 2013: How Digitisation Is Shaking Up IT Outsourcing," ComputerWeekly.com, September 10, 2013, http://www.computerweekly.com/news/2240205134/Gartner-Outsourcing-Summit-2013-How-digitisation-is-shaking-up-IT-outsourcing.

21. Rosenbush, Steve, "Kleiner's Ted Schlein on Cyber Risk: 'It Only Gets Worse,'" *Wall Street Journal*, February 4, 2014, http://blogs.wsj.com/cio/2014/02/04/kleiners-ted-schlein-on-cyber-risk-it-only-gets-worse/.

22. Kuchler, Hannah, "Adobe Says 38m Customers Hit by Cyber Security Breach," *Financial Times*, October 30, 2013, http://www.ft.com/intl/cms/s/0/83e0aa90-417b-11e3-9073-00144feabdc0.html#axzz2xAvlKJlp.

23. Ibid., Kuchler.

24. Kuchler, Hannah, "Cyber Criminals Target Smaller Companies," *Financial Times*, February 10, 2014, http://www.ft.com/intl/cms/s/0/3bb5e5b2-901a-11e3-aee9-00144feab7de.html#axzz39B66hbCN.

25. Pritchard, Stephen, "Moral and Legal Points Weigh on Information Use," *Financial Times*, March 25, 2014, http://www.ft.com/intl/cms/s/0/2507750c-adb5-11e3-9ddc-00144feab7de.html?siteedition=intl#axzz2xAvlKJlp.

26. Kuchler, Hannah, "Investors Flock to Cyber Security Start-ups," *Financial Times*, March 12, 2014, http://www.ft.com/intl/cms/s/0/f5c87808-a883-11e3-b50f-00144feab7de.html#axzz2xAvlKJlp.

27. Dempsey, Michael, "CIOs Must Face Op to 'Off-Radar' Spending on Online Services," *Financial Times*, January 28, 2014, http://www.ft.com/intl/cms/s/0/dd064c6c-81c5-11e3-87d5-00144feab7de.html#axzz39B66hbCN.

28. Patel, Zarna, "Survey: Majority of Employees Ready to Break BYOD Policies," Bank Systems and Technology, October 24, 2013, http://www.banktech.com/survey-majority-of-employees-ready-to-break-byod-policies/d/d-id/1296657.

29. "Surge in Mobile Malware Affects 11.6 Million Devices," Tripwire, January 29, 2014, http://www.tripwire.com/state-of-security/top-security-stories/surge-mobile-malware-affects-11-6-million-devices/.

Chapter 11

1. Waxer, Cindy, "Big Data Blues: The Dangers of Data Mining," *Computerworld*, November 4, 2013, http://www.computerworld.com/s/article/9243719/Big_data_blues_The_dangers_of_data_mining?taxonomyId=18&pageNumber=3.

2. Rainie, Lee, "Anonymity, Privacy, and Security Online," Pew Research, September 5, 2013, http://www.pewinternet.org/2013/09/05/anonymity-privacy-and-security-online/.

3. "High Profile Data Breach Hits Experian, Equifax & Trans Union," Data Breach Watch, March 13, 2013, http://www.databreachwatch.org/high-profile-data-breach-hits-experian-equifax-trans-union/.

4. "Conservatives of Every Hue," *The Economist*, April 5, 2014, p. 27.

5. Doyle, Eric, "ICO to Investigate UK Effects of Sony Data Breach," *TechWeek Europe*, April 28, 2011, http://www.techweekeurope.co.uk/news/ico-to-investigate-uk-effects-of-sony-data-breach-27748, and Armerding, Taylor, "The 15 Worst Data Security Breaches of the 21st Century," CSO, February 15, 2012, http://www.csoonline.com/article/2130877/data-protection/the-15-worst-data-security-breaches-of-the-21st-century.html.

6. "T. J. Maxx Parent Company Data Theft Is the Worst Ever," *Informationweek*, March 29, 2007, http://www.informationweek.com/tj-maxx-parent-company-data-theft-is-the-worst-ever/d/d-id/1053522.

7. Krehel, Ondrej, "10 Worst Government Data Breaches," MSN Money, December 10, 2012, http://money.msn.com/identity-theft/10-worst-government-data-breaches.

8. NuWave Backup web site, last accessed July 15, 2014, http://nwbackup.net/wordpress/computer-security/.

9. Mizroch, Amir, "UK Firms Increasingly Hit by Data Theft, But Aren't Reporting It," Wall Street Journal Digits, April 29, 2014, http://blogs.wsj.com/digits/2014/04/29/uk-firms-increasingly-hit-by-data-theft-but-arent-reporting-it/.

10. Valentino-DeVries, Jennifer, "They Know What You're Shopping For," *Wall Street Journal*, December 7, 2012, http://online.wsj.com/news/articles/SB10001424127887324784404578143144132736214?mod=WSJ_WhatTheyKnowPrivacy_LeftTopNews&mg=reno64-wsj&url=http%3A%2F%2Fonline.wsj.com%2Farticle%2FSB10001424127887324784404578143144132736214.html%3Fmod%3DWSJ_WhatTheyKnowPrivacy_LeftTopNews.

11. Bartlett, Jamie, "iSPY: How the Internet Buys and Sells Your Secrets," *The Spectator*, December 7, 2013, http://www.spectator.co.uk/features/9093961/little-brothers-are-watching-you/.

12. Steel, Emily, "Data Brokers Change Labels Describing Poor," *Financial Times*, March 28, 2014, http://www.ft.com/intl/cms/s/0/a6a0783e-b107-11e3-bbd4-00144feab7de.html#axzz2xGUZ9o4B.

13. Pearson, Sophia, "CVS Accused in Suit of Selling Customer Data to Drugmakers," Bloomberg, March 9, 2011, http://www.bloomberg.com/news/2011-03-09/cvs-accused-in-suit-of-using-customers-pharmacy-data-for-drug-companies.html.

14. Rosenfeld, Steven, "4 Ways Google Is Destroying Privacy and Collecting Your Data," *Salon*, February 5, 2014, http://www.salon.com/2014/02/05/4_ways_google_is_destroying_privacy_and_collecting_your_data_partner/.

15. "Cookies on Mobile 101," iab, November 2013, http://www.iab.net/media/file/CookiesOnMobile101Final.pdf.

16. Newman, Nathan, "Why Google's Spying on User Data Is Worse Than the NSA's," *Huffington Post*, July 1, 2013, http://www.huffingtonpost.com/nathan-newman/why-googles-spying-on-use_b_3530296.html.

17. Jones Harbour, Pamela, "Careful! Your Company May Be a Defacto Data Broker: Are Privacy Regulators Going for Broke(rs) as Part of the 2014 Legislative and Privacy Enforcement Agenda?," *Data Privacy Monitor*, January 10, 2014, http://www.dataprivacymonitor.com/enforcement/careful-your-company-may-be-a-defacto-data-broker-are-privacy-regulators-going-for-brokers-as-part-of-the-2014-legislative-and-privacy-enforcement-agenda/.

18. Bradshaw, Tim, "Snapchat settles privacy complaint," *Financial Times*, May 8, 2014, http://www.ft.com/intl/cms/s/0/a831c9a6-d6d6-11e3-b95e-00144feabdc0.html?siteedition=uk#axzz3E9wqxy6T.

19. Everson, Eric, "Big Data, Big Privacy Concerns, and Big Settlements," Lexology, April 10, 2013, http://www.lexology.com/library/detail.aspx?g=16e512fa-666f-4242-9e9d-7b93dc27204e.

20. Popken, Ben, "FTC Fines Data Broker for Suggesting Potential Hires Were Sex Offenders," NBC News, April 10, 2014, http://www.nbcnews.com/business/consumer/ftc-fines-data-broker-suggesting-potential-hires-were-sex-offenders-n77071.

21. "A Second Front in the Privacy Wars," *New York Times*, February 23, 2014, http://www.nytimes.com/2014/02/24/opinion/a-second-front-in-the-privacy-wars.html.

22. Ibid., Jones Harbour, and Steel, Emily, "Senators Seek New Rules for Data Brokers," *Financial Times*, February 23, 2014, http://www.ft.com/intl/cms/s/0/06a78f5e-94b3-11e3-9146-00144feab7de.html#axzz39B66hbCN.

23. Machanavajjhala, Ashwin, "Big Privacy: Protecting Confidentiality in Big Data," Duke University, last accessed July 15, 2014, http://www.cs.duke.edu/~ashwin/pubs/BigPrivacyACMXRDS_final.pdf.

24. Bolle, Justin, "Mapping, and Sharing, the Consumer Genome," *New York Times*, June 17, 2012, http://www.nytimes.com/2012/06/17/technology/acxiom-the-quiet-giant-of-consumer-database-marketing.html?pagewanted=3&_r=0.

25. Jeffries, Adrianne, "FICO May Start Including Your Facebook Presence in Your Credit Score," *The Verge*, January 9, 2014, http://www.theverge.com/2014/1/9/5292568/fico-may-start-including-your-facebook-presence-in-your-credit-score.

26. Duhigg, Charles, "How Companies Learn Your Secrets," *New York Times*, February 19, 2012, http://www.nytimes.com/2012/02/19/magazine/shopping-habits.html?pagewanted=all&_r=1&.

27. "Consumers, Big Data, and Online Tracking in the Retail Industry: A Case Study of Walmart," The Center for Media Justice, November 2013, http://centerformediajustice.org/wp-content/files/WALMART_PRIVACY_.pdf.

28. Fung, Brian, "OkCupid reveals it's been lying to some of its users. Just to see what'll happen," *Washington Post*, July 28, 2014, http://www.washingtonpost.com/blogs/the-switch/wp/2014/07/28/okcupid-reveals-its-been-lying-to-some-of-its-users-just-to-see-whatll-happen/).

29. Bump, Philip, "Larry Ellison, NSA Database Supplier, Approves of NSA Surveillance," *The Wire*, August 13, 2013, http://www.thewire.com/business/2013/08/guy-who-provides-nsa-databases-loves-nsa-surveillance/68280/.

30. Dembosky, April, "Silicon Valley Rooted in Backing from US Military," *Financial Times*, June 9, 2013, http://www.ft.com/intl/cms/s/0/8c0152d2-d0f2-11e2-be7b-00144feab7de.html#axzz2xAvlKJlp.

31. Kenney, Martin, "Silicon Valley's Spy Problem," Project Syndicate, print, July 2, 2014, http://www.project-syndicate.org/commentary/martin-kenney-warns-that-the-nsa-s-actions-are-undermining-the-american-it-sector-s-global-dominance#pg3dSfs7aHpy5JFP.99.

32. Lee, Timothy B., "Here's Everything We Know about PRISM to Date," *Washington Post*, June 12, 2013, http://www.washingtonpost.com/blogs/wonkblog/wp/2013/06/12/heres-everything-we-know-about-prism-to-date/.

33. Jopson, Barney, "Amazon Gets Clearance to Provide More Cloud Services to Pentagon," *Financial Times*, March 26, 2014, http://www.ft.com/cms/s/0/22a91a08-b504-11e3-9166-00144feabdc0.html#ixzz2xAwV5Cqs.

34. Harris, Derrick, "Under the Covers of the NSA's Big Data Effort," *Gigaom*, June 7, 2013, http://gigaom.com/2013/06/07/under-the-covers-of-the-nsas-big-data-effort/.

35. Perez, Sarah, "Sqrrl Raises $5.2M to Provide Deeper Granularity for NSA-Born Database Technology," Techcrunch, October 21, 2013, http://techcrunch.com/2013/10/21/sqrrl-raises-2-5m-to-provide-deeper-granularity-for-nsa-born-database-technology/.

36. Heath, Thomas, "NSA Revelations Put Booz Allen Hamilton, Carlyle Group in Uncomfortable Limelight," *Washington Post*, June 11, 2013, http://www.washingtonpost.com/business/economy/nsa-revelations-put-booz-allen-hamilton-carlyle-group-in-uncomfortable-limelight/2013/06/11/8f4d9138-d2ca-11e2-a73e-826d299ff459_story.html.

37. Borger, Julian, "Booz Allen Hamilton: Edward Snowden's US Contracting Firm," *The Guardian*, June 9, 2013, http://www.theguardian.com/world/2013/jun/09/booz-allen-hamilton-edward-snowden.

38. Shachtman, Noah, "Exclusive: U.S. Spies Buy Stake in Firm That Monitors Blogs, Tweets," *Wired*, October 19, 2009, http://www.wired.com/dangerroom/2009/10/exclusive-us-spies-buy-stake-in-twitter-blog-monitoring-firm/.

39. Mac, Ryan, "CIA-Funded Data-Miner Palantir Not Yet Profitable But Looking for $8 Billion Valuation," *Forbes*, August 16, 2013, http://www.forbes.com/sites/ryanmac/2013/08/16/cia-funded-data-miner-palantir-not-yet-profitable-but-looking-for-8-billion-valuation/.

40. Babcock, Charles, "Amazon Again Beats IBM for CIA Cloud Contract," *InformationWeek*, November 8, 2013, http://www.informationweek.com/cloud/infrastructure-as-a-service/amazon-again-beats-ibm-for-cia-cloud-contract/d/d-id/1112211.

41. Ibid., Jopson, Barney.

42. Thomas, Daniel, "Cisco boss calls on Obama to rein in surveillance," *Financial Times*, May 18, 2014, http://www.ft.com/intl/cms/s/0/a697c292-de80-11e3-9640-00144feabdc0.html#axzz3E9wqxy6T.

43. Fontanella-Khan, James, "Microsoft Cloud System Wins EU Privacy Regulators' Approval," *Financial Times*, April 10, 2014, http://www.ft.com/intl/cms/s/0/aeeb7350-c0a1-11e3-a74d-00144feabdc0.html#axzz2yaArjflI.

44. Waxer, Cindy, "Big Data Blues: The Dangers of Data Mining," *Computerworld*, November 4, 2013, http://www.computerworld.com/s/article/9243719/Big_data_blues_The_dangers_of_data_mining?taxonomyId=18&pageNumber=3.

45. Greenberg, Andy, "How A 'Deviant' Philosopher Built Palantir, A CIA-Funded Data-Mining Juggernaut," *Forbes*, August 14, 2013, http://www.forbes.com/sites/andygreenberg/2013/08/14/agent-of-intelligence-how-a-deviant-philosopher-built-palantir-a-cia-funded-data-mining-juggernaut/3/.

46. Ibid., Waxer, Cindy.

47. Bartlett, Jamie, "iSPY: How the Internet Buys and Sells Your Secrets," *The Spectator*, December 7, 2013, http://www.spectator.co.uk/features/9093961/little-brothers-are-watching-you/.

48. Carr, Paul, "AOL Sites Will Now Track You, Whether You Like It or Not," PandoDaily, August 18, 2014, http://pando.com/2014/08/18/aol-sites-will-now-track-you-whether-you-like-it-or-not/, and Brodkin, Jon, "Yahoo Is the Latest Company Ignoring Web Users' Requirements for Privacy," ARS Technica, May 1, 2014, http://arstechnica.com/information-technology/2014/05/yahoo-is-the-latest-company-ignoring-web-users-requests-for-privacy/.

49. Madrigal, Alexis C., "I'm Being Followed: How Google—and 104 Other Companies—Are Tracking Me on the Web," *The Atlantic*, February 29, 2012, http://www.theatlantic.com/technology/archive/2012/02/im-being-followed-how-google-151-and-104-other-companies-151-are-tracking-me-on-the-web/253758/.

50. Ibid., Waxer, Cindy.

51. Biegelsen, Amy, "Unregulated FICO Has Key Role in Each American's Access to Credit," The Center for Public Integrity, May 17, 2011, http://www.publicintegrity.org/2011/05/17/4628/unregulated-fico-has-key-role-each-americans-access-credit.

52. Internet Policy Task Force web page, National Telecommunications and Information Administration, last accessed on July 15, 2014, http://www.ntia.doc.gov/category/internet-policy-task-force.

53. "We Can't Wait: Obama Administration Unveils Blueprint for a 'Privacy Bill of Rights' to Protect Consumers Online," White House Press Release, The White House web site, February 23, 2012, http://www.whitehouse.gov/the-press-office/2012/02/23/we-can-t-wait-obama-administration-unveils-blueprint-privacy-bill-rights.

54. Ibid., The White House web site.

55. Ibid., Madrigal.

56. Ibid., The White House web site.

57. "Senate Bill No. 568, Chapter 336, California Legislative Information web site, last accessed July 15, 2014, http://leginfo.legislature.ca.gov/faces/billNavClient.xhtml?bill_id=201320140SB568.

58. Hern, Alex, "Google Faces Lawsuit over Email Scanning and Student Data," *The Guardian*, March 19, 2014, http://www.theguardian.com/technology/2014/mar/19/google-lawsuit-email-scanning-student-data-apps-education.

59. Ibid., Biegelsen.

60. Bachman, Katy, "Senate Commerce Report Says Data Brokers 'Operate Behind a Veil of Secrecy,'" Adweek, December 18, 2013, http://www.adweek.com/news/technology/senate-commerce-report-says-data-brokers-operate-behind-veil-secrecy-154579, and Steel, Emily, "Data Brokers Change Labels Describing Poor," *Financial Times*, March 23, 2014, http://www.ft.com/intl/cms/s/0/a6a0783e-b107-11e3-bbd4-00144feab7de.html#axzz2xGUZ9o4B.

61. Consumers, Big Data, and OnlineTracking in the Retail Industry: A Case Study of Walmart," *The Center for Media Justice*, November, 2013, http://centerformediajustice.org/wp-content/files/WALMART_PRIVACY_.pdf.

62. Ahmed, Murad, "Google adopts 'soft power' Europe lobbying," *Financial Times*, September 18, 2014, p. 20.

63. Jopson, Barney, "Amazon cloud seeks to revamp corporate IT," *Financial Times*, September 25, 2012, http://www.ft.com/intl/cms/s/0/d822679c-0694-11e2-abdb-00144feabdc0.html?siteedition=intl#axzz3E9wqxy6T.

64. Pritchard, Stephen, "Data Privacy: US Revelations Put Heat on Business," *Financial Times*, February 23, 2014, http://www.ft.com/intl/cms/s/0/8ef6af94-94b2-11e3-9146-00144feab7de.html#axzz39FQ2PJDb.

65. Reno, Jim, "Big Data, Little Privacy," CA Technologies, 2012, http://www.ca.com/us/~/media/files/articles/ca-technology-exchange/big-data-little-privacy-reno.aspx.

66. "Commission Proposes a Comprehensive Reform of Data Protection Rules to Increase Users' Control of Their Data and to Cut Costs for Businesses," Press Release from the European Commission, Europa Press Releases Database, January 25, 2012, http://europa.eu/rapid/press-release_IP-12-46_en.htm?locale=en.

67. "Review of the Impact of the ICO's Civil Monetary Penalties," UK Information Commissioner's Office, last accessed July 15, 2014, http://ico.org.uk/about_us/research/data_protection.

68. Greenleaf, Graham, "Global Data Privacy Laws 2013: 99 Countries and Counting," *Privacy Laws & Business International Report*, Issue 123, UNSW Law Research Paper No. 2013-58, June 2013, http://ssrn.com/abstract=2305882).

69. "Welcome to the U.S.-EU & U.S.-Swiss Safe Harbor Frameworks," Export.gov, last accessed July 15, 2014, http://www.export.gov/safeharbor/, and "International Safe Harbor Privacy Principles," Wikipedia, last accessed July 15, 2014, https://en.wikipedia.org/wiki/International_Safe_Harbor_Privacy_Principles.

70. Baker, Jennifer, "EU Will Not Suspend Safe Harbor Data Privacy Agreement with the US," *PCWorld*, November 27, 2013, http://www.pcworld.com/article/2067480/eu-will-not-suspend-safe-harbor-data-privacy-agreement-with-the-us.html.

71. Moyse, Ian, "Cloudy Data Sovereignty in Europe (part two)," Cloudtech, September 28, 2012, http://www.cloudcomputing-news.net/news/2012/sep/28/cloudy-data-sovereignty-europe-part-two/.

72. Vasagar, Jeevan, "Axel Springer Accuses Google of Seeking Digital 'Superstate,'" *Financial Times*, April 16, 2014, http://www.ft.com/intl/cms/s/0/41507d26-c575-11e3-89a9-00144feabdc0.html#axzz2zWpfUGkS.

Index

C

D

E

F

G

J-K

L

M

N

O

P

Q-R

S

T

U

V

W

X-Y

Z